Stories

Also by John D. Roth

Beliefs: Mennonite Faith and Practice

Engaging Anabaptism: Conversations with a Radical Tradition (editor)

JOHN D. ROTH

Stories

How Mennonites
Came to Be

Herald Press
Scottdale, Pennsylvania
Waterloo, Ontario

Library of Congress Cataloging-in-Publication Data
Roth, John D., 1960-
  Stories : how Mennonites came to be / John D. Roth.
    p. cm.
  ISBN 0-8361-9338-5 (pbk. : alk. paper)
  1. Mennonites—History. 2. Anabaptists—History. I. Title.
  BX8115.R68 2006
  289.709—dc22

                            2006020989

STORIES: HOW MENNONITES CAME TO BE
Copyright © 2006 by Herald Press, Scottdale, Pa. 15683
    Published simultaneously in Canada by Herald Press,
    Waterloo, Ont. N2L 6H7. All rights reserved
Library of Congress Catalog Card Number: 2006020989
International Standard Book Number: 0-8361-9338-5
Printed in the United States of America
Book and cover design by Beth Oberholtzer
Maps by Kerry Jean Handel
Cover photo by Wayne Gehman
The sculpture, *Seeds of the Martyrs*, by Esther Augsburger

12 11 10 09 08 07 06   10 9 8 7 6 5 4 3 2 1

To order or request information, please call
1-800-759-4447 (individuals); 1-800-245-7894 (trade).
Web site: www.heraldpress.com

*With gratitude to mentors at Goshen College
who demonstrated in their teaching and writing
that the discipline of history can serve the church:*

*Lee Roy Berry Jr., James Hertzler, Alan Kreider,
John S. Oyer, Theron F. Schlabach,
Shirley H. Showalter, and Nelson Springer.*

Contents

Introduction

Conflict and Renewal in the Church Tradition

The past is never dead. It's not even the past.
—William Faulkner, *Requiem for a Nun*

One afternoon my middle-school-aged daughter—generally a happy and even-keeled child—came home from school clearly out of sorts. Almost immediately, she got into a major squabble, first with one sibling, then another. Then followed a loud and unedifying dispute with her parents, and soon it seemed the whole world was rapidly unraveling around her. Eventually, after a rather fierce conversation, we called a truce and things quieted down. But the tension was still present.

Later that evening, I knocked on her bedroom door to see if we could make amends. I found her sitting on the floor, deep in thought, hunched over a set of family albums, looking at pictures of herself from long ago. Though she didn't actually say it, I think I know what was going through her mind: Who *was* I back then? Who am I now? Where do I fit in this family? What am I to do with these memories? Are the family stories gathered in these albums something to cherish or a burden from which I must be freed? Where is all this heading for me?

I had intended to revive the themes of our dispute. But without really being aware of it, my eye caught a picture of a particularly memorable moment: a family camping trip when it rained for three straight days. Looking at the picture, we began remembering the story together, reliving the details of our soggy misery in the camper and then the stunning beauty of the national park and our long hike up the mountain. An hour or two later, we hugged each other, said goodnight, and went to bed—the argument long forgotten.

It would be nice to end there and conclude that telling stories—remembering together our shared past—resolves all our conflicts and enables us to move into the future united by a common storehouse of memories. But that would be only partially true. Looking at the family album together did serve to defuse the tensions and shift our focus to warm memories of challenges met and conquered together. But the more troubling questions that my daughter was likely asking when I walked into the room are not yet fully resolved.

Like all of us, she encounters the stories of her family in two different ways. On the one hand, the memories preserved in the family album provide a source of comfort and grounding. When the world feels chaotic and unhinged, we turn to the narratives from the past to remember who we are. This is the power of the biblical stories: they remind us amid the confusion of our culture that we are part of a much larger story, one that connects us with the early church and the lives of Jesus, Sarah and Abraham, Miriam, Moses, David, and the prophets. This impulse is as true for groups as it is for individuals. When we tell the collective stories of our congregations, our denomination, or the larger faith tradition, we are looking for points of continuity that join us to that past. Family resemblances in the accounts of those who have gone before us are a source of comfort. Recollections of a shared past reassure us that those common experiences will keep us anchored in times of conflict and change.

As with my daughter, however, there are also occasions when we hear those stories inherited from the past and wonder what they could possibly have to do with us. Are they really my stories? What about all those stories I feel deep within me that have not yet been told? Will they have a place in this album? Will they fit in the three-by-five slots that we have for the other pictures?

Even as we look to the past for the reassurance of the familiar, we also recognize deep within that our relation to history is more complicated than this. The stories of the past are never "possessions" that are passively received. Instead, in remembering the past we are constantly asking ourselves how we are going to participate in the ongoing story of the present—actively transforming the story in the process. In the words of the great American novelist William Faulkner, "The past is never dead. It's not even the past."

The Storyteller's Assumptions

This book offers readers a brief history of the Anabaptist-Mennonite tradition. Some of the stories I sketch below will likely bring comfort and reassurance, reminding readers that the challenges the church faces today are not that different from those faced by earlier generations. However, other stories may be surprising or even disturbing. I think both reactions are appropriate. Just as the biblical story has the power to console as well as challenge, so too our encounters with the past can both soothe and unsettle us.

Since every storyteller shapes the narrative from a particular point of view, it might be helpful to alert readers in advance to the filters and lenses that serve as an organizing framework for the history that follows. Three assumptions are especially important for understanding the structure of this book.

1. History matters. I begin with the assumption that history matters—that stories from the past are a valuable resource for understanding the present and for helping Christians discern God's will for the future. Not everyone believes this. As a practicing historian, I am keenly (sometimes painfully!) aware that for some people the subject of history is likely to evoke a yawn. In a fast-paced culture that celebrates change and focuses on the future, stories from the past can easily seem irrelevant or boring. History in the popular imagination is mostly about kings and diplomats, dusty archives, and the mindless memorization of names and dates that seem to have little bearing on the pressing issues of today. Those in the church often regard the past as an obstacle to faith—the "dead weight" of tradition that keeps Christians bound to legalistic habits or to the eccentric quirks of an ethnic subculture. For many, attention to history seems like an obstacle to interested onlookers from other traditions or cultures, a barrier that gets in the way of mission.

These concerns deserve to be taken seriously. Historians can become obsessed with gathering dusty facts. Tradition can become a burden that stifles. Stories from the past can become tools of exclusion. But Christians whose faith is grounded in the Bible know that God has always acted in specific times and places. From Genesis to Revelation—from the story of creation to the apocalyptic vision of Christ's return—Scripture records the history of God's miraculous presence in the lives of his people. For two thousand years, Christians have found their true identity by telling and retelling these biblical stories. For two thousand years, these narratives have provided spiritual comfort, moral clarity, and hope-filled inspiration. In remembering these stories, we are reminded that God was present in the past, is active in the present, and will not forget us in the future.

2. We remember selectively. But even if we agree that history matters, we still need to ask questions about what *kind* of history we should be telling. In his short story "Funes the Memorious," writer Jorge Luis Borges tells of a character named Ireneo Funes, who was knocked unconscious after falling off a horse. Unlike most people who lose a portion of their memory when they are hit on the head, just the opposite happened to Funes: he lost his ability to forget. After the accident, he remembered every single detail of his life. Not just "what happened," but the intricate details of what he saw and how he felt.

> He knew the forms of the clouds in the southern sky on the morning of April 30, 1882, and he could compare them in his memory with the veins in the marbled binding of a book he had seen only once, or with the feathers of spray lifted by an oar on the Rio Negro on the eve of the Battle of Quebrancho. Nor were those memories simple—every visual image was linked to muscular sensations, thermal sensations, and so on. He was able to reconstruct every dream, every daydream he had ever had. Two or three times he had reconstructed an entire day; he had never once erred or faltered, but each reconstruction had itself taken an entire day. . . . The truth was, Funes remembered not only every leaf of every tree in every patch of forest, but every time he had perceived or imagined that leaf.

What seemed like a remarkable gift quickly turns out to be a curse. Funes becomes so immobilized by his recollections that he can neither function in the present nor think about the future. In fact, he does nothing but lie on a cot in the dark, paralyzed by his memories.

The story of Funes is fictional, of course, but it captures well a crucial point: namely, our memory of the past is always selective. A 1:1 scale map of the past, of the sort that afflicted Funes, is not only impossible to construct, it is also useless.

So the stories we tell are always "maps of the past," representations of the terrain that we hope will help keep us oriented amid the potential chaos of the present.

Still, the question remains: out of all the rich details and many layers of the past, which stories do we choose to highlight and which do we choose to ignore? This question is particularly sensitive for those in the Anabaptist-Mennonite tradition. For most of the past five centuries, it was Lutheran, Reformed, and Catholic authorities who told the "official" story of the Anabaptists. These scholars, writing from the perspective of the powerful, established state churches, tended to regard Anabaptists as either a minor footnote or, more frequently, as a heretical blemish in the history of the church. Anabaptists were worth mentioning only to denounce them as an aberration from orthodox Christianity.

With few exceptions, it was not until the early twentieth century that Mennonites began writing their own history. When they did, their impulse was to describe their past in rather simplistic and heroic terms. The early Anabaptists, the story often went, were the most faithful Christians of the Reformation era. They alone had the courage to follow Scripture—especially the teachings of Jesus—consistently, even to the point of bearing the cross of persecution. For understandable reasons, the stories Mennonites tell about their past are nearly always accounts of courageous faithfulness and perseverance, of hardworking pioneers in close-knit communities, and of God-fearing Christians who remained true to their convictions. Of course, most Mennonites know that they are not perfect. But we assume that public accounts of our past should be upbeat and inspiring. These stories make us feel good, and they strengthen our group identity. We also hope that heroic accounts of Christian virtue will inspire contemporary Christians to act in similar ways.

Yet such sanitized, carefully filtered accounts of the past can hide as much as they reveal. A nostalgic, gilt-edged version of history may offer a momentary escape from the present, but it does not provide a useful resource for those of us who are struggling for clarity amid the messy complexities of daily life. Even worse, a history that focuses only on moments of heroic perfection creates the illusion that our ancestry is "pure and spotless" and evokes a self-righteous attitude that is neither historically accurate nor theologically healthy.

3. We can learn from conflict. All this leads to a third basic assumption I bring to this book: that stories of conflict are as much a part of our past as accounts of heroic faithfulness and that the

presence of God is revealed even within those conflicts that have
seemed so troublesome within our tradition.

Here it is important to be clear. I am not interested in stories of
conflict because I take cynical pleasure in exposing the shortcomings of all ideals. Moreover, I am painfully aware that many of the
world's bloodiest conflicts are kept alive by the memories of
ancient grievances. Closer to home, stories of family disputes or
congregational conflicts sometimes fester for generations, creating
lingering mistrust and tension long after anyone can recall the
details of the original grievance. There is no merit in giving undue
attention to the conflicts that divide us.

But the solution to our contemporary conflicts will not be
found in pretending they do not exist or by writing them out of our
history. Messy stories of the past remind us that conflict is deeply
rooted in the human experience. Part of the power of the biblical
narrative is the fact that the people we encounter there are complex
characters who struggle mightily with their own sinfulness. Even
heroes like David or Esther or Peter were flawed human beings
within whom God worked nonetheless. Recounting stories of
human frailties and foibles can help guard against the temptation
to think that there was once a golden age when life was simple,
Christians were faithful, authority was undisputed, and the church
was fully united in its beliefs and practices.

At its best, conflict is the inevitable by-product of an earnest
search for truth, the consequence of careful and critical conversation in which committed Christians strain to hear the voice of an
unchanging God amid the noisy static of our changing culture.
When we discover that congregations in earlier times struggled
over appropriate forms of worship or embraced competing strategies for mission or interpreted biblical texts in contradictory ways,
we may be less inclined to cling to our particular claims with white-
knuckled certainty. Hearing the voices of struggle from the past
may bring a bit more humility to our own quest for faithfulness, as
we recognize that all ages—including our own—are equidistant
from God.

Patterns of the Past: From Renewal to Structure to Idolatry

Every congregation, especially those in the midst of conflict, is tempted to think that its circumstances are unique. And in a sense, this is true. Yet across the sweep of church history—in the narrative of the Anabaptist-Mennonite tradition, in the history of local congregations, and in the spiritual life of individuals—a distinctive pattern of church life becomes visible that helps to put the particular details of local conflict into a broader perspective.

The pattern goes something like this: A movement for change and renewal springs up, energized by the living, dynamic, and mysterious presence of the Holy Spirit. This movement challenges the organizational structures and theological assumptions of the status quo. It brings a new sense of freedom, energy, and excitement to the church, resulting in new expressions of the Spirit's presence.

Over time, however, renewal movements threaten to fragment into a dozen different directions. So people begin to create structures that give order and form to these new insights. Gradually, even in the most "spiritualist" or charismatic movements, certain patterns and routines emerge that provide a framework of shared assumptions about such things as leadership, worship style, biblical interpretation, and group identity. The Spirit, it turns out, is never "free floating." Instead the Spirit is always "embodied" in particular, culturally specific forms. The language and music we use to express our faith, the spaces of our worship, the way we acknowledge the authority of individuals or sacraments or Scripture all give necessary shape and form to the Spirit's presence. This tension between Spirit and structure is an inevitable—and healthy—dynamic in the history of the church.

Yet, at the same time, structures can become an end unto themselves, squelching the movement of the Spirit. This points to a third, more troubling, stage in the pattern. Frequently, Christians have come to identify the structures of their faith with territorial boundaries, ethnic identity, or political power. Throughout history,

Christians have always been tempted to define God as an extension of their own self-interest, reducing God to a tribal deity who blesses whatever it is that Christians happen to be doing. In short, if our structures become an end in themselves we can easily commit the ancient sin of idolatry, using the name of God in ways that can become exclusive, destructive, and violent.

These patterns of Christian behavior—woven into two thousand years of church history—rarely occur in their pure forms. They are usually visible as emphases or tendencies rather than as clearly defined categories. Nonetheless, being attentive to these patterns helps us to recognize the deeper dynamics at work within specific congregational or personal conflicts. I note these patterns as a reminder that the stories that shape Anabaptist-Mennonite history have an echo in the history of the larger church. Although the details differ in important ways, the themes of Anabaptist-Mennonite history are not unique to that tradition alone.

The Word Made Flesh

In the end, behind all the assumptions that structure this book, the attentive reader will discover an even deeper unifying theme: the mystery and the reality of the incarnation.

In Jesus Christ, Christians confess that God became one with humanity. As John writes in the opening words of his Gospel: "The Word became flesh and lived among us, and we have seen his glory" (John 1:14 NRSV). In Jesus, the creator and sustainer of the universe entered into human history, took on bodily form, and experienced life just as we experience it. Indeed, all of church history since the time of Christ can be read as the story of how Christians have sought to bear witness to the mystery of "the word made flesh." As the living "body of Christ," the church is called to bring word and flesh together in its public witness, embodying God's presence amid the inevitable flux of history and culture. The story of that effort is one filled with hope as well as failure.

Scope of This History

The opening chapters of this book establish a context for Anabaptist-Mennonite beginnings by tracing several general themes in the history of the church, from the dramatic story of Pentecost to the development of the Catholic Church in the Middle Ages that led to the Protestant Reformation in the early sixteenth century. Chapters 4 and 5 focus on the emergence of Anabaptism as a Spirit-inspired movement of radical reform that gradually assumed more structured and enduring forms in the Mennonite, Hutterite, Swiss Brethren, and Amish traditions. Chapters 6 and 7 tell the story of how Anabaptist groups migrated out of Europe during the eighteenth and nineteenth centuries. As these newly established communities took root and began to flourish in the Russian empire and in North America, they also faced enormous pressure to become defined by territory or ethnicity. Chapter 8 details ways in which the Mennonite church in North America has been renewed by the gift of ethnic and cultural diversity during the course of the twentieth century. Chapter 9 extends the scope of this cross-cultural transformation to survey the emergence of a truly global Anabaptist-Mennonite church. The final chapter of the book steps back to reflect on how this distinctive Anabaptist-Mennonite tradition has understood its place within the broader Christian church.

Although the story recounted here begins with the early church of the New Testament and ends with the global community of the twenty-first century, it does not pretend to be comprehensive. A full telling of the story would require many volumes, and it would still be incomplete! What I offer instead is an outline of several main themes in the Anabaptist-Mennonite story, illustrated with stories from specific times and places, and told with a particular eye to the enduring tensions that have given this tradition its distinctive shape.

Because memory is always selective, the framework for the story that follows will inevitably reflect something of my own particular context and experience, which is grounded more firmly in the history of Mennonites in the United States than in Canada or in the growing number of congregations in the Southern Hemisphere. My telling of the story also reflects a worldview shaped more deeply by the Swiss-German Mennonite tradition than that of the Russian Mennonite.

I write this book because I am deeply committed to the health, well-being, and ongoing renewal of the Anabaptist-Mennonite church. Yet I am keenly aware that Mennonite history cannot be read in isolation from the history of the broader church. Clearly ours is not the only story of Christian faithfulness. Our tradition has benefited enormously from the insights and inspiration of other Christian brothers and sisters. Although the story recounted here draws heavily on a narrative from one small corner of God's kingdom, the convictions that motivate our conflicts and frame our sometimes wayward journey are not unique to our tradition.

So I hope this book could be read with profit by all Christians, including those beyond Mennonite circles. And I hope that all readers, regardless of denominational background, will come to a deeper understanding of their own faith by reflecting critically and appreciatively on the Anabaptist-Mennonite story.

1

A Newborn Church

From Movement to Structure

*When the day of Pentecost came, they were all together
in one place. Suddenly a sound like the blowing
of a violent wind came from heaven and filled
the whole house where they were sitting. They saw what
seemed to be tongues of fire that separated
and came to rest on each of them. All of them were filled
with the Holy Spirit and began to speak in other tongues
as the Spirit enabled them.*

—Acts 2:1-4

So begins the dramatic story of the Christian church.

For nearly three years the disciples had put their careers on
hold as they followed Jesus on the dusty roads of Judea. Along the
way they had listened to his teachings and struggled to understand
the kingdom he was proclaiming. They had witnessed his miracles,
occasionally even participating in the "signs and wonders" of healing. Confused, fearful, and disappointed, they had watched as their
master was arrested and crucified.

Three days later, they discovered he had risen from the dead.
And then, suddenly, Jesus was gone—ascended into heaven. Now

this colorful assortment of fishermen, tax collectors, laborers, and revolutionaries who had been his disciples gathered once more in Jerusalem to sort out the meaning of their encounter with Jesus. What were they to make of the past three years? What were they to do now that Jesus was no longer with them? Did the movement to which they had given their lives have a future?

It was there in Jerusalem, at the Jewish festival of Pentecost, that their questions were answered, and their lives suddenly took a remarkable turn.

For nearly two thousand years, Christians have tried to understand the meaning of what happened to that group of men and women who gathered in an upstairs room during the time of Pentecost. Many Christians, perhaps most, are inclined to ignore the strange details recounted in Acts 2:1-4 or regard them as a unique event in the history of the church that has no bearing on the faith of contemporary Christians. For others, the images of wind and tongues of fire have become powerful symbols reminding believers that the Spirit of God comes in ways that surprise and transform us. And for some, the story of Pentecost offers proof that "speaking in tongues" is a requirement for all true Christians.

Yet the primary theme of the Pentecost story as it unfolds in the book of Acts is not really the "tongues of fire" or a personal experience of holiness or the ecstasy of speaking in an unknown language. Rather, the subsequent chapters make it clear that the lasting and tangible result of the Spirit's presence among the disciples was the formation of a new community—one Christians have come to describe as the "church."

According to the account in Acts, immediately after their dramatic encounter with the rushing wind and tongues of flame, the disciples move from cowering behind locked doors to a public proclamation of the resurrection of Christ. They astounded a group of foreigners with their miraculous ability to speak in all the languages of the Mediterranean world. Then the apostle Peter preached a powerful sermon to the crowd that had gathered, after which some three thousand Jews were baptized "in the name of Jesus Christ."

By the end of the second chapter of Acts, the disciples had created a functioning community in which new believers gathered regularly for preaching and teaching, ate communal meals in each other's homes, prayed and worshipped together, and shared freely of their possessions. The passage concludes, "The Lord added to their number daily those who were being saved" (Acts 2:47).

By the fire of the Spirit, a diverse, confused, and uncertain gathering of disciples was transformed into a cohesive community with an identity and purpose greater than the sum of its parts. People who had once been divided—by language, class, culture, gender, and religion—were now suddenly joined together into a new kind of family.

According to the book of Acts, this is the gift of the Spirit: the resurrected Christ lives on in the new community of his followers. At Pentecost, God's word was once again made flesh; Jesus is present once more in the visible form of the church.

The Early Church as a 'Movement'

For most modern Christians the church is a building, the place we attend on Sunday mornings for worship, preaching, singing, and praying. Or we might describe the church as a set of committees, mission programs, and support groups. Or perhaps we think of the church as the theological traditions, rituals, and institutions of a particular denomination.

All of these associations are appropriate. The church can indeed be a place, a program, or a profession of theological identity. Yet these were not the most significant characteristics of the early church as it emerged among the believers of the first generation following Christ's resurrection. The church as it is first described in the book of Acts was not so much a building or a program or a denomination as it was a "movement"—a gathering of committed believers drawn together by a common set of convictions and determined to live out their vision of an alternative way of life. By its very nature, a movement is fluid; its boundaries and exact shape are often hard to define. Movements tend not to have handbooks or organizational charts. Their structures shift from day to day, adjusting to the circumstances of the moment.

Such was the case with the early church. Those who joined this emerging community were attracted by a compelling vision—anchored in the life, death, and resurrection of Jesus—that pointed toward an alternative way of life. Like the first disciples who dropped their nets to follow Jesus, the new members of the church in Jerusalem joined the movement without understanding exactly what they were getting into. And, as in most movements, the earliest leaders had no fixed traditions or established structures to provide a blueprint for the shape this new community would take.

But the energy and excitement that propelled this movement forward did draw on a common set of resources that gave it a coherent message. For example, virtually all its earliest members were Jews steeped in the Hebrew scriptures and inspired by the vision of the prophets that God was still at work in human history (see Acts 7:1-53). Members of the early church were convinced that Jesus was the long-awaited Messiah, the "anointed one" who ushered in a new age in human history. They believed that his life and teachings fulfilled—even superseded—the Law of Moses and that in his death and resurrection lay salvation for all who chose to follow him. Members of the early church had a keen sense that they were empowered by the Holy Spirit to continue Christ's ministry of preaching, healing, and baptizing.

Very quickly, these shared commitments gave a form to the early Christian community that distinguished it from the Jewish tradition and from the pagan religions of the day. That distinctive identity can be summarized by six characteristics.

1. Voluntary membership. Most of the early believers in Jerusalem had been born into the Jewish religion. Their Jewish identity was a birthright; they had been raised in Jewish families, instructed in Jewish synagogues, and steeped in the cultural and religious practices of the Jewish tradition. Joining the Christian movement therefore demanded a conscious decision. This decision was formalized in the ritual of baptism, a symbolic statement of allegiance. As Paul and the other apostles began to preach in non-Jewish cities in the territories between Jerusalem and Rome, many people—including those from outside the Jewish tradition—were attracted by the convictions and practices of the new community. What united participants in this movement was not an inherited ethnicity, genealogical pedigree, or cultural tradition but rather the conscious choice they had each made to follow Jesus Christ.

This was not a decision to be taken lightly. Followers of Jesus challenged assumptions of status, allegiance, and power that the Roman Empire valued highly. They refused to offer sacrifices to Caesar, insisting instead that "Jesus is Lord." And for many, the commitment to follow in the way of Jesus meant they would also share the same fate as Jesus: persecution, suffering, and even death. This was not child's play. Membership in the early church was a conscious choice, and a dangerous one.

2. *Sharing of possessions.* From the very beginning of the movement, participants in the new community assumed that each member shared in the responsibility of caring for the physical and material well-being of the other members. The New Testament word used to describe this mutual concern is *koinonia.* Koinonia suggests a community defined by generosity, sharing, active participation, and fellowship. Koinonia begins with the recognition that none of our possessions—neither our physical resources nor our time, talents, and desires—are truly ours. Rather, they come to us on loan, as it were, from God. And since all that we have belongs to God, we are freed to share those possessions lavishly and joyfully with others. The book of Acts describes it this way: "All the believers were one in heart and mind. No one claimed that any of his possessions was his own, but they shared everything they had" (4:32). Indeed, so central was the concept of koinonia to the early church that when two members attempted to hoard wealth for themselves, an angel of the Lord struck them dead! (See Acts 5:1-11.)

3. Accountability to each other. The story of Ananias and Sapphira points to another, closely related expression of community life: the practice of mutual accountability. Christians today are used to thinking about themselves as accountable to God on the final day of judgment and perhaps to the inner voice of their conscience. But Christians tend to be squeamish about the idea of accountability to each other in matters of religious beliefs or ethical practices. Faith, we are apt to argue, is a personal and private matter between God and ourselves. Whatever passes between us and God is no one's business but our own.

Yet part of the appeal of the early church—and one reason for its missionary success—was the way in which members of the community took responsibility for each other's spiritual and emotional well-being. The commitment to mutual accountability was not an invitation to gossip or an excuse to wield power over weaker members. Instead, if a member had a concern about someone else that person should begin with a private face-to-face conversation, as Jesus taught in Matthew 18. If the matter was not resolved and the counsel was rejected, the concern should be brought before a group of two or three other members. Only as a last resort did the issue become a matter of discussion for the entire community.

At each level, the purpose of confronting questionable beliefs or conduct was to nurture the spiritual health and well-being of the individual and to mend frayed relationships with God and fellow members. Paul's letters are filled with examples of this sort of fraternal challenge and encouragement. Although church discipline today has taken on negative connotations in our individualistic culture, among the early Christians it was a mark of participation in a community of friends who cared enough about each other to address issues of conflict honestly.

4. Commitment to nonviolence. From the beginning, members of the Christian movement refused to settle disagreements with violence. With very few exceptions they also refused to carry lethal weapons as police or soldiers in the Roman army. The teachings of the early Christians were antithetical to the ruthless violence of the

Roman army. They understood themselves to be servants first of Christ and only secondarily as subjects of the Roman emperor. Jesus, they insisted, was their Lord—not Caesar. Whereas the *pax Romana* (peace of Rome) was based on the sword, the peace of Christ was based on the resurrection and the triumph of love over the power of fear and death. Christians claimed that true peace came from compassion and service. They practiced the principles of "turning the other cheek" and "going the second mile" and loving one's enemies that Jesus taught in the Sermon on the Mount. Although soldiers who converted to Christianity may have taken up noncombatant roles rather than resign their positions immediately, there is virtually no evidence that Christians actively participated in the Roman military during the first three centuries of the church's history.

5. *A distinctive culture.* Members of the early church not only rejected imperial violence, but they also came into conflict with Roman culture in other ways. Members of the newly established community, for example, often refused to participate in pagan holidays; they protested against the gladiatorial contests; and they boycotted plays featuring Roman gods and mythology. Christians resisted the cultural assumptions of their time not only in what they rejected, but also in more positive ways by what they affirmed. The early church earned grudging respect from its opponents for the way it cared for widows, orphans, and the poor; it also challenged Roman society with new perspectives on the human dignity of slaves and the equitable treatment of women. Early Christians gained a reputation for being honest and trustworthy; they were generous with their possessions and noted for their hospitality. Since Christ broke down the dividing walls of hostility, all human beings—slave and free, male and female—could sit at a common table to eat together.

6. *Mission-minded.* As the events after Peter's sermon made clear, one consequence of the Spirit's presence at Pentecost was the rapid growth of the Christian community. Part of this growth was the result of the tireless work of two gifted preachers: Peter, whose primary

focus was on the Jewish community, and Paul, who embarked on a series of missionary journeys to the Greek-speaking Gentile peoples along the eastern coast of the Mediterranean Sea. Both of these men were persuasive preachers, and they convinced many people to join the movement as it radiated outward from Jerusalem.

But the growth of the early church was not only the result of powerful sermons. New members joined the community because of the quality of life they saw among the early Christians. In their worship and praise, in their care for each other, and in their willingness to live out their convictions, followers of Jesus attracted the curious and the spiritually hungry to become part of a new way of life. The decision to follow Christ resulted in transformed lives. Members of the early church were healers mending broken bodies and shattered spirits. Here those who were used to living at the margins of respectable society could find a new sense of dignity and hope.

A description of the earliest practices of the Christian community suggests that mission was as much a by-product of koinonia as it was an intentional goal or strategy. As recorded in Acts, "Every day they continued to meet together in the temple courts. They broke bread in their homes and ate together with glad and sincere hearts, praising God and enjoying the favor of all the people. *And the Lord added to their number daily those who were being saved*" (2:46-47, emphasis added).

Historians estimate that by the end of the third century as much as 10 percent of the population of the Roman Empire professed faith in Jesus and had been baptized into the Christian church.

The Movement in Conflict: Separating Essentials from Peripherals

The message of the early church was exciting and attractive, and the movement grew rapidly. Yet the very success of the church's outreach also became the source of a series of conflicts that nearly destroyed the community.

Every movement faces the challenge of defining those principles that are essential for membership. As people from diverse cultural, social, religious, and ethnic backgrounds joined the Christian community, questions began to emerge as to which beliefs and practices were core to the Christian faith and which were peripheral. Almost from the start, for example, leaders in the church disagreed with each other about issues related to non-Jewish converts in the movement. Jesus had ministered almost exclusively within the Jewish community. The texts he preached from—the Bible of his day—were Jewish scriptures (what Christians today call the Old Testament); his sermons and parables frequently referred to the Law of Moses or to Jewish subgroups like the Pharisees and the Sadducees; and his earliest followers believed him to be the Messiah—the one promised by the Hebrew prophets who would usher in a new reign of God.

Since many of the early Christians regarded their decision to follow Jesus as simply a deeper and fuller expression of their identity as Jews, they continued to follow the rituals of Jewish worship and to practice distinctive Jewish traditions like circumcision, seeing no reason to throw out these religious customs simply because the Messiah had come. But for Gentile believers—the Greek-speaking converts who did not grow up with these traditions—Jewish practices seemed irrelevant to the deeper message of love, compassion, and forgiveness that Jesus had taught. They wished to become followers of Jesus, not adherents to Jewish traditions.

The simmering tension between Jewish Christians and Gentile Christians soon boiled over. Acts 15 describes the confrontation between leaders of the two groups in Jerusalem. After a series of tense exchanges, they finally agreed that most of the Jewish rituals, including the practice of circumcision, would not be essential features of the Christian community, though no one would be rejected for choosing to maintain these customs.

The council at Jerusalem seems to have resolved the immediate crisis. But the larger challenge remained. The dynamic energy of a movement comes from a common vision, not a list of rules. But as new members join, the nature of that common vision inevitably needs more precise definition. How does the community keep the energy of the movement on track while preventing it from spinning off in a dozen different directions? Which teachings and practices would be nonnegotiable? Which would be optional?

The questions refused to go away, especially as church leaders continued to encounter issues that Jesus had not explicitly addressed. How should the church respond, for example, to members who recanted under the pressure of persecution but wanted to rejoin the church? Should they be given a second or third chance? What about those Christians who tried to avoid persecution by pretending to conform to Roman demands—offering sacrifices to the Roman gods, for example—while privately continuing to profess allegiance to Jesus? Perhaps most vexing of all were the questions related to the person of Jesus himself. Was Jesus a human being who had Godlike characteristics, or was he actually God who only appeared to take on human form? Had Jesus existed before Creation or only since the moment of his conception or birth?

The Church Responds: From Movement to Structure

The Christian community responded to these challenges by introducing a number of changes that helped to address these questions and to give the church greater definition and form. In short, what began as a movement slowly evolved into an institution. Some later observers have pointed to these changes as the downfall of the early church—the loss of its initial zeal and the muting of the presence of the Holy Spirit. Others have insisted that these transformations were both inevitable and necessary for the church's long-term survival.

Formal patterns of leadership. Though the early church stressed the fundamental equality of all members, the apostles quickly recognized the need to affirm specific gifts and to acknowledge the authority of certain individuals over that of others. So, for example, the church in Jerusalem appointed a special group of people called "deacons" for the task of gathering food and other material goods to ensure that widows, orphans, and poorer members had adequate provisions. Elsewhere in the New Testament, we find references to elders or overseers, sometimes called bishops, who were charged with the task of providing spiritual leadership to local congregations. In time, some bishops—notably those in Jerusalem, Antioch, Constantinople, Alexandria, and Rome—assumed even broader authority over a cluster of congregations within a certain region. Eventually, the bishop at Rome asserted his authority over all the other bishops by claiming that Peter, the disciple to whom Christ had entrusted the "keys of the kingdom" (see Matthew 16:16-20), had passed his spiritual authority on to church leaders of Rome prior to his execution there around AD 67. That authority, first given by Jesus to Peter, was then passed along in an unbroken chain of "apostolic succession" down through the centuries, establishing the basis for the current pope's claim to be the legitimate heir of Peter as the head of the church. Regardless of the merits of that particular argument, the fact remained that the early church needed some sort of leadership. And so the roles of deacons, bishops, elders, and overseers emerged as a practical response to this need.

Rituals: baptism and communion. Just as these specific leadership positions clarified roles and authority within the early church, a number of ritual practices also developed over time to help the community distinguish between true members of the movement and the crowd of curious onlookers that gathered around it. One of these rituals, initiated by John the Baptist at the outset of Jesus' ministry, was baptism. In baptism the new convert symbolically died to his or her old life of sin and was "reborn" into a new life in Christ. The ceremony began with new believers literally removing the clothes of everyday life and being immersed in the waters of "rebirth." When they emerged again, they were dressed in clothes of white, symbolizing new life in a new community. The ritual of baptism served as a clear boundary that gave public witness to the believer's desire to follow Christ; equally important, it marked one's initiation into the family of the church—a community of love, intimacy, nurture, and support.

A second ritual of the church was the sharing of a common meal—sometimes called the Lord's Supper or communion—that evoked the living presence of Christ in a special way. Like baptism, the Lord's Supper had been instituted by Jesus (see Matthew 26 and Luke 22). Later believers who participated in this common meal saw it as an occasion to remember the suffering and death of Christ and as a way to express the intimate nature of their relationship to Christ and to each other as the "family of Christ." Since participation in the meal symbolized this commitment, to be "excommunicated" meant that a wayward member no longer shared a seat at the table of the community.

These rituals of baptism and the Lord's Supper brought structure to a movement that was in danger of flying apart—baptism by initiating new believers into the community of faith and the Lord's Supper as a celebration of the presence of Christ and the unity of believers.

Canonical texts: the "New" Testament. The only scriptures available to Jesus and to members of the early church were the texts that Christians today refer to as the Old Testament. Those scriptures had been translated into Greek three centuries before Christ (a text known as the Septuagint) and into Latin (the Vulgate) by the end of the fourth century. Throughout the history of the church, Christians have regarded the Old Testament as foundational to our understanding of the faith. It records the creation story, God's covenant with Abraham, the account of the children of Israel, and the powerful message of the prophets. Still, it was not the final authority for the early church. Christians believed that Jesus represented the fulfillment of the Old Testament; his teachings fulfilled and transcended the Law of Moses. Indeed, the revelation of God in the person of Jesus marked a new age in human history. So the story of Jesus, his teaching, and the movement he initiated needed to be told.

Within a century of Jesus's death and resurrection, various texts recounting stories from his life had begun to circulate among Christians. Soon thereafter, writings from key leaders in the early church, especially letters written by the apostles to encourage or admonish newly established congregations, also began to find a readership beyond their original audience. Over a much longer period and as a result of intense conversation and debate, a collection of those writings gradually emerged that would become recognized as a standard, or canon—an authoritative guide for testing new teachings and doctrines.

Christians today sometimes imagine that the New Testament appeared suddenly, as a fully written text that was immediately accessible to all believers. In fact, it was not until the Council of Carthage in 397 that we find a list containing all twenty-seven books that comprise the New Testament today. And Christians continued to debate vigorously well into the sixteenth century as to whether or not the "apocryphal writings" (or "intertestamental" texts) should be added to the canon. In any case, the Bible as we know it was not available to the earliest believers. Instead it came into being only through a process of sifting and sorting as the church made the transition from movement to structure.

Authoritative doctrine: the creeds. Once it did emerge, the canon formulated by the early church contained no less than four different accounts of the life and teaching of Jesus. In most respects, Matthew, Mark, Luke, and John are in close agreement with each other. Yet each of these books also reflects the particular perspective and emphasis of its author. For example, Matthew was a Jewish tax collector whose telling of the story is directed especially to a Jewish readership; by contrast, Mark seems to have had a Gentile audience in mind. Whereas Luke's gospel is full of parables, the book of John makes no reference at all to these pithy stories and tends to focus instead on more abstract theological concerns. We can be grateful to the early church for preserving such diverse accounts. At the same time, the differences evident in the four Gospels make it clear that the early church itself was not completely unified in its interpretation of Christ's teachings or its understanding of his nature and purpose.

The Jesus we discover in the Gospels was not a systematic theologian. He tended to prefer illustrative stories over precisely formulated doctrinal statements. Because of this, the early church needed to clarify several basic theological principles that Jesus did not directly address, questions related to his divinity, for example, and the relationship between Jesus, God, and the Holy Spirit. The early church struggled with these—and many other questions—as it sought to define itself amid the competing claims of various groups.

Not until the fourth and fifth centuries, after a series of councils, did a body of formal Christian doctrines begin to emerge. Thus, in 325, the Council of Nicea sought to bring an end to the ongoing debate about the nature of Christ by insisting that Jesus was *both* "fully human and fully divine." The Council of Constantinople in 381 addressed the difficult question of the Trinity, using extremely precise Greek language to express such nuances as Jesus being "begotten, but not born" of the Father. Such theological statements clearly went beyond Jesus' specific teachings and the writings of the apostles in the New Testament (for example, the Bible offers no fully developed explanation of the Trinity). Nevertheless, the church recognized these creeds as authoritative for its life and practice and used them as a means of distinguishing Christian orthodoxy from non-Christian heresy.

Conclusion

When the followers of Jesus gathered in Jerusalem at Pentecost, they had no clear picture of the future. The dramatic presence of the Spirit—made visible in tongues of fire, the gift of speech, miracles of generosity, and healing—forged these confused and frightened men and women into a movement. That movement dedicated itself to bear witness to Christ's resurrection through word and deed. Its message was powerful, attracting Jews and Gentiles alike to join in a new community. And the koinonia of life together offered a vibrant witness to the living "body of Christ."

Over time, structures emerged—formal leadership patterns, rituals like baptism and the Lord's Supper, a canon of authoritative texts, and theological doctrines—that were intended to keep this Spirit-infused movement on track. To be sure, few of these new structures had been part of the community's original vision. The impulse to define essential beliefs and develop greater organizational clarity emerged as a practical response to the centrifugal forces that threatened to divide the church into a dozen different factions.

This shift in the character of the early church from movement to structure was probably inevitable and even necessary. But it also contained the seeds of great danger. Structures tend to become ends in themselves. Institutional forms and routines can easily stifle the freedom that makes a movement so attractive and dynamic. Doctrines, rituals, and authoritative Scriptures can become tools of power in the hands of leaders interested only in maintaining their own authority. In the process, the calling of Christ to faithful discipleship can be forgotten.

For the first three centuries of its history, the church lived in creative tension, trying to establish a healthy balance between movement and structure. In the fourth century, the delicate interplay between movement and structure was overwhelmed by an even larger dynamic. A redefinition of the church in terms of power and territory transformed the very identity of early Christianity and had profound consequences for the history of the church.

2

A Catholic Church

Constantine and the Christian Empire

In the fall of AD 312, on a battlefield just outside the city of Rome, an event occured that would change the course of world history. For nearly a decade, the Roman Empire had been embroiled in a bloody civil war that had been triggered by the surprise resignation of Emperor Diocletian. At one point, no fewer than seven different generals battled with each other for the emperor's crown. Now an army led by Flavius Valerius Aurelius Constantinus—better known to history as Constantine the Great—had advanced to the Milvian Bridge that crossed the Tiber River into Rome. At this strategic location, his army encamped and prepared for a final assault on the imperial city. On the night before the decisive battle, Constantine walked among his troops, offering encouragement and planning his strategy. Suddenly, according to his biographer, the sky above Constantine lit up and he saw emblazoned there the symbol of the Christian church: the Greek letter *chi* superimposed on the letter *rho*. Then from the starry heavens he heard a voice say, "In this sign, conquer!"

Skeptics have justifiably questioned whether Constantine's vision was authentic or an imaginative fiction created by his biographer. What we do know is that Constantine and his army won the battle of the Milvian Bridge in 312. Even more important, we know that Constantine publicly attributed his victory to the Christian God and claimed God's favor as he ascended to the throne as emperor of Rome.

Almost immediately, Constantine set out to reverse Roman policies that had violently repressed Christianity for three hundred years. Under Constantine and his successors, Christianity went from the persecuted religion of a minority to the state religion of the Roman Empire. Virtually overnight, Christian bishops who had recently feared for their lives were treated as honored guests in the emperor's palace. Indeed, by the end of the century, Roman emperors were no longer content merely to grant special concessions to Christians; they now began to issue edicts that made Christianity the *only* acceptable religion of the empire and turned the armies that had once persecuted Christians against anyone who refused to submit to Christian beliefs. The shift could not have been more dramatic. Indeed, its consequences are still reverberating today. But was this sudden turn of events really a sign of God's blessing and favor? Or did it mark a transformation within Christianity that would compromise the church's very character?

The Persecuted Church

As we have seen, the disciples who gathered in Jerusalem at Pentecost had been transformed by the Holy Spirit into a powerful movement that had established itself in small fellowships in cities throughout the eastern Mediterranean region. As the church grew in numbers, however, opposition to it also increased. Some of the resistance came from Jewish authorities who regarded the upstart faith as a disruptive threat to their teachings and practices. Already in the days after Pentecost, Jewish elders and teachers in Jerusalem had tried unsuccessfully to silence Peter and John (see Acts 4:5-18). Stephen had been stoned to death by members of the synagogue (see Acts 7:54-60). Even Paul, who later became a leader of the church, spent the early years of his career as a zealous persecutor of Christians (see Acts 9:1-19; 22:4ff.; 26:12ff.).

By the middle of the first century, however, the most severe threat to the Christian movement came not from Jewish religious leaders but from Roman authorities. Roman emperors were quite tolerant of the diverse religions represented in their far-flung colonies. They generally allowed traditional practices to continue unmolested on the condition that local priests include the Roman emperor within their pantheon of gods and offer an occasional sacrifice to acknowledge his divinity. This, however, was a concession that Christians stubbornly refused to make. In their minds, Jesus alone was Lord, and offering sacrifices to Caesar was idolatry.

The first systematic persecution of Christians began in AD 64 during the reign of Emperor Nero, who blamed Christians for a fire that destroyed much of Rome. The violent wave of repression following the disaster resulted in the gruesome deaths of hundreds, perhaps thousands of Christians, including the apostles Peter and Paul. In the decades that followed, persecution tended to be sporadic and pursued more aggressively in some parts of the Roman Empire than others. During the middle of the third century, Emperor Decius renewed a systematic policy of persecution against Christians that resulted in the death of hundreds and drove thousands more into hiding.

Yet the observation of the Christian writer Tertullian that "the blood of the martyrs is seed" proved true. Even as violence against Christians intensified, their persistent witness in the face of imprisonment, torture, and death only heightened interest in the movement. The last serious wave of persecution came under Emperor Diocletian (284-305) and was a blistering campaign that sought to stamp out Christianity altogether. Although it too proved unsuccessful, the experience of persecution was still vivid in the minds of Christians when Constantine began his sudden rise to power.

On the one hand, it was tempting to interpret Constantine's conversion as a miraculous act of God. Just as God had softened the heart of Pharaoh, maybe he had intervened once again on behalf of his people and moved the hard hearts of the Roman emperors. After all, Constantine brought an end to persecution, granted Christians the freedom to worship in public, and allowed bishops to have a hand in shaping imperial policies.

But not all of the consequences of Constantine's conversion were positive. The adoption of Christianity as the "official" religion of the Roman Empire had a profound impact on the character of the church. For example, after Constantine, the decision to become a Christian was no longer voluntary. Now *everyone* within the territorial boundaries of the empire was compelled to be a Christian. Indeed, there are reports of Constantine marching whole armies through a river in a mass baptism that signaled their "conversion." Since Christian faith was no longer an individual decision, it now made sense to baptize infants. This innovation found theological justification in the writings of the church father Augustine (354-430) and was widely practiced by the sixth century. Bishops could now impose church discipline by force, calling on the coercive power of the Roman army if necessary. Furthermore, if everyone, including soldiers in the Roman army, was by definition a Christian, then the principles of pacifism and love of enemy ceased to be meaningful characteristics of the Christian community. The same was true of nonconformity. Now that the entire Roman Empire was Christian, the church no longer represented an alternative to the broader culture. And since infant baptism made everyone a Christian from infancy, missions also became unnecessary, at least within the territories controlled by Rome.

From the perspective of the early church, the new circumstances were clearly a mixed blessing. To be sure, the church was no longer persecuted. But what was happening to the character and witness of the church?

Remembering the Early Church: Compromise and Faithfulness

Many leaders of the church recognized the problematic nature of their new relationship to the empire and struggled to resolve these troubling questions. In time, several compromises emerged that enabled the church to retain some of its deepest ideals while adjusting to the political realities of a Christian empire.

Monasticism. One solution led to the creation of a new institution intended to keep the distinctive characteristics of the early church alive, at least for a select group of highly motivated individuals.

Already in the first century after Christ, there are reports of individual Christians who took to heart Christ's admonition to "be perfect, therefore, as your heavenly Father is perfect" (Matthew 5:48). Since it was difficult to live in the ordinary world according to these standards of perfection, these earnest followers of Jesus retreated from the temptations of human society to the desert in the hopes of following Christ more completely in prayer and solitude. But these hermits—sometimes called anchorites, or desert fathers—were isolated cases. It was only after Constantine's conversion that monasticism emerged as a clearly structured institution.

Around 525 Benedict of Nursia drew up the essential principles of monasticism. The Rule of Saint Benedict became the charter for dozens of monasteries established in the eighth and ninth centuries and served as the blueprint for the entire monastic tradition.

Today we tend to associate monasteries with tonsured, brown-robed monks chanting plainsong or with sisters of charity caring for the poor. Or perhaps we remember that monasteries were centers of medieval scholarship, preserving manuscripts and literacy during the Middle Ages. These are all accurate images of monastic life. But in the broader history of Christianity, the most significant aspect of monasticism was its attempt to maintain the distinctive features of the early church at a time when they were being lost by the alignment of the broader church with the interests of the Roman Empire.

The similarities between monasticism and the early church are remarkable—and they are not accidental. As in the early church, the monastic vocation was *voluntary:* no one was born a monk or a nun. Rather, each novice made a conscious decision to enter the monastery, recognizing that this was a choice with lifelong consequences. Like the early Christians, monks and nuns cultivated the practice of *mutual aid,* vowing to give up their claims to private property and trusting the community to care for their material needs. Members of the monastic community committed themselves to a life of spiritual discipline and *mutual accountability,* according to the expectations outlined in Benedict's Rule.

Like all clergy, the monks and nuns were dedicated to *nonviolence;* in times of warfare, monasteries were considered safe havens for soldiers and noncombatants alike. Furthermore, in their distinctive dress and way of life, monks and nuns *set themselves apart from the dominant culture.* Sometimes this took the form of care for the sick; sometimes it was kindness to strangers or hospitality to weary travelers. But always the monastic commitment to following Christ had a visible expression.

Finally, the monasteries kept alive the tradition of Christian *missions.* In the centuries after the collapse of the Roman Empire, it was the monks who continued to witness to Christ and his church among the various Germanic, Frankish, and Anglo-Saxon peoples of northwestern Europe. In all these areas the institution of monasticism preserved essential features of the early church, features that were rapidly disappearing following the marriage of church and empire after Constantine.

However, monastic life was understood to be an option for only a minority of Christians—those spiritual "athletes" who felt called to this special vocation. It was not a standard all Christians were expected to follow. So even while monasticism preserved the ideals of the early church, it also introduced into the Christian tradition a two-tiered understanding of faithfulness. On the one hand, there was the mass of believers, saved by virtue of their baptism as infants and called to follow Christ as best they could, knowing that most would fall short of that ideal. On the other hand, a tiny minority continued to live by standards that everyone recognized as the ideal but dismissed as too difficult for most Christians.

Just war. Christian leaders also made a second important compromise in the centuries following Constantine that left a deep impact on the history of the church. Few Christians today glorify violence or war. Nonetheless most insist that under certain circumstances Christians can in good conscience kill other people. These arguments supporting the Christian use of lethal force are summarized in the Christian doctrine of "just war." Actually, it was the Roman philosopher Cicero, writing several centuries before Christ, who gave the first clear defense of the just war. The Christian tradition did not pick up his arguments until the century after Constantine, and with good reason. For the first three centuries after Christ, the church had taught that Christians should love all people, including their enemies. But when Christians suddenly became active in the Roman government, charged with maintaining political order and defending the boundaries of the empire, their commitment to nonviolence shifted. Now leaders in the church struggled to align the commandments of Christ with the necessary and inevitable violence associated with running a country.

Their solution was to define a set of specific circumstances under which Christians could legitimately wield the sword. Thus Augustine and other church fathers claimed Christians could participate in war only if it was "justified" under a prescribed set of conditions. For example, the war had to be in response to an attack or in defense of a weaker neighbor. It had to be conducted by "proper authorities"; private feuds or barroom brawls were never permitted for Christians. Christians should always use "proportionate means" in war; that is, the level of violence against the enemy should always be in proportion to the level of the threat posed. And, though it sounds absurd, Christians were instructed to kill "in love." In other words, the Christian soldier should never dehumanize the enemy or think of the opponent as an animal, unworthy of life. In short, the Christian should kill with regret and restraint, never out of anger or hatred for the enemy, and in the knowledge that the larger good required this sacrifice of human life.

By seeking to minimize human violence and by recognizing that Christians could participate in war only in exceptional circumstances, the doctrine of the just war retained a clear link to the teachings of the early church. At the same time, the just war logic that continues to dominate mainstream Christianity today is a result of the changes following Constantine's conversion. It emerged as a direct consequence of the church's willingness to accept its new role as "chaplain" to the Roman Empire rather than remain a countercultural alternative. If Christians were going to enjoy their favored status in the empire, the teachings of Jesus would need to be set aside or modified in the interests of political stability and the well-being of the Christian state.

'Christendom' in the Middle Ages

The Christianity of medieval Europe drew heavily on the Gospels and the story of the early church for its highest ideals. But because the institutions of the Roman Catholic Church and the political interests of the Holy Roman Empire dominated, the public face of Christianity looked quite different than it had at the time of the apostles. The shorthand term for Christianity in the Middle Ages is "Christendom."

Christendom refers to the fusion of religion, politics, and culture set in motion by Constantine's conversion. Its basic logic ran something like this: Before Christ ascended into heaven, he passed his spiritual authority on to the apostles and by extension to the early church that spread out from Jerusalem. The church thus became the living "body of Christ" on earth. Its spiritual authority, like that of Christ, was quite literally universal (or "catholic"). There was no place in the universe where the authority of the Catholic Church was not already present. As the "body of Christ," the church assumed a physical form in institutions like the papacy, cathedrals, monasteries, and parish churches, and was organized according to a divinely ordained hierarchy. At its head was the pope—the vicar of Christ (in medieval society, a vicar was the representative of an absentee feudal lord who wielded the lord's full authority). Under the pope, a hierarchy of spiritually endowed offices—the *sacerdotum*—extended from the cardinals and archbishops all the way down to parish priests. This hierarchy preserved clear organizational lines of accountability and authority.

Contrary to popular opinion in the sixteenth century, the primary purpose of the sacerdotum was not to collect tithes. Rather, the sole reason for the institutional church, at least in theory, was to administer the *sacraments;* that is, the church existed so that ordinary people could enter into the presence of God. The most common sacrament, of course, was communion, or the Eucharist. Once the priest consecrated the wafer, common peasants could, at least for a moment, literally witness (and ingest) the physical presence of God, the word become flesh. Other sacraments of the church included such rituals as baptism, marriage, and ordination, each of which bridged the reality of God's transcendent presence with the world of time and space. It is important to note here that the sacraments "worked"—that is, had spiritual power—only if administered by a priest invested with spiritual authority through the hierarchy of the church. In other words, the sacraments were not legitimate—there was no salvation—apart from the intermediary of the church.

The spiritual presence and authority of the church was evident in virtually every aspect of medieval daily life. Its monasteries were the centers of cultural preservation, its universities the arbiters of knowledge, and its cathedrals the standard of architectural style and aesthetic taste. In the village, the church's spire dominated the horizon. The bells of the church announced baptisms, weddings, and funerals: their ringing brought divine protection from hail and floods. Saints days and religious festivals punctuated the calendar. Likewise, the natural world was also infused with religious significance. The village priest blessed the fields with prayers at planting time. A bountiful harvest was a measure of God's favor, while famine or plague were equally clear signs of divine displeasure.

Two traditions were especially important to maintaining political and religious order in medieval Christendom. Since both of these traditions marked the intersection of divine and earthly authority—again, the "word made flesh"—these two rituals emerged as potent symbols of an entire worldview. And since the Anabaptist movement incurred the wrath of those in power by rejecting or redefining these rituals, they deserve closer attention here.

Infant baptism was one crucial point of intersection between spiritual and political order in the Middle Ages. According to Augustine and the church tradition that followed him, the reason for baptizing infants was rooted in the doctrine of original sin. Since babies bore the stain of sin from the moment of their conception, only the saving sacrament of baptism could spare them from eternal damnation. It was assumed that adolescents would receive instructions in the faith, but salvation before God was a transaction effected by the church, not a personal decision of the individual.

Baptism also had an important political dimension. The ritual not only marked the entrance of the child into the spiritual communion of the saints, but it also signaled membership in the civic community of the local village and territory. In feudal society, baptism was the moment when a newborn child took on a political identity and was entered into the tax rolls as a subject of the local feudal lord.

The oath was another ritual that became crucial to religious and social order in medieval Europe. In a culture of unstable political alliances, agreements were almost always sealed with an oath— a formal promise to fulfill specific obligations with the threat of divine retaliation if the promise was broken. By appealing explicitly to God's authority ("may God strike me dead if I break this vow" or "so help me God"), oaths brought a measure of order to the political chaos of the feudal era. They were the glue that held medieval society together. To be sure, oaths were occasionally broken or ignored; but no one doubted that they were an essential— and divinely sanctioned—part of medieval life.

These then were Christendom's essential features: a church that claimed universal authority to mediate between humans and God; a church whose presence was deeply integrated into the cultural fabric of medieval society; and a church whose identity was welded firmly to the political interests of feudal lords and the early modern state. Although most Christians today regard religious liberty and the freedom of conscience as essential principles that scarcely need defending, the culture of Christendom assumed that a healthy society would have only one religion and that the church could rely on the coercive power of the state to enforce religious orthodoxy.

Conclusion

In most histories of the church, the Emperor Constantine is recognized as "Constantine the Great"—the man who brought an end to the persecution of Christians, supported the construction of new churches, convened several major church councils, and restored some glory to the collapsing Roman Empire by rebuilding the ancient city of Byzantium (which he renamed Constantinople). But perhaps the "greatness" of Constantine deserves a closer look.

In the first centuries of its existence, the church struggled to find an appropriate balance between the movement of the Spirit and the need for structure. In the fourth century, that balance was lost and the church was transformed into a "territorial" institution, firmly wedded to the interests, power, and prestige of the state. The "Constantinian shift" altered the very identity of the church. It preserved the distinguishing characteristics of early Christianity, but only by redefining them as an option for a small number of clergy who accepted a special calling to the vows of poverty, chastity, and obedience.

After Constantine, the fusion of church and state meant that most Christians no longer regarded the practice of patient, suffering, nonresistant love as central to their faith. In a similar way, Christians adjusted to the new practice of infant baptism—recognizing that territorial boundaries now defined one as a Christian rather than a voluntary commitment to Christ—and they made their peace with oath swearing, calling on the name of God as a guarantee of political obedience. Understandable enough from a historical perspective, these developments nonetheless fundamentally altered the character of Christianity.

Though they did not all agree in the substance of their critiques, the reformers of the sixteenth century shared in a passionate desire to transform Christian thought and practices inherited from the Middle Ages. It is to those reformers—both Protestant and Anabaptist—that we now turn.

3

A Protestant Church

Revolt, Reform, Renewal

In the summer of 1520 a young Augustinian monk from the German territory of Saxony wrote a public letter to Pope Leo X that appeared as the preface to a small booklet called *The Freedom of a Christian.* Martin Luther began his letter by assuring the pope of his unwavering allegiance. But as Leo X read the substance of the message, he might have had good reason to doubt the sincerity of that claim. "The Roman church," Luther asserted, "has become the most licentious den of thieves, the most shameless of all brothels. . . . Its corruption surpasses beyond all comparison the godlessness of the Turks so that it is now an open mouth of Hell. Not even the Antichrist himself could think of anything to add to its wickedness!" If those words were not offensive enough, even more audacious claims followed. "Furthermore," Luther wrote, "*I will accept no fixed rules for interpreting Scripture,* since the Word of God, which teaches freedom in all matters, must not be bound."

It is conceivable that Leo X might have acknowledged and even remedied the specific abuses in the church that Luther found so offensive. But when Luther rejected any rules for interpreting Scripture, he undermined the very foundation of Catholic tradition. By insisting on the freedom to read Scripture without "fixed rules"—independent of the authoritative teachings of the church—he set in motion a chain of events that not only divided the church, but ultimately shattered it.

From a modern perspective, it is tempting to look on the Protestant Reformation as being somehow inevitable. We are so accustomed to thinking about salvation as an individual experience, so quick to assume the right of each person to a "personal" faith, that Luther's challenge to the monopoly of the Catholic Church over God's forgiveness seems self-evident.

Yet those who participated in the Reformation of the sixteenth century did not see it that way at all. After all, the Catholic Church rested on one thousand years of history. It had a highly organized administration supported by long traditions that were deeply inscribed into the memories of the common person. For faithful Catholics, the thought of a divided church was almost inconceivable. Even if it occasionally suffered from ill health, the body of Christ was a living organism, not a fragmented corpse. Throughout the Middle Ages, only heretics and fools argued that salvation could be found apart from the sacraments of the church. And those who challenged the church's authority could expect to encounter imprisonment, a sharp sword, or a fiery pyre.

Problems in the Catholic Church of the Late Middle Ages

The universal church of the late Middle Ages was a divinely ordained institution—God's authority made visible on earth.

At least, that was the theory. In reality the church's actual authority in late medieval society was more tenuous than it liked to admit. Consider, for example, the role of the pope. In traditional Catholic understanding, the pope was the "head" of the church—God's representative on earth who would speak on behalf of Christ until the time of the Lord's return. Such claims to absolute authority reached their pinnacle in 1302 when Pope Boniface VIII went so far as to claim that salvation depended entirely on one's willingness "to be subject to the Roman pope." Yet increasingly the church's sweeping claims to power were coming into conflict with the more worldly interests of Europe's princes and kings.

In 1303, a year after Boniface's bold announcement, France's King Philip the Fair, sent his armies to Rome when the pope refused to allow him to tax the French clergy. Amid the confusion and fear caused by the presence of a foreign army in Rome, Pope Boniface suddenly died. Under the ominous shadow of the French army the cardinals who elected Boniface's successor chose a French-speaking pope. To the astonishment of Catholics throughout Europe he moved the papal residency from Rome to Avignon, a provincial town on the southern coast of France. For nearly seventy years—a period that later Catholic historians have sometimes called the "Babylonian Captivity" of the church—papal offices remained in Avignon under the watchful eye of the French kings.

In 1378, the papacy finally returned to Rome. But soon thereafter the situation worsened when several of the French cardinals, frustrated by the independent spirit of Pope Urban II, returned to Avignon and elected their own French pope, Clement VII. So for nearly forty years, Europe had not one pope but two, each claiming to be the true "vicar of Christ," each appointing bishops as vacancies occurred, each asserting the right to collect church tithes, and each issuing statements on matters of faith. In 1409, a council met in Pisa and resolved the issue by deposing both popes and electing their own. But when the popes in Avignon and Rome refused to step down, the Catholic Church was suddenly in the very awkward position of having three popes!

It took another decade before the matter was finally resolved. But the damage had been done. A century of disputes over papal authority left faithful Catholics deeply troubled about the institutional church. Questions lingered about the validity of the sacraments, and kings and princes in Europe were emboldened to act independently, sometimes in open defiance of the pope.

Trust in the church was further eroded in the fifteenth century as authorities began to appoint their friends and relatives to church offices—people who supported their political interests rather than people who were spiritually qualified for the job. It even became common to sell church offices outright to the highest bidder. Since many offices brought with them the right to collect certain tithes, some individuals began to hold multiple offices to maximize their income. The person holding these offices did not have to be a member of the clergy. Instead he could hire a priest to conduct the spiritual tasks of the position—and enjoy the considerable surplus revenue for himself. Although the specifics of these practices varied from region to region, there were enough examples to make the local population increasingly cynical and resentful.

Historians have described the broad wave of resentment generated by such abuses as *anticlericalism*. It was not that people in fifteenth-century Europe were resisting Catholic theology or demanding an entirely new faith. In fact, anticlericalism often reflected an earnest desire on the part of laypeople for church leaders to become *better* Catholics. Yet the deeper consequences of anticlerical sentiment were profound. The burden of ecclesiastical tithes, the immorality of the parish clergy, and the worldly interests of the church administrators raised nagging doubts about the integrity of the church. If salvation was to be found only in the church, and the church showed so many signs of corruption and decay, could one be sure that the sacraments—infant baptism, for example, or the ritual of communion—were trustworthy?

One tangible expression of this uncertainty about the sacraments was a growing hunger among laypeople for forms of faith that bypassed the sacramental system. Thus the late fifteenth century witnessed a sharp rise in pilgrimages, new expressions of devotion to the Virgin Mary, and the growing popularity of books like Thomas à Kempis's *The Imitation of Christ*, which emphasized practical forms of Christian discipleship.

Reform Initiatives Prior to the Reformation

Even before this rise of anticlericalism in the late Middle Ages, other voices within the church had been calling for renewal. These voices were almost always silenced, but they shared many of the same concerns that would lead to the cataclysmic upheavals of the sixteenth-century Reformation. Among these concerns were a deep interest in reading the New Testament, a desire that faith be relevant to daily life, and an emphasis on a spirituality free from institutions and accessible to all Christians regardless of education or social status.

One such reform initiative, that of Francis of Assisi in the twelfth century, was quickly absorbed into the Catholic Church in the form of a new monastic movement: the Franciscan Order and its female counterpart, the Sisters of Clare. By turning Francis's reform initiatives into a monastic order, the church effectively resisted his critique of material wealth and his call for all Christians to depend on God and each other. His ideals were not so much explicitly rejected as blunted by turning them into an option only for the spiritual elite.

Another reformer, roughly contemporary with Francis, did not fare as well. In 1170 Peter Waldo, a merchant from Lyon, France, gave his possessions to the poor and began a traveling ministry preaching the gospel of discipleship to Jesus. Authorities were troubled less by Waldo's emphasis on voluntary poverty than by the fact that his followers were distributing copies of the Gospels to an eager reading audience. Unlike Francis, Waldo was excommunicated by the church. In 1250, his followers, the Waldensians, were condemned as a heresy and for the next three centuries were severely persecuted.

The same themes emphasized by Francis and Waldo emerged again a century later, this time in England among the followers of John Wycliffe. Like Waldo, Wycliffe called for the translation of Scripture into the language of the people, and he sent out dozens of itinerant lay ministers who taught a simple faith, following in the example of Christ. In 1399 the English Parliament passed a law permitting the execution of heretics, and it was not long before Wycliffe's followers were being burned at the stake. His spiritual descendants, known as the Lollards, were forced underground, where they tenaciously survived until the coming of the Protestant Reformation in the 1520s.

Other reformers met with a similar fate. All of them had in common a desire to recover the simple gospel of Jesus and the radical movement of the Spirit evident in the early church. They started with a voluntary commitment to follow Jesus, a commitment that inevitably led to the formation of communities whose members shared freely of their possessions, were mutually accountable to each other, taught nonviolence, practiced nonconformity, and spread their teachings with a missionary zeal. The radical social and political implications of their teachings, combined with their view of the Bible as the Christian's highest authority, made both political and church authorities very nervous.

Even as the church denounced these reform initiatives as heretical, many loyal Catholics were becoming open to some measure of reform. In Spain, for example, Cardinal Ximenes began a campaign to weed out corrupt bishops and to raise the standard of education and morality among local priests. At the Lateran Council of 1512, representatives from throughout the Catholic Church expressed deep concern about abusive practices, such as the sale of church offices, and committed themselves to sweeping reforms.

So when Martin Luther, an obscure German-speaking lawyer-turned-monk from the backwater region of Saxony, began a campaign for church reform in the fall of 1517, there was little reason to think it would lead to anything other than early death for Luther.

But circumstances in Europe in the early sixteenth century had changed since the days of Francis, Waldo, and Wycliffe. The invention of the printing press in the 1450s meant that ideas could be spread quickly and cheaply. Moreover, the first texts coming off the Gutenberg press in Mainz were Bibles. Within only a few decades, the demand for the Scriptures—both in Latin and in the common languages of Europe—had made it profitable for printers to issue dozens of new editions. As a consequence, popular access to Scripture was growing in Europe at precisely the moment Luther appeared on the scene.

Luther himself recognized the revolutionary potential of the printing press. His own German translation of the Bible became an instant bestseller, and he quickly adopted the new technology as a tool for disseminating his ideas to a broad audience. Even though the great majority of peasants in Europe were still illiterate at the beginning of the sixteenth century, traveling preachers attracted large audiences, and local reading circles made it possible for villagers to read and discuss Scripture in their own language.

Luther also had the good fortune of pushing for church reforms at a time when the German princes were seeking greater economic and political independence from the authority of the pope in Rome and from the political oversight of the Holy Roman Emperor. When Luther's own prince, Frederick of Saxony, decided to defend the fiery reformer, he did so less out of deeply held religious convictions and more for political reasons—to demonstrate his independence from the pope and the emperor.

All of these factors—anticlericalism, the impact of the earlier reform efforts, broader access to Scripture, new technologies, and a growing sense of nationalism—helped to create conditions in Europe that were favorably disposed to change. The tinder was dry and well prepared for the spark that Luther ignited.

Martin Luther: A Church Divided

The man whose sharp critique of Catholic theology brought about the Reformation came to his convictions as a result of a personal crisis of faith. As a bright university student, Luther seemed destined for a successful career as a lawyer. But in the summer of 1505, as he was returning from the University of Erfurt with his newly minted law degree, his plans suddenly changed. As Luther recalled the event much later in life, he was passing through the small German village of Stottenheim when a summer storm began to rage overhead. Out of the dark clouds a lightning bolt suddenly flashed next to him, throwing him violently to the ground. Fearing death, Luther cried out, "Saint Anne, help me! I will become a monk!"

Luther survived and, against the wishes of his father, made good on his promise. Virtually overnight he switched careers and entered an Augustinian monastery, where he set about to become an exemplary monk. In good monastic fashion, Luther rigorously followed the routines of prayer, work, study, and fasting. He regularly confessed his sins to the abbot of the monastery and followed the prescribed acts of penance that would bring forgiveness for his offenses.

But despite all his earnest efforts, Luther did not find spiritual comfort. He was particularly troubled—even obsessed—by the thought of God's justice and God's righteous wrath. If God was truly *just,* he reasoned, punishing us according to what we deserve, then there was nothing human beings could do that would ever satisfy God's awesome standard of holiness and justice. Plagued by fears and doubts, Luther redoubled his efforts to purge himself of his unrighteousness. He spent countless hours in the confession booth; he prayed and fasted rigorously; he whipped himself in his monastic cell in an effort to subdue his fleshly desires. And yet he still trembled at the thought of a righteous God—a God, Luther later recalled, "I came to hate!"

Then in 1516 as Luther, now a professor of theology at the University of Wittenberg, was preparing lectures on the book of Romans, he was suddenly struck by an insight that would become the basis of his theology for the remainder of his life. In Romans 1:17, Luther read the phrase "the just shall live by faith"—that is, humans can claim to be just before God only by virtue of their *faith.* That insight gained additional power when he joined it to another passage, where the apostle Paul writes, "For by grace are ye saved through faith; and that not of yourselves . . . lest any man should boast" (Ephesians 2:8-9 KJV).

These simple verses struck Luther with the same force as the lightning bolt had a decade earlier. God grants us salvation not because of anything we do that might earn God's forgiveness; rather, salvation is a completely free gift of God's love. The contrast between this free gift of grace—given by God without strings attached—and the Catholic system of confession and penance could not have been clearer. And with this insight Luther felt a huge burden of guilt fall away. He later wrote, "It was as if I had entered through the gates of Paradise itself."

Almost immediately, Luther began to reflect on the practical consequences of this insight for the common peasants and artisans who lived in his small parish. One of his first concerns was the sale of indulgences. An indulgence is the release of the time a soul would spend in purgatory—the spiritual realm between heaven and hell where Catholics believe Christians reside after their death to atone for their sins. Since the Catholic Church held the "keys of the kingdom," it reasoned that it had control over when a soul departed purgatory. The practice to which Luther and others objected concerned the selling of documents that promised to release the buyer (or a designated friend or relative) from some of their time in purgatory. For simple peasants and artisans an indulgence offered some measure of control over the uncertainty of the afterlife. For the Catholic Church, indulgences served as an effective means of raising money, in this case for the construction of St. Peter's Cathedral in Rome.

As a theologian and village priest, Luther resented the sale of indulgences. The practice both deprived poor people of their hard-earned money, and it promoted a flawed understanding of faith that turned one's relationship to God into a commodity that could be bought and sold. Because the sale of indulgences encouraged people to think that their salvation depended on their actions, it challenged the essence of Luther's new understanding of grace. So, in the fall of 1517, he denounced indulgences by posting ninety-five arguments in Latin against their sale, and he invited his colleagues on the theological faculty at Wittenberg to an academic debate on the subject.

Luther probably did not imagine that he was starting a revolution; after all, posting arguments for academic debate was a common practice among university professors at the time. But his Ninety-Five Theses quickly drew widespread attention. Within a short time, translations of his theses began appearing in Europe's major cities, and news of his critique soon reached the papacy in Rome. Some saw his arguments as an attack on the exploitation of peasants; others, as an assertion of national independence from the pope's meddling; still others, as a theological manifesto striking at the foundations of the church's authority. In any event, the posting of the Ninety-Five Theses marks the symbolic beginning of the Reformation.

Official reaction to the document—and to Luther's unrepentant defense of it—was swift. The pope demanded that Luther and others who were sympathetic to his views appear before a board of inquiry, which firmly rejected the teachings. A series of further debates over the next two years only served to harden the battle lines. In October 1520, when Luther received word that his teachings had been officially condemned and that he had been excommunicated as a heretic, he responded by denouncing the church for teaching false doctrine and by building a bonfire where he and his students burned the papal decree and texts of church law.

In that same year Luther published three pamphlets—one aimed at winning the support of the German nobility, one challenging the doctrine of the sacraments, and one detailing the essential themes of salvation by grace alone—that generated widespread interest and almost guaranteed that reconciliation with the church would be impossible. Among other things, Luther clarified in these pamphlets his understanding of the crucial question of religious authority. If the church was going to debate him on these matters, Luther insisted, the only acceptable basis of argument would be Scripture, not the traditions of the church or the dictates of the pope, who had long claimed the last word in theological matters. Thus Scripture alone (*sola scriptura*) became a central theme in Luther's reform effort, one that was to have fateful consequences for the future of the Reformation and the history of the Christianity.

A year later, in April 1521, the authorities gave Luther one last chance to retract his arguments and return to the Catholic fold. In a dramatic showdown at Worms before a large gathering of

Europe's religious and political leaders, Luther held his ground. "Here I stand," he reportedly said, "I can do no other; I cannot go against the dictates of my conscience. So help me God!"

For many Christians today, the image of Luther defending the freedom of conscience—standing up to a thousand years of tradition, the political power of the Holy Roman Emperor, and the spiritual authority of the "universal" church—is a heroic moment indeed. Modern people are inclined to celebrate such acts of resistance, especially because expressions of individual freedom and the assertion of religious liberty have become the bedrock of contemporary pluralistic society.

Yet Luther's arguments resulted in consequences far beyond what he originally intended. To be sure, the principle of *sola scriptura*, combined with his redefinition of salvation as a personal experience of grace, posed a powerful challenge to traditional Catholic theology and practices. But to Luther's dismay, the forces of change that he helped to unleash quickly moved in directions beyond his control and in ways that he strongly opposed.

Consequences and Problems of Luther's Theology

As a reformer, Luther needed to establish a basis of authority that would enable him to challenge the church's monopoly on spiritual power. He did so by insisting that religious differences were to be resolved by Scripture alone and apart from any "human-made rules" such as those fixed by tradition or the rulings of the pope. Luther believed that the Holy Spirit would inevitably lead all honest seekers of truth to the same understanding of the text.

What he had not anticipated was that this same argument could be used just as readily, and with the same authoritative certainty, against Luther himself. Indeed, by rejecting the weight of tradition and teaching of the Catholic Church, Luther had unwittingly opened the door to a crisis of authority that would lead to the splintering of the reformers into dozens of competing groups, each claiming its doctrine to be the true Word of God. And that is exactly what happened. Almost immediately, Luther came into conflict with his colleague and mentor in Wittenberg, Andreas von Karlstadt, over understandings of the Lord's Supper. Each man cited Scripture to defend his particular interpretation. These early skirmishes with Karlstadt were a foreshadowing of more serious disputes to come. Within a decade of his initial break with the Catholic Church, Luther found himself embroiled in a host of bitter debates with other reformers, some of whom even shared many of his theological perspectives.

Luther's dramatic speech before the Diet of Worms points to another problematic legacy of the Protestant Reformation, namely, its individualistic and subjective character. Note how frequently in his famous speech at Worms Luther spoke in the first person pronoun: "Here *I* stand"; "*I* cannot go against the dictates of *my* conscience; so help *me* God." Luther insisted that because we are saved by God's grace alone, and because there is nothing in our outward actions that has any bearing whatsoever on God's saving initiative, Christian faith is essentially an inward, personal, subjective experience of God's action in our hearts.

In the standard Protestant language of today, we are saved not by good works but by "accepting Jesus Christ as our Savior." Although Luther soon found it necessary to qualify the individualism implicit in his argument, his theology of "grace alone" pointed toward a Christianity that could easily be reduced to an inward experience or to vague language about God's action in our hearts. Thus, for many Protestants today, salvation is a private matter that happens independently of the external institutions or rituals of the church.

Although Luther did not intend this, the individual nature of "salvation by grace" meant that anyone could legitimately claim his or her interpretation of scripture and experience of God's presence was as true as anyone else's. One outcome of this new approach was the shattering of the universal church into the colorful mosaic of denominations that now make up the Christian church. Today more than fifteen thousand different Christian groups compete with each other in the marketplace of religious ideas for converts and resources, each claiming, like Luther, to be following Scripture alone, true to the dictates of their own conscience.

The Reformation Turns Radical, the Reformer Turns Conservative

As a result of his refusal to recant at the gathering in Worms, Luther became a wanted man subject to arrest and execution as a heretic. Fortunately, he found a protector in his prince, Frederick the Wise of Saxony. Before agents of the pope could arrest Luther, Frederick arranged to have him whisked off to the isolated fortress of Wartburg. There Luther immersed himself for the next two years in writing tracts, corresponding with friends, and the Herculean task of translating Scripture into German.

Meanwhile, some of the consequences of Luther's radical arguments were becoming apparent. In 1522, radicals in Wittenberg, following the principle of "Scripture alone," began to "cleanse" the local Catholic church of its "idols" by smashing religious images and destroying stained-glass windows, statues, and relics. Concerned about maintaining the political stability of his territory, Frederick asked Luther to come out of hiding long enough to denounce these actions and to provide assurances that future reforms would move slowly, without posing a threat to political order.

However, peasants in other parts of Germany did not share Luther's conviction that the reforms should be introduced incrementally. Unrest among rural peasants and urban artisans had been building in the German territories for decades. Angry at the imposition of new feudal dues, frustrated by the immorality of local priests, and fearful of the economic and demographic changes unfolding around them, a diverse coalition of peasants and artisans began to demand a hearing for their grievances.

Luther's arguments fit perfectly with their goals. Not only did he provide a model of heroic opposition to Europe's most powerful leaders, he also offered them a rationale for denouncing the authority of tradition. Thus when Luther proclaimed in his early pamphlets that the Christian is "freed from the law," the peasants understood him to mean this *literally*—that they were freed from oppressive feudal laws. When Luther said that the only true authority for the Christian was Scripture, the peasants took him at his word. They claimed that their demands for economic and social reform were nothing more than an attempt to structure their communities around the principles of the gospel. For example, nowhere in the gospel could they find justification for feudal labor obligations, the elaborate tangle of church tithes, or the traditional restrictions on their hunting and fishing rights. In 1524 and 1525 peasants and artisans throughout the German territories began to rally around the Twelve Articles—a program of sweeping social and political reform explicitly based on Scripture—and launched a campaign of bloody uprisings against their feudal overlords.

Luther was aghast. This was not the kind of reform he had intended. In the spring of 1525 he dashed off an angry pamphlet entitled "Against the Robbing Murderous Hordes of Peasants." In it he called on the princes and lords of Europe to unite in repressing the peasant uprising, sparing no one in their righteous cause. God, Luther thundered, is a God of order.

The nobility obliged. At the Battle of Frankenhausen in May 1525, knights fighting on behalf of the princes and nobles slaughtered the largest of the peasant armies. Less than a year later, the Peasants' War, and with it the Twelve Articles, came to a bloody and decisive defeat.

The events of 1525 marked a crucial shift in the course of church reform. In the aftermath of the Peasants' War, the future of the Reformation was placed firmly in the hands of the princes, its direction shaped as much by a concern for political order as by the principle of "Scripture alone." Moreover, the union of church and state introduced by Constantine more than a thousand years earlier remained essentially unchanged by the Reformation. The new churches that emerged in Protestant territories continued to baptize infants, they blessed the decisions of their princes, and they provided theological arguments to justify their wars. Indeed, in many Protestant territories the prince took the title of "supreme bishop" (*summus episcopus*), and in the middle of the sixteenth century the principle of "whose region, his religion" (*cuius regio, euius religio*) established the legal right of every prince to determine the religion of the people within his territory.

It was within this fascinating and complex context that the Anabaptists—the spiritual forerunners of the Mennonites—emerged as a new expression of religious reform. As we shall see in the following chapter, the Anabaptists were people of their times, fully integrated within the economic and political upheavals of the sixteenth century. The movement they started drew heavily on the teachings of late medieval reformers (with their emphasis on the Spirit and on following Jesus in practical ways) as well as on the insights of the Reformation (with its challenge to traditional religious institutions and its elevation of Scripture as the ultimate authority for Christian faith and practice). And the first generation of Anabaptists could not help but be shaped by the concerns that gave rise to the Peasants' War and its goal of creating godly communities structured around the teachings of Jesus and the early church.

Yet the Anabaptists also renounced the violence of the Peasants' War, and they rejected the long-standing assumptions of Christendom—unchallenged by Luther and the other reformers—that aligned the church firmly with the state. In so doing, the Anabaptists cut against the grain of both late medieval Catholicism and the early Reformation. As a consequence, authorities on all sides responded with fierce opposition, including the death penalty.

Nevertheless, against great odds, the Anabaptist movement endured as a distinctive movement, charting an independent path among traditional Catholicism, reforming Protestantism, and the utopian dreams of the peasant revolutionaries.

4

An Anabaptist Church

A Third Way Emerges

Like most Protestant reformers of his day, Luther detested the Anabaptists. Claiming to base their teachings on his own principle of *sola scriptura,* they were to him wolves in sheep's clothing—heretical in their theology and seditious in their social teachings. Luther's understanding of the Anabaptists was actually quite limited; but his worst fears would likely have been confirmed if he had encountered Margret Hottinger, a young peasant from the village of Zollikon just outside the Swiss city of Zurich.

Though the Hottingers were people of limited means, the family was well known in the region for their interest in reading the Bible and their readiness to criticize the church on the basis of biblical teachings. In 1523, for example, authorities had arrested Margret's father, Jakob, following a heated argument with a local priest on the subject of communion. Soon thereafter, a story circulated that he had made disparaging comments about the Mass, richly illustrated with barnyard metaphors. The following year Catholic authorities from neighboring Luzern arrested Margret's uncle, Klaus Hottinger, for the crime of destroying a crucifix at a local shrine. He was beheaded for the deed, becoming one of the first martyrs of the Swiss reformation.

Margret herself became the focus of an investigation in February 1525 when she took the radical step of receiving baptism as an adult, an act the Zurich city council had denounced as a crime a few weeks earlier. According to her court testimony, she understood her baptism to be a natural application of Luther's principle of "Scripture alone." Margret assured authorities that she would gladly recant "if they could prove from Scripture that infant baptism is correct," but she did not find their arguments persuasive.

A month later, following an unsuccessful effort to extract a recantation, Margret and several others were sentenced to prison in the New Tower and given "nothing more than bread and water to eat, and straw to lay upon." "Thus let them die in the tower," the judgment concluded, unless they "are willing to desist from their opinion and error and be obedient." In May 1526, Margret appears to have recanted. She was released, but immediately afterward she began to preach and teach again, this time in the region of St. Gall, where she reportedly was even heard to prophesy. For the next several years Margret disappears from the record. Then in 1530 she and several colleagues were captured while attempting to flee to Moravia. This time the authorities showed no mercy: the last recorded notice of Margret Hottinger is a report of her execution by drowning.

This bare-bones account of Margret's short life raises many interesting questions. What, exactly, was it that she and her friends were teaching? Why did these new doctrines so terrify the authorities? And what compelled people like Margret to persist in their convictions, even to the point of death?

Anabaptist Beginnings in Switzerland

Margret Hottinger was part of a grassroots reform movement in the sixteenth century that opponents labeled *Anabaptist* (*Wiedertäufer,* or rebaptizers). Whereas Catholics and Protestants alike baptized infants, the Anabaptists insisted that true Christian baptism assumed a conscious commitment to follow Jesus—

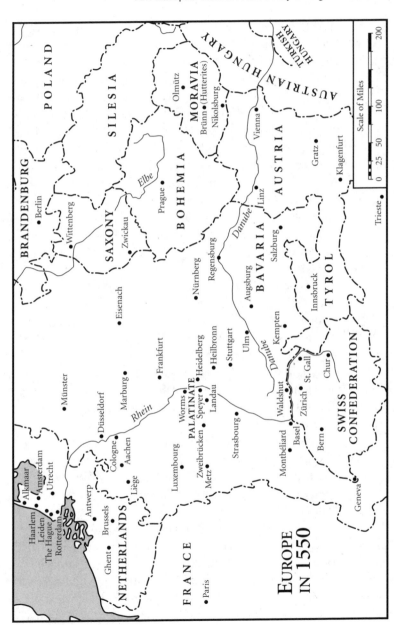

EUROPE IN 1550

something no infant could do. Members of the movement generally referred to themselves as "Brethren" (*Brüder*)—or later by the more descriptive term "Baptism-minded" (*Taufgesinnten*)—since in their minds they were not *re*baptizing, but rather baptizing correctly for the first time. Yet the name stuck, in part because "rebaptism" had long been a criminal offense in the Holy Roman Empire, punishable by death. Despite its negative overtones in the sixteenth century, *Anabaptist* has since become an accepted term for all Reformation groups who practiced believers (rather than infant) baptism, and the denominations descended from them such as the Amish, Mennonites, and Hutterites.

Anabaptist teachings represented something new and dangerous in early modern European society. By calling on Christians to refrain from swearing oaths, participating in lethal violence, or serving in magisterial offices, they seemed to threaten the foundations of political stability. The Anabaptist model of economic sharing and social equality unsettled those in positions of power. And by defining the church as a voluntary community, separated from the "fallen world," the Anabaptists raised doubts about whether Europe was entitled to call itself a "Christian" society.

Although these teachings do not sound so radical today, authorities in the sixteenth century thought they were both heretical (a threat to the church) and seditious (a threat to the state). Indeed, the theologians and princes of Europe were so troubled by Anabaptist teachings that they agreed the Anabaptists must be silenced. During the course of the sixteenth century, at least two thousand Anabaptists were executed for their convictions. Thousands more were imprisoned, tortured, and exiled.

It is tempting for the spiritual heirs of the Anabaptists to impose greater clarity on the beginnings of the movement than the historical facts permit. Anabaptism was clearly a product of its time, indebted to the religious heritage of the late Middle Ages and the swirling currents of reform unleashed by the Reformation. All of the earliest participants in the Anabaptist movement started out as Catholics—baptized as infants and raised in the rituals, images, and stories of late medieval Catholicism. But they also were caught up in the ferment and excitement of the Protestant Reformation. They read the pamphlets of the early reformers; they shared Luther's enthusiasm for Scripture; and they participated eagerly in lay Bible studies, always asking how Scripture might be applied to their lives.

Some converts to Anabaptism had been active in the Peasants' War and were disillusioned by its failure to transform social and political realities according to a biblical template. Others reflected the apocalyptic mood of the times, drawing from the prophetic writings of Daniel and Revelation a message of God's imminent judgment. Still others were gripped by the teachings of Jesus and assumed, naively perhaps, that the Sermon on the Mount and the story of the early church offered a kind of blueprint for contemporary Christians.

Like many grassroots movements, the early Anabaptists struggled to reach agreement on the principles that would distinguish the group's core membership from the fringe teachings of a few inspired eccentrics. As a whole, members of the movement were somewhat suspicious of formal theology, emphasizing instead concrete practices of Christian discipleship within the context of the local congregation. In addition, most of the first generation of educated leaders were executed very early. That painful fact, combined with the ongoing threat of persecution, made communication among Anabaptist leaders difficult, and it complicated efforts of the various Anabaptist groups to reach consensus in matters of belief and practice.

Over time, however, a coherent movement emerged. Its identity was forged, in part at least, by the need to respond to several basic challenges. First, in response to accusations of heresy by religious and political authorities in the first half of the sixteenth century, Anabaptists were quick to define themselves as faithful, Bible-believing Christians. Second, militant voices within their number who were ready to impose social and religious change with violence forced Anabaptists to clarify their identity as peaceful, law-abiding, nonresistant Christians whose only weapon was love. And finally, in the face of spiritualist dissenters who favored an internal religious experience that could avoid theological disputations and go undetected by authorities, Anabaptists were compelled to defend the public and visible nature of the church.

Despite the diversity of theology and practice evident in the first generation of Anabaptists, three coherent groups had emerged by the 1540s: the Swiss Brethren in the German-speaking territories; the Hutterites in Moravia; and the Mennonites of the Netherlands and North Germany who were organized around the leadership of Menno Simons. Although these groups differed in important ways, they nonetheless recognized each other as members of the same religious tradition, so that their internal disagreements often took the form of a family quarrel.

This chapter outlines the beginnings of these three Anabaptist groups—the Swiss Brethren, the Hutterites, and the Mennonites—amid the tumult of the sixteenth-century Reformation. The formation of an enduring institutional identity with traditions, doctrinal statements, and church structures will be the primary focus of the next chapter.

The Swiss Brethren in Switzerland and South Germany

The earliest forms of Anabaptism appeared in Zurich in the first half of the 1520s as an extension of the broader Reformation.

In 1519 the Zurich city council invited Ulrich Zwingli, a university-educated Catholic priest, to assume the pulpit of the Grossmünster Church. Zwingli shared with Luther a commitment to the principle of "Scripture alone" and a strong interest in church reform. Soon after his arrival in Zurich, he introduced a disciplined pattern of Bible study to a group of bright young students who were eager to read the New Testament in the original Greek and to apply its teachings to the renewal of the church. Zwingli also began to preach daily, captivating large audiences by his systematic study of the Gospels and the epistles, always searching for the contemporary relevance of the particular text.

In the course of their study, Zwingli and his students were quickly struck by the absence of a biblical basis for a host of traditional Catholic practices. Initially, their questions focused on the Mass. Why, for example, was the Mass in Latin? And why were common people permitted to receive the bread in communion but not the wine? Doubts also emerged about the biblical basis for such things as monasticism, clerical celibacy, and religious relics and images. In January 1523, as religious controversies of all sorts swirled throughout Europe, the Zurich city council held a formal debate about the city's religious future. Zwingli's appeal for reform won the day. The city council voted to break ties with the Catholic Church and declare the city for the "evangelical" cause. What that meant in practical terms, however, was still quite unclear.

In the meantime, other Bible study groups had begun to form, especially among villagers like the Hottinger family in the small towns and hamlets scattered around Zurich. As with Zwingli's circle, these groups were emboldened to criticize church traditions that could not be directly defended on the basis of Scripture. But their critique soon became even more radical. For example, where in the Bible could one find justification for the host of church tithes that peasants were expected to pay? On what basis were local congregations denied the right to select their own pastors? And most revolutionary, what was the biblical justification for infant baptism?

Gradually, a coalition formed between leaders of the rural Bible studies and the more radical elements in Zwingli's own study circle. Among the leaders of that inner circle were Conrad Grebel, a humanist scholar and son of a prominent Zurich family; George Blaurock, a former Catholic priest, noted for his hot temper; Felix Mantz, fluent in Latin, Greek, and Hebrew; and Simon Stumpf, one of the most radical of the group, who would be banished from the region already in December 1523.

Given the city council's expressed openness to "evangelical" reforms, the coalition began to pressure Zwingli to implement these changes immediately. In October 1523, the city council met again to consider arguments regarding the content and pace of church reforms. Aware that radical reforms, introduced suddenly, could lead to social and political upheaval, the council called for moderation. When Zwingli agreed with this decision, the first signs of division emerged.

Simon Stumpf, a spokesman for the radicals, challenged Zwingli directly: "You have no right to refer these questions to the council," Stumpf insisted. "The matter is already settled; the Spirit of God has decided." That claim—that the authority of Scripture and the Spirit trumped the authority of tradition, church hierarchy, and political expedience—marked the first use of an argument that the Anabaptists would return to again and again. And it was an argument they learned directly at the feet of Luther, Zwingli, and the other reformers.

In the year that followed, tensions between Zwingli and the more radical reformers continued to mount. The heart of the debate focused especially on baptism, though it seems that the radicals were also questioning the biblical basis for the oath and the Christian use of the sword. When some of the radicals refused to baptize their newborn babies—arguing that Christ's instructions in the great commission implied that teaching should precede baptism (see Matthew 28:19)—the city council responded fiercely. On March 7, 1524, it resurrected an ancient law that made "rebaptism" a capital offense.

First 'rebaptisms.' In January of the following year, the council issued an ultimatum demanding that the radicals baptize their infants or risk expulsion from the city. In defiance of the mandate, a small group gathered at the home of Felix Mantz's mother—a stone's throw away from the Grossmünster church—to plan a response. There, on January 21, 1525, George Blaurock, a former priest, asked Conrad Grebel to baptize him with water for the remission of his sins. According to an account preserved in the Hutterite *Chronicle,* Blaurock then baptized others at the meeting, thereby marking a symbolic beginning to the Anabaptist tradition.

Already by the next day, reports had begun to trickle into the city of additional baptisms in Wytikon and other villages surrounding Zurich. The rebaptism movement was spreading. Conrad Grebel was soon discovered baptizing new converts in Schaffhausen; George Blaurock went on a mission campaign into the Tyrol, southwest of Zurich; and Hans Brötli began baptizing in Hallau, as did Lorenz Hochrütner in St. Gall.

According to Sebastian Franck, a chronicler sympathetic to the Anabaptists, the movement "spread so rapidly that their teachings soon covered the whole land and they secured a large following and also added to their number many good hearts who were zealous toward God." Some details of Franck's account—his report of 1,500 baptisms in the Swiss city of Appenzell, for example—may have been an exaggeration. But the angry response of Zwingli and the Zurich city council suggests that they regarded the baptizing movement as a serious threat.

As with the early church, rapid growth was both a strength and a weakness of the Anabaptist movement. Clearly, the Anabaptist commitment to following Christ in daily life appealed to the hearts of many who were dissatisfied with Catholicism and the options offered them by the Protestant reformers. At the same time, however, it quickly became clear that not everyone shared the same understanding of what baptism actually meant.

Take, for example, Balthasar Hubmaier, a university-trained theologian and close friend of the Zurich radicals. Of all the early Anabaptists, Hubmaier was far and away the most articulate defender of adult baptism. In public debates with Zwingli and in his numerous publications, he consistently presented powerful biblical arguments in favor of the practice. However, Hubmaier did not necessarily link adult baptism with a voluntary, separated church, nor was he convinced that Christians should be nonresistant. Thus, in the spring of 1525, Hubmaier baptized virtually the entire town of Waldshut in one fell swoop. At the same time, he vigorously promoted the Twelve Articles of the Peasants' War and encouraged the citizens of Waldshut to arm themselves for battle against the Austrian government. Clearly, Hubmaier still held to a traditional Christendom view of society, one in which rebaptized believers might serve as magistrates and use violence to defend the "godly community" against evil-doers.

The Waldshut baptisms are a good illustration of the confusion about Anabaptist theology during these early years. In sharp contrast to Hubmaier, other early Anabaptist leaders insisted that true Christians could not swear oaths, serve as magistrates, or use coercive violence, even against their enemies. Some, following the example of the early church, taught a radical view of property that called on Christians to share their wealth with all in need. But in the very earliest phase of the Anabaptist movement, few of these teachings were held unanimously.

Although the Zurich radicals agreed that infant baptism and other aspects of medieval Catholicism were not scriptural, they were still a long way from consensus on the exact shape of the new church they were introducing in its place. The Spirit might indeed be "making all things new," but no one was quite certain just yet what these new things would look like.

The Schleitheim Confession. In the spring of 1527, two years after the first baptisms, a group of Anabaptists met in the small town of Schleitheim, a day's walk north of Zurich. There, under the leadership of Michael Sattler, a former Benedictine abbot, they agreed on seven principles that were basic to their understanding of faith. The Brotherly Union of Schleitheim—sometimes called the Schleitheim Confession—was not intended to be a systematic or comprehensive statement of Christian faith. The document was composed hurriedly, under the threat of imminent arrest and execution, and some of the original Zurich radicals—Hubmaier, for one—openly rejected the statement. But the written agreement provided a useful summary of shared convictions. In the century that followed, the central themes of the Schleitheim Confession, and occasionally the text itself, continued to resurface within many German-speaking Anabaptist congregations.

At the heart of the Schleitheim Confession is a view of the world in which the forces of good and evil are aligned against each other in a spiritual struggle. As actors in this cosmic battle, human beings are faced with a genuine choice: to act according to their natural impulses of greed, selfishness, and violence, or to pledge allegiance to Jesus, who teaches the principles of love, generosity, and peace. Baptism marks a transfer of allegiance, a "crossing over," from the kingdom of darkness (the world) to the kingdom of light (the church). Those who are baptized should separate themselves from the sinful practices of the world and promise to hold each other accountable for their actions and attitudes, following the pattern laid out by Christ in Matthew 18. The Lord's Supper should be understood as a symbol of the unity of believers in their commitment to Christ. Leaders are to wield their authority as gentle shepherds, not coercive kings. Christ's followers should respect governing officials but abstain from using the court systems or any form of violence to defend their rights. Likewise, believers should not serve in government positions that require the use of coercive force, but must instead treat all human beings—including enemies—with love. Finally, in keeping with the words of Jesus in the Sermon on the Mount, the Anabaptists at Schleitheim rejected the swearing of oaths, agreeing to keep their speech simple and to always speak the truth.

In short, the 1527 Schleitheim Confession affirmed a view of the church as a voluntary community separated from society at large and united by its commitment to Christ and the practices of obedience and discipline.

To modern Christians, these claims may not sound overly radical. But to the sixteenth-century authorities, the convictions expressed in the Schleitheim Confession posed a serious threat to religious and social order. From the perspective of Protestants and Catholics alike, the Anabaptists' refusal to baptize infants seemed callous, even cruel. Their claim to being a "separated" community—identifying everyone outside their fellowship as part of the fallen world—sounded arrogant. Civil authorities were especially troubled by the Anabaptist rejection of the civic oath and their suggestion that good Christians could not serve as magistrates or defend the territory against its enemies. With memories of the Peasants' War still fresh in mind, such arguments sounded like a formula for anarchy—as if Christians need not be concerned with social justice or political order.

In January 1527, two years after the first baptisms, the city council approved the execution by drowning of Felix Mantz. Mantz was the first Anabaptist to die in Zurich. His execution would soon be followed by the death of hundreds of other Anabaptists, and the arrest, interrogation, imprisonment, and torture of thousands more.

The Hutterites in Moravia

The seven articles of the Brotherly Union of Schleitheim were an effort to unify a movement that was in danger of spinning off in many different directions. But just as Luther was forced to recognize that a commitment to "Scripture alone" did not inevitably lead to unity, the radicals who broke with Zwingli in Zurich quickly discovered that a seven-point statement did not automatically result in broad agreement on all Anabaptist beliefs or practices. The Hutterites are a good case in point.

On the surface, the group that eventually became the Hutterites shared a great deal with the Swiss Brethren. Indeed, the Hutterites looked on the first adult baptisms in Zurich as the beginnings of their tradition, and they included the Schleitheim Confession among their treasured texts. Yet the combustible mixture of personalities, historical context, and new readings of Scripture created a Hutterian form of Anabaptism distinct from that of the Swiss Brethren.

The spiritual and genealogical roots of the Hutterites began in the Tyrol, a region southeast of Zurich under the jurisdiction of Archduke Ferdinand of Austria. As an ardent defender of the Catholic faith, Ferdinand did not hesitate to bring the full weight of his authority to bear against heretics of any sort, and especially against the Anabaptists.

In the face of the archduke's persecution, many Anabaptist converts in the Tyrol left their homes (and sometimes their families) and immigrated eastward to Moravia—a territory east of Austria now divided into Slovakia and the Czech Republic. Although the lords of Moravia were technically under the authority of the Hapsburg emperors, they had long ignored imperial edicts against religious dissidents. For more than a century—since the religious reforms of John Hus and the Czech Brethren in the early fifteenth century—the Moravian nobility had jealously guarded their liberties and privileges, including control over local religious life. Even though Hus was burned at the stake in 1415, his followers—the Hussites—were allowed to remain in Moravia, charting their own course in matters of religion. As a result, the region had gained a reputation for tolerating dissident religious groups. Toleration of religious minorities was a way for the local nobility to assert their independence in the face of Ferdinand's efforts to impose his control over the region. Thus, Moravia became a destination for thousands of Anabaptists refugees and a safe haven where they could practice their faith in relatively safety.

Hans Hut. George Blaurock, instigator of the original adult baptisms in Zurich, was one of the first Anabaptist missionaries to the Tyrol. Here and in other parts of Austria, the Anabaptist movement soon took on its own distinctive character, one heavily influenced by the experience of intense persecution, the currents of late medieval mysticism, and apocalyptic preaching oriented to Christ's imminent return. A key figure in all this was Hans Hut, a traveling book peddler, preacher, and close friend of Thomas Müntzer—the fiery preacher of social reform who had led the peasant army to its disastrous defeat at Frankenhausen in the spring of 1525. Hut was present at the battle and deeply shaken by the catastrophic end of the peasant uprising. But he did not give up on his vision of a renewed Christian social order.

Instead Hut reformulated his message in language that echoed nearly all the themes of Swiss Brethren Anabaptism, albeit with a distinctive mystical and apocalyptic twist. For example, Hut shared the Swiss Brethren emphasis on following Jesus in the suffering of the cross as well as in the glory of his resurrection; but the language he used to describe this—with numerous references to yieldedness (*Gelassenheit*), suffering, and purification—sounded very much like late medieval mysticism. Like the Swiss Brethren, Hut rejected violence, but only as a temporary measure until Christ returned to lead his followers in a final decisive battle against the forces of evil. In a similar way, Hut, like the Swiss Brethren, baptized adults (hence, he was a "rebaptizer"). But he did so by marking converts on their foreheads with the "sign of the Thau," a spiritual symbol that would distinguish the 144,000 elect mentioned in Revelation from the ungodly on the day of judgment.

When Hut's confident prediction that Christ would return at Pentecost 1528 did not come to pass, he accepted the counsel of other Anabaptists to cease speculation about the date of the judgment day. Still, the mystical and apocalyptic themes in Hut's preaching hints at the range of expressions evident among the first generation of Anabaptist leaders.

In May 1527 Hut's travels took him to Nikolsburg, Moravia, a thriving commercial city where hundreds of Anabaptists and other religious dissidents had found refuge under the benevolent protection of the Lords of Liechtenstein. Before Hut's arrival in Nikolsburg, Balthasar Hubmaier had won over the local prince, Leonard of Liechtenstein, to the Anabaptist cause, albeit with the understanding that a Christian magistrate could legitimately serve in government and use the sword. Hut, by contrast, publicly rejected the idea of a Christian magistrate, denounced all forms of lethal violence, and reiterated his themes of suffering as the Christian calling.

Not surprisingly, Hut's teachings quickly came into conflict with Hubmaier, who insisted on a formal disputation to resolve their differences. Just as predictably, the Lords of Liechtenstein, who adjudicated the debate, ruled against Hut. As a result he and some two hundred of his followers—who called themselves *Stäbler* (or "staff bearers") to distinguish themselves from the *Schwertler* ("sword bearers")—were forced to flee Nikolsburg in the dead of winter.

Just outside the city they laid out a blanket and asked everyone to pool their possessions. Historians differ as to whether the decision behind the radical step of "community of goods" was based primarily on Scripture or whether it was the result of economic necessity. Clearly, the concept of mutual aid had been an important part of Swiss Anabaptism from the start. But this gesture of sharing by Hut's followers moved beyond an occasional and voluntary act to an explicit rejection of all private property. Whatever the motivation, the group continued to share their material goods, even after finding safe haven in the nearby town of Austerlitz, and the practice became a defining feature.

The social and economic equality practiced by Hut's followers at Austerlitz quickly attracted hundreds of curiosity-seekers and converts, drawn by a combination of religious ideals and the prospects of economic security. In December 1530, Wilhelm Reublin, one of the earliest radicals in Zurich, arrived at Austerlitz eager to witness a functioning model of radical Christian community. His expectations, however, were soon dashed. According to his account, leaders of the Austerlitz community were authoritarian (imposing marriages on unwilling couples, for example), and they were taking the best food and accommodations for themselves. When Reublin began preaching and holding Bible studies on his own, the leaders tried to silence him. In response, he convinced a splinter group of some 150 discontented Austerlitzers to form a new settlement in the Moravian city of Auspitz. No sooner had Reublin's group established itself in Auspitz then a colleague revealed that Reublin himself had hidden a private sum of cash, despite the fact that the community was desperately short of resources. Reublin departed in disgrace.

Jacob Hutter. Over the next two years, the Auspitz group struggled mightily to sort through issues of leadership and organization. Finally, in 1533, a successful missionary preacher from the Tyrol named Jacob Hutter assumed leadership and brought a new sense of administrative order, especially in the area of community of goods. Although Hutter would be martyred only two years later, the stability he imparted to the group is reflected in the fact that the Auspitz community adopted his name, becoming the Hutterites. Shortly thereafter, Peter Riedemann, another gifted leader, produced a lengthy statement on Hutterite beliefs. Although it did not prevent disagreements in later years, Riedemann's *Account of Our Faith* provided the Hutterites with a theological foundation for their community.

Complex though it may sound, the story of Hutterite origins recounted here is actually a simplified version of the events that unfolded between 1527 and 1533. However, enough of that narrative has been told to make it clear that the Hutterites, like the Swiss Brethren, did not emerge instantaneously as a fully formed community based only on a simple reading of the New Testament. Like most Spirit-led movements, the Hutterites were born in the midst of fluid, sometimes messy circumstances. Clarity of leadership, organization, and theology emerged only gradually as a result of intense debates about the precise form the movement would assume.

This same challenge—discerning how the "word is made flesh"—was a central theme in the story of a third branch of Anabaptism that took shape in North Germany and the Netherlands.

The Melchiorite/Münsterites in the Netherlands

As the Hutterites were moving toward a form of Anabaptism characterized by tightly structured communities in which members shared all their possessions, Anabaptists in North Germany and the Netherlands were moving in a rather different direction. In northern Europe the early Anabaptist movement was dominated by Melchior Hoffman, a zealous evangelist and self-styled prophet whose teachings made a profound impact on the character of the Anabaptist movement in the region.

As a young man, Hoffman was attracted to the teachings of Luther, and he began to promote Lutheran doctrine as a traveling preacher in Catholic regions. Like many early reformers, Hoffman associated faith with an intimate encounter with the Holy Spirit.

Because God was Spirit, he reasoned, and because Christians were to worship God "in spirit and in truth" (John 4:24), everything external and "nonspiritual" (religious images, for example) was an impediment to true faith. So he traveled throughout North Germany and Sweden, preaching fiery sermons against Catholic religious statues, images, altars, and relics, and leading several rampages through churches and monasteries aimed at destroying "idols."

Hoffman's anticlerical message and the promise of a new, purified Christian order was especially appealing to the poor. Not surprisingly, his actions also aroused the hostility of local authorities and other reformers. Even though Luther had once written a letter recommending Hoffman for a pastorate, by 1529 he firmly distanced himself from any association with his teachings and actions.

Eventually, Hoffman's travels took him to Strasbourg, a city on the Rhine located in present-day France. In the sixteenth century Strasbourg was an independent city and a haven for all sorts of religious dissidents. There Hoffman was won to Anabaptism, and he began to preach and practice adult baptism. At the same time, his biblical studies—drawing especially on the books of Daniel and Revelation—increasingly focused on the end times, leading to confident assertions regarding Christ's imminent return. Hoffman began to preach that he was the first of two witnesses prophesied in Revelation 12, called directly by God to gather 144,000 of the elect to await the second coming.

Like Hut, Hoffman understood baptism as a spiritual seal that marked the believer as a member of the elect. He also began teaching his own distinctive understanding of the incarnation, namely, that Jesus had a "heavenly flesh" untainted by any human physical qualities. Though born of Mary, Jesus passed through her "like water through a tube," thereby retaining his divine character.

When Dutch authorities, under pressure from the Habsburg emperor, began to crack down on Hoffman, he quickly incorporated the experience of suffering into his apocalyptic vision. That is, until December 1531, when one of his converts, Jan Volkerts

Trijpmaker, was executed as an Anabaptist. The experience so sobered Hoffman that he backed away from all external sacraments, including baptism, and urged his followers to practice a secretive and spiritualist faith.

Hoffman also spread the word that Christ would return directly to Strasbourg on Easter 1533. The Strasbourg city council, tired of such claims and the Anabaptist movement as a whole, ordered that Hoffman be thrown into prison when he returned to the city in anticipation of Christ's second coming. In the spring of 1533 the appointed date of the Lord's return came and went with Hoffman languishing behind bars. Ten years later, he died in prison—broken, ignored, and irrelevant.

Even though Hoffman was gone from the scene, his teachings nevertheless continued to live on. One disciple, Jan Matthijs, a baker from Haarlem, argued that Hoffman had been wrong only about the place and the date of Christ's return. Claiming to be the second witness prophesied in Revelation 12, Matthijs called on Hoffman's disappointed disciples and other new converts to leave their homes and join him in the north German city of Münster. There they would form the vanguard of a holy army that would destroy the wicked and godless when Christ returned in glory. As believers began to make their way to Münster, rumors swept through the Netherlands, inspiring hope among ordinary churchgoers and fear among the authorities. At one point, a group of Melchiorites ran through Amsterdam, waving swords and calling out warnings about the imminent wrath of God.

Several weeks later, in a mixture of apocalyptic fervor and street theater, another group took off their clothes and ran naked through the streets of Amsterdam, calling on the citizens of the city to repent and join their cause. Then in March 1535, a band of some three hundred armed Melchiorites marched in the direction of Münster but were detained by local authorities. They resisted arrest and holed up in the Oldesklooster, a local monastery. Following a siege of the cloister, a bloody battle broke out in which half of the group lost their lives.

The Münster Tragedy. Meanwhile, initiatives in the city of Münster for religious reform had brought the guilds into conflict with the Catholic Church as both struggled for control of the city council. Initially, the council sought to maintain a neutral position, but slowly civic support shifted in favor of the reformers. Leading the reform movement was a former Catholic priest named Bernhard Rothmann. Rothmann had come under the influence of Melchiorite teaching and began to implement believers baptism—a radical step for the city council since rebaptism was an imperial crime. When voices on the council called for restraint, Rothmann's Anabaptist supporters managed to gain a majority during the February 1534 elections, effectively taking control of the city.

The events that followed were both tragic and farcical. In response to the rising power of the Anabaptist party, the Catholic Bishop of Waldeck raised an army to retake the city by force. In the meantime, Matthijs moved into Münster with many of his followers and began to prepare the inhabitants for a violent confrontation. He announced that Münster was the New Jerusalem and initiated a program of radical reform that included mandatory baptism, enforced community of goods, and preparations for Christ's return on Easter 1534 to vanquish the godless. As with Hoffman, the events Matthijs had predicted failed to materialize. Undaunted, he led a small squad of armed men in a wild charge against the besieging army. Matthijs was killed immediately; his head was cut off and mounted on a pike where all the inhabitants of the city could see it.

Matthijs's sudden death and the failure of the prophecy led to still more radical measures. Leadership now fell into the hands of twenty-four-year-old Jan of Leiden, an actor who was more at home with the pageantry of Old Testament kingship than with the New Testament gospel. Jan saw himself as the reincarnation of King David. He replaced the elected council with twelve elders; introduced polygamy; proclaimed the Anabaptist Kingdom of Münster, complete with its own currency; and in September 1534, declared himself "King of the New Israel and of the whole world." In the face of dissent, Jan resorted to public executions and dramatically staged demonstrations of his absolute authority.

By the spring of 1535, the faithful who had gathered in Münster were hungry and exhausted. They had come to the city convinced that they were players in the fulfillment of a divine plan. Now they were tired and disappointed. On June 25, 1535, allied Protestant and Catholic troops stormed city. The bloody massacre that ensued brought a decisive end to the Anabaptist Kingdom of Münster. Leaders who survived the battle were interrogated, tortured with red-hot tongs, and then executed—their bodies exposed to the public in three iron cages hoisted to the top of the bell tower of the Lamberti church. The cages can still be seen to this day. Indeed, centuries after the ill-fated event, the story of the so-called Anabaptist Kingdom of Münster continues to live in the European imagination as the only Anabaptist story that really mattered. In the eyes of many, the tragic events revealed the true character of the Anabaptist movement: fanatical, heretical, and dangerous.

Keeping a Movement on Track

Like all good stories, the account of Anabaptist beginnings amid the tumultuous upheaval of the sixteenth-century Reformation is filled with a host of colorful characters, an intricate storyline, and numerous complex subplots. Yet overarching the sound and the fury of these details, the traces of a coherent narrative can still be found.

The Swiss Brethren, Hutterites, and Melchiorites all emerged out of the same soil. They all drew deeply on forms of piety inherited from late medieval Catholic spirituality; they all were indebted to the Protestant reformers of their day for a new awareness of the power of Scripture as the "Word of God"; and they all reflected something of the utopian vision of the peasant revolutionaries who tried, unsuccessfully, to restructure medieval village life around a New Testament blueprint. With few exceptions, the first generation of Anabaptist leaders shared a commitment to the radical principle of voluntary, or believers, baptism. They envisioned the church as a gathered community of true believers, followers of Christ who were ready to leave behind the safety of tradition and assumptions of Christendom to shape an alternative community.

Yet despite these shared convictions, the shape of this new community could vary widely, as we have seen, depending on local circumstances and the influence of key leaders. By the 1540s the Swiss Brethren, the Hutterites, and the Melchiorites were reasonably well-established as distinctive expressions of Anabaptism. Yet they all faced a similar challenge, the same challenge the early church confronted soon after Pentecost: how to move beyond the initial excitement of a radical movement to more stable and enduring forms of community. That story, the shift from movement to structure, is the focus of the following chapter.

5

Mennonites in Europe

New Reforms, New Structures

In 1648 Arent Dircksz Bosch, a well-to-do Mennonite merchant in Amsterdam, built a retirement home (*hofje*) consisting of eight apartments for impoverished widows in his congregation. At the same time, he established an endowment to ensure that they would enjoy some measure of financial security in their old age. Bosch was a wealthy man; yet, like many other Dutch Mennonites of his generation, his fortune was earned, not inherited. As a young man, Bosch had borrowed money to invest in the wholesale grain trade that was flourishing in the port cities of the Netherlands. He then parlayed those profits into contracts with the lucrative Baltic shipping industry. Finally, drawing on his network of family and church contacts, Bosch invested heavily in real estate, building several large warehouses and a luxurious home located in a prestigious section of Amsterdam. Throughout his life, he remained closely connected to his Waterlander Mennonite congregation. For more than forty years he served as a deacon of the church, a role that brought him into regular contact with the very poorest members of the congregation. The retirement home Bosch built for the widows of his church—still standing today—represents only a fraction of his philanthropic efforts on behalf of the needy in his community.

Part of what makes Bosch's story so remarkable is the very fact of its ordinariness. By the middle of the seventeenth century, the descendants of the Anabaptists in the Netherlands had undergone a dramatic transformation from a movement of persecuted, impoverished artisans living in the shadow of the debacle at Münster to an established church claiming among its membership some of the wealthiest people in the country. Though Mennonites, as they were known in the Netherlands, were forced to meet in "hidden churches" and still excluded from prominent political positions, their members played a leading role in the seventeenth- and eighteenth-century renaissance of Dutch economic, artistic, and intellectual life known as the Dutch Golden Age, all the while remaining fully committed to the Anabaptist-Mennonite faith tradition.

The Nature of the New Struggles

By the middle of the sixteenth century, the Anabaptist movement had crystallized into three distinct groups: the Dutch Mennonites in the Netherlands and North Germany; the Hutterites in Moravia; and the Swiss Brethren in Switzerland and South Germany. Despite significant differences, each of the groups faced a similar challenge, a challenge deeply rooted in the biblical story and the history of the Christian church. How can a movement of radical renewal maintain its identity into the second and third generations?

For the first generation of Anabaptists, baptized as infants and raised in Catholic homes, rebaptism implied a radical break with the past. By the middle of the sixteenth century, however, a new generation of children had been born to Anabaptist parents and raised in settings predisposed to Anabaptist doctrines and practices. For them, the context of their decision regarding faith was quite different from that of their parents.

The world had shifted politically as well. In the aftermath of the tragedy at Münster, second- and third-generation Anabaptist leaders went to great lengths to persuade government officials that they were "harmless" and "defenseless" Christians who posed no threat to political stability. Moreover, Anabaptist communities sought to demonstrate their social and economic usefulness to their neighbors by becoming exemplary models of hard work, self-discipline, and moral rectitude. These characteristics—harmlessness, productivity, discipline—became hallmarks of all Anabaptist groups in Europe between 1550 and 1800.

The desire for respectability is also suggested in the new labels that Anabaptist groups adopted for themselves. Since the term *Anabaptist* (*Wiedertäufer*) was both technically inaccurate (they were not "rebaptizing" but baptizing correctly for the first time) and so closely associated with the episode at Münster, later generations took great pains to identify themselves by other names. Thus the Dutch Anabaptists preferred the term *Doopsgezinden* (Baptism-minded) or Mennonite, after their influential leader, Menno Simons. The Anabaptists who practiced community of goods in Moravia became known as the Hutterites, in recognition of Jacob Hutter. The group that formed around the Schleitheim Confession adopted the name Swiss Brethren, despite the fact that their congregations were scattered far beyond Switzerland and many of their members were of German rather than Swiss descent.

New systems of authority, clearer theological guidelines, and more routine forms of congregational life provided each of these groups with needed stability. But all of these changes, which were crucial to the long-term survival of Anabaptism, also created new problems. For example, as Anabaptists sought to convince their neighbors that they posed no threat to social order, they became less zealous in their missionary outreach and more likely to make compromises with the culture around them. As Anabaptists moved into the second generation, their children were raised within the boundaries of a religious subculture, raising new questions about the principle of "voluntary" baptism. As Anabaptists became wealthier and more integrated into the larger economy, the gap between the rich and the poor in their congregations began to widen. And the desire to prove themselves as trustworthy subjects led some Anabaptist groups to soften their position on nonresistance.

Anabaptist-Mennonite history from 1550 to 1800 is the story of this tension and the challenge to remain faithful stewards of a radical tradition within the context of institutionalization and acculturation. The account of Arent Dircksz Bosch at the outset of this chapter is a reminder that finding a balance between these opposing forces is not destined to failure. But the ongoing struggle to clarify the path of faithful discipleship was real. At their best, the Mennonites, Hutterites, and Swiss Brethren managed to hold these tensions in a creative balance; at their worst, they allowed their distinctive witness to disappear altogether as they were absorbed into the surrounding culture.

Dutch Mennonites: Between Affluence and Stewardship

From Münster to Menno. Without a doubt, the formative moment in the early history of Anabaptism in the Netherlands and North Germany was the tragedy that unfolded in Münster in 1534 and 1535. The collapse of the Anabaptist Kingdom of Münster left hundreds of people dead and thousands more deeply disillusioned, either as a result of Jan of Leiden's tyrannical "justice" or from the fighting that ensued between the city's defenders and the besieging troops. On a larger scale, the episode confirmed the worst fears of the government and the church, namely that the Anabaptists were seditious, wild-eyed revolutionaries who recognized no authority other than themselves and were determined to turn the world upside-down. As a result, a new wave of anti-Anabaptist persecution rolled across Europe.

Yet out of the ashes of Münster, a new Anabaptist group emerged. Led by Menno Simons (1496-1561), a Catholic priest turned radical reformer, Anabaptism in northern Europe regained its theological moorings. To a movement of uneducated peasants and disillusioned artisans, Menno brought a renewed commitment to Scripture, anchoring the distinctive themes of the radical reformation within the broader categories of orthodox Christianity. The group that gathered around his energetic leadership was dedicated to a biblicism shorn of apocalyptic visions, to an ethic of suffering love in all human relations and to a vision of a disciplined, visible church committed to Christian discipleship in daily life.

Reformer on the run. Menno was born in 1496 in the small town of Witmarsum in Friesland. The son of a farmer, he attended grammar school at a monastery, where he likely learned Latin and gained some familiarity with the early church fathers. At the age of fifteen, Menno entered a novitiate for the priesthood. Five years later he became a deacon in the Catholic Church, and soon thereafter he began his first formal assignment as a vicar in Pingjum, his father's native village.

Even as a young priest, Menno had doubts about his spiritual calling. Like many of his Dutch contemporaries, he had deep misgivings about Catholic teachings on baptism and the sacrament of communion, and he acknowledged that he devoted much of his time to "playing cards, drinking, and frivolities of all sorts." But in 1531 the martyrdom of Sicke Freeriks Snijder—"a god-fearing, pious hero," beheaded as an Anabaptist in nearby Leeuwarden—drove Menno to reread the Bible. "I examined the Scriptures diligently," he wrote later, "and pondered them earnestly, but could find no report of infant baptism."

Still, Menno wavered. Though intrigued by the Anabaptist movement, he nonetheless accepted a promotion as a priest in his home church at Witmarsum in 1531 and continued to carry out the duties of that office for the next three years, all the while struggling with the tension between his understanding of Scripture and the Catholic tradition he had inherited.

In the end, it was not a new theological insight that led Menno to break with the church, but rather the fanatical excesses of the Anabaptist movement itself. In the spring of 1535, as the horrors of the Münsterite kingdom unfolded, Menno penned his first surviving tract—a polemic against Jan of Leiden, in which he denounced the visions and violence of the Münsterites and advocated a method for interpreting Scripture based firmly on the teachings of Christ. For the next nine months, Menno preached his new message of practical Christianity from the pulpit of his parish church in Witmarsum.

Finally, on January 20, 1536—just as public sentiment against the Anabaptists reached a crescendo—Menno resigned his priestly office, gave up the salary, status, and security of his former identity, and publicly aligned himself with the Anabaptist cause. "Without constraint," he wrote, "I renounced all my worldly reputation, name, and fame, my unchristian abominations, my masses, my infant baptism, and my easy life, and I willingly submitted to distress and poverty under the heavy cross of Christ." Shortly thereafter Obbe Philips, leader of the beleaguered pacifist remnant of Dutch Anabaptism, ordained Menno as an Anabaptist pastor.

Immediately, Menno set out to rebuild the scattered and dispirited fellowship. For the next three decades, he and his wife, Gertrude, traveled almost constantly—preaching, baptizing, and instructing new believers in the faith. Somehow he managed to evade capture, despite a sizeable bounty offered for his arrest. Along the way, Menno wrote dozens of letters, commentaries, admonitions, and refutations, publishing them in secret presses. His most systematic theological writing, *The Foundation Book* (1539), went through several revisions in the following decades and eventually appeared in German in 1575.

No other foundation. Menno was among the first Anabaptist theologians to publish his thought in print, giving his teachings considerable influence beyond his own circle. His focus was consistently on Christ, both the practical teachings of Jesus and his saving work in the cross and resurrection. Indeed, these themes were so central to Menno's thought that the title page of every book he published included the inscription "For no one can lay any foundation other than the one already laid, which is Jesus Christ" (1 Corinthians 3:11).

The transformation of the Christian into a "new creature," Menno argued, is made possible only through Christ's atoning sacrifice. But in the very next breath, he insisted that this new birth was more than simply an opportunity to have one's sins forgiven. The gift of grace must lead to a life of Christian discipleship. It will not "help a fig," he wrote, "to boast of the Lord's blood, death, merits, grace or gospel if the believer is not truly converted from his sinful life." Becoming "like minded with Jesus" implied a commitment to actually live like Jesus. Menno wrote, "True evangelical faith cannot lie dormant. It clothes the naked, it feeds the hungry, it comforts the sorrowful, it shelters the destitute, it serves those that harm it, it binds up that which is wounded, it has become all things to all people."

Many of Menno's writings sought to describe the characteristics of the church. He argued that the true body of Christ would be found not in the state-dominated churches of Christendom, but in the voluntary gathering of believers who pledged themselves to study Scripture, follow Jesus in daily life, and practice mutual aid. This community was an alternative society where violence and coercive force had no place. Here discipline practiced according to the teaching of Jesus in Matthew 18 could happen in Christian love. By presenting itself as the bride of the risen Christ "without stain or wrinkle or any other blemish" (Ephesians 5:27), the church offered the world a collective witness to the resurrected Christ. The church was Christ's body made visible.

The violence at Münster had also convinced Menno of the profound danger of confusing Christian convictions with the power of the sword. Thus, in all his writings, Menno challenged his readers to reconsider Christ's teachings on peace and particularly the alliance medieval Christians had made with the political order. God offered the gift of unconditional love, Menno insisted, while humans were still enemies of God, alienated from him (see Romans 5:8-11). The gift of God's grace has world-transforming power precisely because it enables followers of Jesus to express that same grace-filled love to others, including those who might be considered their enemies. "The Prince of Peace is Jesus Christ," wrote Menno. "We who were formerly no people at all, and who knew of no peace, are now called to be . . . a church . . . of peace. True Christians do not know vengeance. They are the children of peace. Their hearts overflow with peace. Their mouths speak peace, and they walk in the way of peace."

Even though Menno was clear in renouncing lethal violence, his own writings frequently took on a polemical tone as he defended Anabaptists against attacks from without (such as the Reformed theologians John a Lasco, Martin Micron, and Adam Pastor) and heresy from within (such as David Joris, on the question of prophetic visions).

In 1557 a painful conflict divided his own group over the issue of church discipline. Along with his co-workers Dirk Philips and Leneart Bouwens, Menno argued that congregations should not only withhold communion from members under church discipline, but they should also practice social avoidance, or shunning. When Menno insisted that shunning must also apply to married couples—so that one spouse could have no contact with the other—a small group of his followers withdrew in protest. Since many of them came from the low-lying wetlands of northern Holland, they became known as the Waterlanders. The division of 1557 cast something of a shadow on the last years of Menno's life, especially since the schism—and others to follow—persisted until the Mennonites (*Doopsgezinden*) were reunited again early in the nineteenth century.

Menno died on January 31, 1561, at the age of sixty-five in Fresenberg.

The path to toleration. The history of Anabaptism in the Netherlands after Menno's death unfolded against the backdrop of a long war (1568-1648) that pitted the northern Protestant provinces against Spanish armies under the Catholic rule of Philip II, who dominated the southern provinces (now Belgium). When in 1581 the seven northern provinces declared their independence as the Dutch Republic, the newly formed country made the economic well-being of its merchants, whalers, and bankers a higher priority than religious uniformity. The Reformed Church enjoyed a privileged legal status in the new republic, but the new government under William of Orange also established freedoms for minority religious groups, such as the Mennonites, thereby bringing an end to open persecution. To be sure, Mennonites were still not permitted to participate in politics, attend Reformed seminaries, or hold worship services in public. However, they were free to gather for worship in their own "hidden churches," and they were allowed to participate fully in the growing commercial and cultural life of Dutch society. Amsterdam, the republic's center of commerce and culture, quickly gained a reputation as a refuge for Mennonites and many other religious dissidents.

The period from 1600 to 1800 was an era of remarkable religious, cultural, and economic vitality in the Dutch Republic. By the middle of the seventeenth century, Mennonites were participating fully in the creative flourishing of culture of the Dutch Golden Age. In the world of business, for example, their work ethic, frugality, honesty, and network of family and congregational connections made them leaders in a host of profitable industries—especially shipping, salt production, textiles, and the manufacture of decorative tiles—and earned them the nickname "worker bees of the state." Mennonites gained widespread recognition for their engineering skills, harnessing wind power to drain the polders and reclaim fertile farmland from the North Sea.

In the printing industry, Mennonites took the lead as publishers, mapmakers, and compilers of almanacs. Artists like Solomon Ruysdael, Govert Flinck, and Jan Luyken, along with the art historian, Karel van Mander, and the most famous literary figure of the Dutch eighteenth century, Joost von Vondel, were all Mennonites. Barred from the theological faculties of the universities, Mennonites instead frequently sent their most gifted students to medical school. One of the most famous Mennonite physicians, Govert Bidloo (1649-1713), published an anatomical textbook and served as a professor of medicine in the Dutch town of Leiden. Many of these trained physicians in the seventeenth and eighteenth century also served as pastors.

Wealthy Dutch Mennonites were also quick to apply their entrepreneurial and organizational skills to church life. Already in the early seventeenth century, Dutch Mennonites were establishing hostels for the chronically ill, the aged, and members with disabilities. In virtually every congregation, a board of deacons met regularly to consider requests for financial assistance from the poor in their midst. One congregation in Amsterdam even paid a local surgeon a retainer fee with the understanding that he would treat any of its members without additional charge. The physician was to provide his own "salve, plasters, gargling fluid, waters and cooling-draughts," while the deacons provided necessary medicines from the apothecary.

Challenges: divisions and affluence. In the midst of this dynamic cultural and economic growth, Dutch Mennonites struggled to maintain unity within the church, often unsuccessfully. Like the split between Menno's followers and the Waterlanders in 1557, most of the divisions that occurred in the course of the seventeenth century were the result of disagreements over specific church practices rather than debates about doctrine. Thus, for example, Menno's followers divided in the 1560s into the Friesen and the Flemish, with both groups subdividing again at least once more before the end of the century. Efforts at reconciliation often had the paradoxical effect of creating still more divisions, as stalwart defenders broke away from those willing to compromise for the sake of unity.

The energy, resources, and ill will expended in those internal debates clearly diverted the church from its public witness. On the other hand, the church conflicts tended to cultivate committed and articulate leaders who were theologically astute, well-versed in Scripture, and quick to put their thoughts into print. Thus Dutch Mennonite groups published hundreds of confessions of faith, sermons, catechisms, hymns, and devotional literature in the course of the seventeenth and eighteenth centuries, both to defend their own positions and to establish a basis for reconciliation with others. By 1800 some 150 different *Doopsgezinden* hymnbooks had been produced, containing an estimated fifteen thousand songs. The sheer volume of sources related to Dutch Mennonites between 1550 and 1800 overwhelms that of all other Anabaptist groups.

If church divisions had both a shadow and a light side, so too did the phenomenal economic success of the Dutch Mennonites. One positive consequence of Mennonite prosperity occurred in the late seventeenth century when two Waterlander groups—the Lamists and the Zonists, still divided by an intensely bitter conflict in 1664—agreed to pool their resources in a joint Committee for Foreign Relief to assist Swiss Brethren refugees who were being forced out of their homes in Zurich and Bern. Between 1690 and 1694, the committee collected fifty thousand guldens for Swiss Brethren refugees in the Palatinate; and between 1710 and 1711 it helped hundreds of Swiss Brethren and Amish resettle from Switzerland to the Palatinate, the Netherlands, and America. In 1735 Dutch Mennonites used their resources to establish their own seminary, an initiative that eventually became the impetus for the union of most Waterlander and Mennonite groups in 1811 under the umbrella of the General Mennonite Conference (ADS). And in 1847 Mennonites in the Netherlands created the Dutch Mennonite Missionary Association, a cooperative mission outreach that drew support from Mennonites in Russia, Germany, and Switzerland as well. In these, and in dozens of other ways, Dutch Mennonites demonstrated how financial resources and organizational skills could be made to serve Anabaptist principles.

Yet affluence and social respectability were also fraught with ambiguities. For example, in 1572 Dutch Mennonites agreed to contribute one thousand guldens to William of Orange's military campaign against the Catholics, a demonstration of support for the new republic that might have been intended as "protection money" but unavoidably raised questions about their long-term commitment to the principle of nonresistance. Contemporary critics leveled charges of hypocrisy when Mennonites began to build sumptuous residences in the wealthiest parts of town while continuing to espouse principles of simplicity and egalitarianism. When Swiss Brethren refugees found their way into Mennonite churches in Rotterdam and Amsterdam, observers could not help but contrast their simple faith and impoverished condition with the affluence and sophistication of their Dutch Mennonite cousins in the Netherlands. In his preface to the *Martyrs Mirror*—a massive, coffee-table collection of martyr stories—compiler Thieleman van Braght expressed the hope that these stories would help Dutch Mennonites, at the peak of their economic and cultural success, remember that religious commitments could also lead to suffering.

So the Dutch Mennonite story between 1550 and 1800 is something of a paradox. Blessed with religious toleration and civil liberties, Mennonites in the Netherlands entered vigorously into the cultural, economic, and social life of their day. Many used their new-found wealth to support church-related projects that addressed the needs of the poor, supported theological education, and funded numerous other philanthropic initiatives. Yet despite this remarkable display of generosity and organizational zeal, Mennonite identity in the Netherlands became increasingly blurred. Measured in terms of membership statistics, it would appear as if Anabaptism in the Netherlands was not sustainable in the long term. In 1700 Mennonites numbered around 160,000 baptized members, representing 10 percent of the Dutch population. By 1830 that number had fallen to around 30,000 and to 11,000 by 2003.

The precipitous decline of Mennonites in the Netherlands raises a troubling question. Can the Anabaptist tradition be sustained in circumstances of wealth and social prestige? Or were cultural developments—the impact of Enlightenment rationalism, for example—the primary cause of the decline? Should Mennonites regard prosperity, higher education, and social prestige as a sign of God's blessing or as a threat to their deepest convictions? Can a church in the Anabaptist tradition retain its radical witness in the midst of affluence and cultural assimilation?

Hutterites: Between Success and Survival

If the Dutch Mennonites represent one extreme of Anabaptism—prosperity in the midst of a tolerant society—the Hutterites moved in the opposite direction. As the most radical of all the Anabaptist groups, the Hutterites rejected private property, refused to pay war taxes, and adopted a communitarian style of life that drew clear boundaries between their congregations and "the world." The history of the Hutterites is filled with stories of suffering and persecution; indeed, that they survived at all is a kind of miracle. Yet during the middle decades of the sixteenth century, the Hutterites flourished in Moravia. Thanks largely to their economic productivity, Hutterite communities played a crucial role in the regional economy and, for a time at least, led to a remarkable degree of protection from their local lords.

Structure and theology of Hutterite communities. Historians often refer to the second half of the sixteenth century as the Hutterite Golden Age. And with good reason. By the middle of the sixteenth century, the Hutterites in Moravia were going through an organizational revolution. Each Hutterite community was a self-contained economic unit, ranging in size from fifty to five hundred members. Leadership in the community was clearly defined. Servants of the Word, who tended primarily to spiritual matters, shared authority with stewards who were in charge of economic decisions, and with schoolmasters who oversaw the education of children, beginning at age two.

Contemporary descriptions of Hutterite colonies as "beehives" or "dovecotes" were intended to be derogatory. But the Hutterites themselves regarded such metaphors as appropriate descriptions of their well-ordered communities that elevated "common good over personal good." Virtually every aspect of community life was tightly regulated. Each adult in the community had a task to perform, either in domestic labor, in agriculture, or, most commonly, as artisans.

Everyone who joined the Hutterites, regardless of age or status, was expected to learn a trade. Skilled handcrafts were the economic engine of Hutterite communities. Governed by written regulations and modeled after the constitutions of medieval guilds, Hutterite workshops quickly gained a reputation for high standards of craftsmanship. By purchasing raw materials in bulk and by keeping labor costs to a minimum, Hutterite communities were able to produce goods at greater volume and sell them for lower prices than their local competitors—a fact that made them popular among their aristocratic customers but resented by the local population.

Initially, Hutterite workshops focused on producing necessities like pottery, cutlery, mason work, knives, roof thatching, wagons, carpentry, locks, barrels, and leather crafts. By the middle of the sixteenth century, however, Hutterite craftsmen had branched out into luxury items that required highly specialized skills. References to exquisitely decorated porcelain, for example, along with Hutterite-produced crocks, knives, and cutlery regularly appear in the household inventories of the Moravian nobility.

The nobility also looked to the Hutterites as trustworthy scribes and bookbinders. Thanks to Hutterite experience in administering complex organizations, local lords began to hire Hutterites as managers of their landed estates, and they came to rely on the Hutterites as skilled druggists and healers, often granting them positions as court physicians.

Under the leadership of Jacob Hutter, Peter Riedemann and Peter Walpot, the original community at Auspitz spawned dozens of other communities. Each spring Hutterites in Moravia commissioned dozens of missionaries to recruit converts in the German-speaking territories of western Europe. The missionaries focused especially on those regions with established Swiss Brethren congregations, knowing that fellow Anabaptists were more likely to be sympathetic to their message. Although the tactic created a great deal of conflict between Swiss Brethren and Hutterite leaders, it proved to be highly successful. During the second half of the sixteenth century hundreds of poor peasants and artisans, struggling for survival in the midst of abject poverty or impending famine, were inspired by the Hutterite promise of a life in a Christian community that knew no distinctions between rich and poor and promised everyone enough to eat.

Ideals—and reality. During Walpot's tenure as bishop (1565-1578), the Hutterites also began to write their own history. The *Chronicle,* begun by Caspar Braitmichel in the late 1530s, traced Hutterite practices back to the early church and compared the Hutterite martyrs of the sixteenth century with the early Christian martyrs. The *Chronicle* went on to give a year-by-year "salvation history" of the Hutterites, carefully recording God's ongoing redemptive presence in the story of his people.

In Hutterite colonies, membership in the church was inseparable from the economic, educational, and cultural life of the community. The goal, according to the *Chronicle,* was to establish the kingdom of God here on earth: "Everyone, wherever he was, worked for the common good to supply the needs of all and to give help and support wherever it was needed. It was indeed a perfect body whose living members served one another."

That, at least, was the ideal. It is a painful theme in the history of the church that such ideals inevitably seem to run aground on the rocks of reality. A variety of sources—both friendly and hostile to the Hutterites—make it clear that Hutterite communities did not, in fact, achieve Christian perfection. For example, the records show that communities were occasionally forced to deal with leaders who pocketed money from community transactions or were involved in sexual misconduct. Arguments persisted over such basic concerns as the care and discipline of children and the freedom of individuals to enter into marriage. Tempers ran high on the question of whether someone who left the community was entitled to a refund of the money he or she had contributed when joining. The Swiss Brethren bitterly protested the Hutterite habit of targeting their congregations in their mission efforts. In turn, the Hutterites accused the Swiss Brethren of being half-hearted and inconsistent in their commitment to Christ, criticizing especially the economic disparities that existed among Swiss Brethren members.

New conflicts and forced emigration. All of these internal tensions were minor distractions, however, compared to an external crisis at the end of the sixteenth century that threatened to bring the Hutterite Golden Age to a sudden and violent end. In 1593, armies of the Ottoman Turks and their Hungarians allies attacked Habsburg lands in Moravia. When the Hutterites refused to pay war taxes or turn their wagons over to local militia groups, armies on both sides resorted to outright pillaging and looting. The war raged for more than a decade, with the rich holdings of the Hutterite colonies providing a lucrative source of booty for all parties.

After only a brief respite from the Turkish wars, the region was again plunged into political chaos. In 1620 the Catholic armies of the Hapsburg emperor defeated rebellious Protestant nobles at the Battle of White Mountain, an event that marked the beginning of the devastating Thirty Years' War and sealed the fate of religious minorities in the region. Even before a Habsburg edict of 1622 formally expelled the Hutterites from the region, decades of war, forced requisitions, and famine had taken their toll. An entry from 1621 in the *Chronicle* reports that one-third of the entire Hutterite population had died in that year alone.

Those Hutterites who managed to escape settled in scattered colonies in upper Hungary (now Slovakia) or further west in the Siebenburgen region of Transylvania (now Romania), beyond the reach of either the Hapsburgs or the Ottomans. In the middle of the seventeenth century, Hutterites in upper Hungary experienced a brief revival under the energetic leadership of Andreas Ehrenpreis. In the colony at Sobotiste, for example, Ehrenpreis restored the organizational structures of the Golden Age through rigorously disciplined workshops and a centrally managed plan for economic growth. Like Walpot, Ehrenpreis recognized the importance of theological and historical reflection. His *Sendbrief* of 1650—addressed to "the Mennonites, Swiss Brethren and others"—offered a thoughtful, systematic defense of community of goods. Ehrenpreis also attempted to revive the Hutterite missionary tradition by planting new colonies in the Palatinate and North Germany, and he engaged in vigorous ecumenical conversation with the Polish Socinians, a Christian group that shared Anabaptist beliefs on nonresistance and the oath, but denied the doctrine of the Trinity.

In the end, however, the revival proved to be a fading flower. In 1665 a Hutterite scribe entered the last entry in the *Chronicle*—a long letter to the Mennonites in the Netherlands, begging them for financial assistance. By 1685, virtually all of the Hutterites in Slovakia had abandoned the community of goods; ten years later, the Hutterite communities in Transylvania did the same. With the expulsion of the Ottoman Turks from the region in 1700, Jesuit missionaries began to systematically confiscate Hutterite manuscripts, hymnals, and Bibles, and to convert, sometimes forcibly, those who remained.

Hutterite survival in South Russia. That the Hutterian Brethren survive today is a remarkable story of ecumenical cross-fertilization. In the late 1750s, a small group of Lutheran refugees— fleeing persecution in Carinthia—settled in Transylvania, where they encountered the thirty or forty remaining Hutterites still living in the area. Inspired by their texts and by the principle of Christian community, the Lutherans joined with the Hutterite remnant and brought about a revival of Hutterite theology and practice. Eventually, the combined group migrated to the Ukraine, where they found asylum on the estate of a wealthy nobleman. In the middle of the nineteenth century, the descendants of this group encountered Mennonites of Dutch and North German origin who had also come to the Ukraine seeking religious toleration.

With the support of these Mennonites, the group reinstated the practice of community of goods in 1859 and revived the writings of Riedemann, Walpot, and Ehrenpreis. Not long afterward, the newly established Hutterites emigrated from the Ukraine to South Dakota to evade conscription into the Russian military. Since coming to North America in the late 1870s, the Hutterites have flourished in the western United States and Canadian provinces, undergoing a second Golden Age that has led to the formation of some 350 new communities.

Swiss Brethren: Between Compromise and Flight

Still another variation of Anabaptism took shape in Switzerland and South Germany. In sharp contrast to the Dutch Mennonites, the Swiss Brethren survived only at the margins of society, driven out of the urban centers into isolated hamlets in the countryside and mountain valleys. Although most Swiss Brethren were eventually forced to leave Switzerland and resettle in Alsace and the

Palatinate, their survival throughout the seventeenth and eighteenth centuries is a testimony not only to their resilient faith, but also to their willingness to compromise in some of their principles—as had the Dutch Mennonites and the Hutterites.

Official antagonism. Zurich, Bern, and Basel—the regions where the Swiss Brethren were most numerous in the sixteenth century—were all city-states ruled not by a prince but by a city council made up of the leading landowners and merchants. Zurich, home to Zwingli and his influential successor, Heinrich Bullinger, tended to dominate political affairs in the Swiss Confederation and to set the tone for religious policies for the rest of the Protestant territories.

Throughout the sixteenth century, Zurich and the other cities responded harshly to the Anabaptists, executing several dozen believers in the two decades after the first baptisms of 1525. Already by 1530, persecution had eliminated most of the first generation of leaders and driven the movement out of the cities and into the countryside, where small fellowships met secretly in woods, meadows, and caves.

It is clear from the dozens of mandates issued by the authorities against the Swiss Brethren that executions alone were not effective in putting an end to the movement. These mandates typically began with a long warning about the dangers of Anabaptist teachings and expressed a strong hope that the Swiss Brethren could be persuaded to recant their heresy and return to the Reformed faith. Failing that, the mandates set forth a sequence of punishments that Swiss Brethren believers could expect, ranging from fines, beatings, imprisonment, and the confiscation of property to branding, expulsion, galley slavery, and execution.

It was the task of Reformed theologians to persuade the Swiss Brethren of the errors of their ways. To that end, church officials initiated numerous disputations, or formal debates—some twenty-three altogether in the course of the sixteenth century—in which they called the Swiss Brethren to account for their false teachings. Inevitably, the state church theologians set the terms for the debates. The conversations almost always focused on classical themes of Christian theology (for example, the nature of God, the Trinity, sin, and the redemptive work of Christ), and the Reformed theologians who hosted the debates framed their arguments in the technical, highly nuanced language of their university training. The Swiss Brethren were far more interested in practical questions of Christian ethics, and they tended to defend their positions with a literalist approach to New Testament Scriptures that their opponents regarded as naive and simplistic.

Not surprisingly, the two sides often talked past each other. Thus, in 1571, when Reformed theologians at Frankenthal pressed the Swiss Brethren minister Hans Büchel for his views on whether or not the Old Testament patriarchs were saved, he responded, "The Lord knows best when those of old entered heaven. I am not commanded to dispute what took place one or two thousand years ago. I am commanded to do right, and this is my lifelong aim. The secrets which God reserved for himself, I wish to entrust to God." Unimpressed, the exasperated head of the Reformed delegation responded, "Then why debate? You could have just sent the Bible and said 'This is our understanding!'" Büchel's elevation of practical ethics over formal doctrine was typical of the Swiss Brethren approach to theology.

Swiss Brethren religious life. Most of what we know about Swiss Brethren congregational life is suggested by several religious texts which, in addition to the Bible, could be found in virtually all Swiss Brethren congregations during the sixteenth and seventeenth centuries. The first of these—a hymnal known as the *Ausbund*—appeared in 1564. Revised and enlarged in 1583 to include a total of 130 hymns, the *Ausbund* included songs written by well-known Swiss Brethren leaders such as George Blaurock, Felix Mantz, and Michael Sattler. Nearly all of the book's hymns echo a similar set of themes: the world is filled with wickedness; true followers of Christ should expect to endure suffering, even death, on account of their faith; God will not forsake those who remain faithful to the end. Sung slowly and in unison, the hymns of the *Ausbund* anchored

Swiss Brethren identity within the larger biblical story and kept alive memories of suffering and martyrdom in later generations, long after the actual experience of persecution had faded.

In a similar fashion, the *Concordance* (*Concondanzt vnd zeyger*) also reinforced the Swiss Brethren understanding of themselves as actors in salvation history. Organized around sixty-six different topics, the pocket-sized collection of biblical texts allowed users to quickly find scriptural passages relevant to Anabaptist themes (for example, "Separation," "No one can serve two masters," and "Do not follow the crowd"). The *Concordance* was both a devotional guide and a useful tool for preparing church members to defend themselves with biblical arguments in prison interrogations or in public debates.

A third text central to Swiss Brethren religious life—the glue that held their congregations together in the seventeenth and eighteenth centuries—was the Strasbourg Discipline. In 1568 representatives from numerous Swiss Brethren congregations met in Strasbourg to agree on a common church order (*Ordnung*). The document they drew up would shape Swiss Brethren—and later, Amish—congregational life for the following three centuries. Of the twenty-three articles that emerged from the conference, only one focused explicitly on theological concerns. The remainder were devoted to practical matters of church organization and ethical behavior. The Discipline, for example, defined the tasks of a minister and the relationship of a congregation to its leadership; it provided the framework for assistance for the poor within the congregation; and it outlined a structure for church ordinances like communion, baptism, and church discipline. It also admonished the Swiss Brethren to dress simply, and it clarified practices regarding nonresistance and the use of courts.

At first glance, the Strasbourg Discipline of 1568 appears to be somewhat haphazard in its organization and focus. Yet the statement became the basis for all subsequent conversations about Swiss Brethren church life. When a group of leaders met again in Strasbourg in 1607, they began by reaffirming the 1568 document before adding three additional articles. Later meetings of Swiss Brethren ministers (in 1630, 1668, 1688, 1779, 1809, and 1837) all continued this pattern of explicitly reaffirming previous versions of the discipline, even as they amended it to reflect changing circumstances.

More than any confession of faith, these three texts—the *Ausbund, Concordance,* and Strasbourg Discipline of 1568— imparted to Swiss Brethren congregations a shared ecclesiological identity rooted in an ethical understanding of faith.

Revival—and compromise. Even though the Swiss Brethren faced intense pressure from state and church authorities to recant their faith, it appears that their presence in local communities did not arouse the same sort of hostility. By many accounts, their neighbors regarded the Swiss Brethren as honest, upright, hard-working people whose eccentric religious customs posed no threat to the welfare of the community. In the preface to a lengthy book against the Swiss Brethren, Reformed pastor Georg Thormann noted that he was compelled to write the volume because village parishioners in his Reformed church were attracted to the simplicity, the moral convictions, and the New Testament biblicism of the Swiss Brethren. The common people, he observed, had come to regard them as model Christians, "as saints, as the salt of the earth, as the true chosen people and the proper core of all Christians. . . . [They think that] an Anabaptist and a good Christian are the same thing."

Much to the dismay of civil authorities, village pastors in the Reformed church frequently turned a blind eye to the presence of Swiss Brethren in their communities. And some neighbors even went beyond passive acceptance to active support. These people, known to the Swiss Brethren as the Truehearted (*Treuherzige*) or Half-Anabaptists (*Halbtäufer*), did not accept adult baptism or formally join the Swiss Brethren. However, they were deeply impressed by the integrity of their Anabaptist neighbors and were sympathetic to their plight. In times of persecution, many of the Truehearted offered material assistance to Swiss Brethren families, and some even sheltered those who were being hunted by state authorities.

In 1614 Zurich officials—exasperated by the failure of earlier mandates to excise the Swiss Brethren "cancer" in their territories—executed Hans Landis, a well-known Swiss Brethren preacher who had stubbornly refused to be silenced. Although Landis was the last Swiss Brethren martyr, his death suggested a new determination on the part of the government to eradicate all traces of Anabaptism. Consequently, the Zurich city council created an independent police force (Anabaptist hunters, or *Täuferjäger*) with far-reaching authority, including the right to confiscate and sell Swiss Brethren property.

As a result of these and other repressive actions, the Swiss Brethren suffered greatly for their faith. The archival records from these years are filled with detailed accounts of interrogations, imprisonments, property confiscations, and an elaborate network of spies charged with the task of identifying the Swiss Brethren and rooting them out of their hiding places. By the 1640s the new tactics succeeded in driving most of the Swiss Brethren out of the Zurich region into Bern or up the Rhine River into Alsace and the Palatinate.

During the second half of the seventeenth century, officials in neighboring Bern began to use similar tactics in their own campaign against the Swiss Brethren. In a mandate of September 8, 1670, for example, the Bernese government decreed that all Anabaptists who did not swear a general oath of allegiance were to be expelled from the country within two weeks. Those who refused to go were to be whipped, led forcibly to the border, and marked with a branding iron. If they returned, they were to be executed. The following year, more than seven hundred Swiss Brethren emigrants flocked to the Palatinate, seeking refuge among small congregations already established there.

In the decades that followed, hundreds of other Swiss Brethren left their homeland in the Bernese Emmental and Oberland, hoping to find religious toleration in Alsace and the Palatinate. Although estimates vary, in the early 1690s alone, as many as four hundred refugees flocked to the Alsace region, where they joined established Swiss Brethren congregations in the villages of Markirch, Jebsheim, and Ohnenheim under the benevolent protection of the lords of Rappoltsweiler. In 1710 and 1711, Bernese authorities drew yet another dragnet through the region that resulted in the eviction of four boatloads of Anabaptists. A portion of these exiles found new homes in the Low Countries with financial assistance from the Dutch Mennonites. Some continued their journey to join Mennonite settlements in North America.

The overall picture of the Swiss Brethren church in the final decades of the seventeenth century is one of a community in flux. The witness of the Swiss Brethren to a practical and disciplined form of Christian life continued to attract many new converts. At the same time, persecution and migration unsettled Swiss Brethren congregations during the second half of the seventeenth century, as families were divided and impoverished, church leadership weakened, and communication disrupted.

Those who refused to flee seem to have survived only by accepting various forms of compromise. There is ample evidence, for example, that some Swiss Brethren agreed to attend worship services in the state church and to take communion with their Reformed neighbors. Some publicly swore oaths of fealty to their feudal lords, despite the teaching against oath swearing (authorities continued to express concern that they only mumbled the words). And a significant number of Swiss Brethren even allowed their infants to be baptized, arguing that the ritual did no spiritual harm to the infant, though it did ensure that the child would be eligible to inherit property and to be legally married.

It was these strategies of compromise that sparked the greatest internal crisis of the period.

The Amish division. Late in the summer of 1693, Swiss Brethren congregations that had recently relocated to Alsace commissioned Jacob Ammann and several other ministers to make an investigative journey to the Bernese Emmental in order to clarify the position of Swiss Brethren ministers there on certain questions of church practice, especially concerning discipline.

Initial contacts with the Swiss Brethren ministers in the Emmental did not go particularly well. Ammann and his group were aggressive, setting the terms of the discussion and demanding an immediate accounting from the individual ministers they visited. Hans Reist, a senior minister in the region and eventual spokesman for the Emmental brethren, expressed his offense at this intrusion by delaying, then avoiding, a meeting with Ammann's group and by dismissing their concerns as of little importance. When efforts to mediate differences between the two groups met with no success, the disagreements became even more pronounced and the tone of the discussion turned polemical.

The issues at stake in the debate were varied, ranging from frequency of communion (Ammann wanted to celebrate it more often) to disagreements over issues related to church discipline (Ammann called for more consistent application and stricter procedures, including shunning). At the heart of the conflict, however, were different understandings of how sharply the boundaries between the church and world should be drawn. Ammann and his followers, who soon became known as "Amish," were troubled by the many compromises the Reist group seemed to be making in order to avoid friction with the authorities and local villagers. In his view, the basic principles of the Schleitheim Confession, which assumed a stark division between the gathered church and unredeemed society, were being blurred.

Efforts to reconcile the two groups came to naught, and the division between the Amish and the Swiss Brethren has remained ever since. In Europe the two groups lived side by side, though the Amish practiced a stricter form of church discipline and distinguished themselves by their distinctive mode of dress. In North America, the two groups also tended to settle in close proximity and had a great deal of interaction through the end of the nineteenth century. Although differences between the two groups have become much more pronounced during the course of the twentieth century, the Amish and the Mennonites share a common historical and theological legacy prior to 1700.

The quiet in the land. In the decades following the Thirty Years' War (1618-1638), feudal princes in Alsace and the upper Rhineland were anxious to attract able farmers to settle on estates that had been depopulated by the devastation of the war. In return for their skills as farmers and artisans, the Swiss Brethren and other religious refugees were often granted concessions, including the freedom to worship, provided that they paid an annual toleration tax and refrained from proselytizing. In addition, the princes required the Swiss Brethren to meet in homes rather than churches. The princes also limited the number who could settle in a given region, and prohibited the Swiss Brethren from joining guilds or attending universities.

Despite these restrictions, the beleaguered Swiss Brethren, weary of generations of persecution and uncertainty, regarded the offer as a godsend. Wherever they settled in the Rhineland—in Alsace, Kraichgau, or the Palatinate—Mennonite and Amish farmers gained a reputation for being hard-working and intelligent agricultural entrepreneurs. In the Palatinate, for example, a Mennonite farmer from Monsheim named David Möllinger was widely acclaimed as "the father of agriculture in the Palatinate." Möllinger pioneered the use of lime fertilizer and legumes to replenish the soil. He also bred beef cattle, developed a distillery to manufacture liquor from potatoes (the by-products of which he fed to his cattle), manufactured vinegar, and kept careful records of all he did. "No better, more industrious, and competent subjects are to be found," wrote one state official, "who, with the exception of their religion, their faith, and their error, should serve the members of other faiths as an example in morals as well as in working day and night."

Yet this economic success came at a cost. Scattered on isolated estates, dependent on lay leadership, and restricted by the conditions of their toleration, many congregations in the region settled into a kind of spiritual dormancy during the course of the eighteenth century. Although they faithfully preserved church traditions and retained memories of persecution in their hymns, the Swiss Brethren in the upper Rhineland tended to define their congregations more in terms of family genealogy than religious vitality. No longer living in tension with the culture around them or engaging in missions, Swiss Brethren in the eighteenth century became known as "the quiet in the land."

Conclusion

Like the early church, Anabaptism did not emerge fully formed. The Reformation principle of "Scripture alone," and the explosive combination of religious convictions, political interests, and social upheaval, opened the door to a variety of interpretations among the early Anabaptists, shaped by the personalities of key leaders and the circumstances of local contexts.

Anabaptists in the Netherlands successfully recovered from the episode at Münster. Under the gifted leadership of Menno Simons, they reclaimed a sober-minded, and biblically-grounded understanding of the church. In the following centuries, Dutch Mennonites continued to sort through their differences—especially regarding church discipline—as they participated in the commercial and cultural renaissance of an urban setting. Likewise, after surviving several early crises of leadership, the Hutterites emerged in Moravia as a vibrant expression of Anabaptist convictions, determined to keep alive the radical practice of community of goods, even amid the shifting political fortunes in eastern Europe. Meanwhile, the Swiss Brethren also survived and flourished, albeit at the very edges of Swiss society and always under the shadow of state-sponsored persecution.

Despite significant regional differences, each of these Anabaptist groups shared a common set of convictions, rooted in their desire to recover the convictions and practices of the early church. This common theological orientation fostered an ongoing awareness among the groups of a shared identity that pulled them into conversation with each other despite the real differences that separated them.

All three Anabaptist groups shared the conviction that following Jesus—being a disciple—should be a voluntary decision symbolized by believers baptism. All emphasized the sharing of material possessions as an extension of God's generosity to humanity; and all assumed that membership in a voluntary church implied a mutual accountability to the shared convictions and norms of the larger group.

With the obvious exception of Münster, virtually all the Anabaptist groups adopted an ethic that precluded Christian participation in warfare or lethal violence. As a result of these convictions, Anabaptist groups generally took on a cultural form that was in tension with the surrounding culture. Since allegiance to Christ transcended commitments that the individual owed to the prince, the society, or the family, the practices of the gathered church would stand in contrast to the norms and assumptions of the broader culture. This meant that the Anabaptist were, by definition, missionary in their orientation to the world.

Finally, at an even deeper level, the Anabaptists, like the early church, faced the age-old challenge of keeping the energy that animated the beginnings of the movement alive, even as they developed more stable, institutional forms of church life. By the end of the sixteenth century, all the various Anabaptist groups found themselves facing similar pressure to assimilate into the culture around them—to persuade governments of their essential "harmlessness" or to prove their usefulness to the economic well-being of the state. All of them had developed routines and traditions, orthodoxies of belief, and structures of organization that brought a needed sense of stability and order.

Anabaptism demonstrated a remarkable capacity for survival and adaptability in the course of the seventeenth and eighteenth centuries. But these same impulses threatened to weaken those characteristics that gave Anabaptism its distinctive character.

The struggle for identity amid the pressures of compromise and voices of renewal has structured the contours of Anabaptist-Mennonite history ever since. It is to that struggle that we now turn.

6

Mennonites in South Russia

Migration and Assimilation

The image on the worn black-and-white photo is stark and chilling. A huddled group of Mennonite villagers stand silhouetted against the November sky, heavy coats shielding them from late autumn air in Russia. They are peering into an open grave at the remains of eighty murdered friends and family, the bodies wrapped in shrouds of white linen and awaiting burial.

The year was 1919. For more than a century, German-speaking Mennonite immigrants from Poland and Prussia had called South Russia their home. Through hard work, the favor of the tsar, and the grace of God, they had transformed two small settlements along the Dneiper and Molotschna rivers into a flourishing network of colonies that stretched from the rich wheat fields and orchards of the Ukraine to the steppe lands of Siberia. By the beginning of the twentieth century, Mennonites were recognized throughout the Russian empire as innovative and productive farmers. They were pioneers in the selective breeding of sheep, cattle, and horses; their experimental farms yielded new strains of highly productive, disease-resistant wheat. In 1910 Mennonite factories were producing nearly 10 percent of all new agricultural machinery in Russia. Their colonies supported hospitals, orphanages, teacher-training colleges, and even a school for the deaf. And the massive stone churches in the largest settlements gave ample testimony to the wealth and generosity of the community.

When the Russian empire found itself spiraling into anarchy in the years after the Bolshevik Revolution of 1917, Mennonites were utterly unprepared for the horror that was about to befall them. For nearly four years, Mennonite communities in South Russia found themselves in the path of a constantly shifting battle line, with each army—the Whites, the Reds, and the anarchists—looting, destroying, and killing each time they passed through. Late in November 1919, several Mennonites in the colony of Nikolaipol had taken up arms against the intruders. In retaliation, a roving band of anarchists, led by the infamous Nestor Mahkno, descended upon the hamlet of Eichenfeld, massacring most of the men in the village. The mute grief of the survivors—captured in the photo of the mass grave at Eichenfeld—is a heart-wrenching symbol of the suffering Mennonites in Russia were to endure in the decades ahead.

The Mennonite experience in the Russian empire and the Soviet Union spanned two full centuries—from the first immigrations in 1788 following an invitation from Catherine the Great, to the mass exodus of Mennonite descendants to Germany in the 1990s after the collapse of the Soviet Union. Their story is a dramatic narrative of blessing and trauma, prosperity and pain.

On the one hand, Mennonites regarded the opportunity to move to South Russia in the late eighteenth century as a gift from God. For virtually the first time in their history, Mennonites were allowed to practice their faith completely free from the restrictions of princes and the hostile suspicions of religious authorities. Living in isolation on some of the Russian empire's richest farmland, they established peaceful and productive communities.

At the same time, however, the social isolation, political self-sufficiency, and close identification with the land that made the move to Russia so appealing also created a series of profound tensions. Externally, the boundaries separating Russian Mennonites from their neighbors created a legacy of mutual suspicion that would eventually explode into violence. Within the colonies, Mennonites were confronted with a miniature version of the same dilemma that the early church faced following the conversion of Constantine. What happens to the essence of faith if the church is defined primarily in terms of territory? What happens to believers baptism if everyone in the colony is a Christian (or at least a Mennonite) by virtue of their birth? What happens to nonresistance if it is Mennonites who must maintain public order?

In many ways the challenges faced by Mennonites living in Russia between the 1790s and the 1990s were unique, the product of their specific context and a series of world events beyond their control. But as will become clear in following chapters, many of the dilemmas they confronted were no different in principle from those faced by Amish, Hutterites, and Mennonites in North America during the same period or by the 1.3 million Mennonites living in some sixty-six different countries around the world today.

From the Netherlands to North Germany to South Russia

The roots of the Mennonite experience in Russia go all the way back to the story of the Dutch Mennonites in the Netherlands. As we have seen, Mennonites in the Netherlands gained a measure of toleration during the last decades of the sixteenth century, thanks in part to their contribution to the growing Dutch economy. In the expanding markets of northern Europe, Mennonites became well-known as industrious workers, valued particularly for their skills in building dikes and pumping water out of low-lying regions in order to reclaim land for agricultural purposes. During the course of the seventeenth century, government officials in regions to the east of the Netherlands—Friesland, the Danish territory of Friedrichstadt, and the Hanseatic cities of Hamburg, Altona, and Lübeck—were eager to have Mennonites settle in their territories, especially if they brought with them capital, specialized skills, and a reputation for hard work. Although none of these territories had official policies tolerating religious minorities, progressive-minded princes and city councils were often willing to negotiate a special charter (*Privilegium*) that allowed the Mennonites to settle in their territories, albeit with clear restrictions.

The Mennonites who moved into the region around Hamburg and Altona, for example, were granted exemption from military service and were permitted to worship as they pleased. In return, they agreed to be quiet, obedient, and hard-working subjects. Additional restrictions were firm, but not overly burdensome. They were obliged to pay a yearly "recognition" tax; they were not allowed to proselytize or build churches; they were barred from many guilds; and they were restricted in the amount of land they could own.

Initially, the immigrants borrowed heavily from their Dutch Mennonite background, even reproducing the same church divisions that were unfolding in the Netherlands. But over time, Mennonites in North Germany—regions that later became Poland and Prussia—developed their own identity, symbolized by a slow shift in language from Dutch to German (or *Plautdeitsch,* a Low German dialect) and the emergence of their own hymnbooks and catechisms.

On the whole, the Mennonite immigrants to North Germany thrived. In the free city of Hamburg and the neighboring Swedish-controlled city of Altona, they became wealthy ship owners and leaders in the whaling and herring fishing industries. Later immigrants to the Vistula Delta region around Danzig became famous, first for their agricultural prowess and then for their distilleries and textile mills.

At first, the toleration agreements worked reasonably well. But by the middle of the seventeenth century, a familiar scenario began to unfold. As the number of Mennonites steadily grew, the amount of land they were permitted to own remained fixed, thereby creating a class of landless, increasingly impoverished Mennonite day laborers. In addition, hostile clergy petitioned the city councils of Hamburg and Altona to impose sharper restrictions on

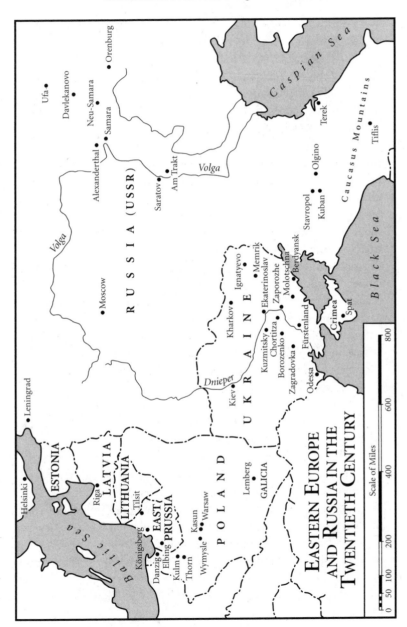

EASTERN EUROPE
AND RUSSIA IN THE
TWENTIETH CENTURY

Mennonites residents, calling attention to their heretical teachings and ambiguous status under imperial law.

Then, in the 1770s, the Danzig region shifted from Polish to Prussian control. The new Prussian government challenged the concept of a privilegium and brought new pressure to bear on Mennonites to conform to the laws of the state, especially in matters of military support.

In the midst of these uncertainties, Catherine the Great, the Russian tsarina, offered a welcome solution. After assuming control of the Russian empire in 1762, Catherine had issued several manifestos inviting German farmers to establish colonies on land in South Russia that had recently been won from the Turks. Although the territory was still occupied by nomadic peoples—especially the Cossacks, the Tatars, and the Nogai—Catherine was eager to bring this rich farmland under cultivation. Within a decade, she had welcomed a colorful variety of more than one hundred colonies, including many religious minorities. In 1788 she extended her offer to the Mennonites in North Germany.

Mennonites in Prussia were initially skeptical about the prospect of settling on this distant and unknown frontier. Nonetheless, Catherine's offer in March 1788 of a privilegium—combined with glowing reports based on investigative journeys and conversations with Russian officials in St. Petersburg—proved persuasive. The terms of the privilegium guaranteed each Mennonite family 175 acres (sixty-five dessiatines) of land in "perpetual possession" and freedom from military service "for all time." Moreover, the Russian government promised Mennonites full religious liberty and nearly complete administrative control over the internal affairs of their colonies. The language of the charter suggested that Mennonite discipline and industriousness might serve as a model for other colonies.

In the spring of 1788 the first group of Mennonite immigrants, most of them poor and landless, left Danzig by wagon. After a difficult journey lasting nearly a year, some four hundred families established a cluster of villages on the western bank of the Chortitza River in the heart of the Ukraine.

The settlers of the Chortitza colony—often called the Old Colony, since it was the first to be established—faced enormous challenges. The Russian government was slow to deliver on its promise of subsidies and supplies; basic principles of self-governance had to be established; the group had no ordained ministers to baptize or to officiate at weddings; tensions with local nomadic groups ran high; and the threat of disease and hunger was always at hand.

Nevertheless, the colony at Chortitza survived, and in 1803 it was joined by a sister colony one hundred miles away called Molotschna, after the river that the settlement straddled. Within a few decades, both colonies numbered over one thousand families residing in dozens of villages. Though the names of the Chortitza and Molotschna colonies remain the most familiar, by the middle of the century, ongoing immigration and rapid population growth led to the creation of some fifty additional colonies spread across the Ukraine, Crimea, Caucasus, and Siberia.

Despite the hardships of pioneer life, the decision to move to Russia seemed a good one. Mennonites gained access to productive land in a setting where they were exempt from military conscription. They were free to worship as they pleased, and the Russian government noted with satisfaction that Mennonites were fulfilling their hopes of establishing productive farms.

Colony Life

The basic organizational structure of the Chortitza and Molotschna colonies defined the contours of Russian Mennonite life for the next century. Within each colony, a cluster of villages emerged, each comprised of twenty or twenty-five families who built their houses along the road, with the farmland extending outward from the village center. Technically, the village held collective title to the land, which was then granted to individual families in a kind of perpetual lease agreement. According to the terms of the privilegium, individual families were not permitted to subdivide their holdings. Each village had its own school and church. A village assembly, made up of male landowners, elected a mayor (*Schulze*) and met regularly to address basic questions of administration and justice. Together the villages elected a governor (*Oberschulze*), who had oversight of the entire colony and served as its representative to the Russian government.

The colonies as a whole enjoyed a remarkable degree of political autonomy. Essentially, they functioned as self-governing Mennonite commonwealths, virtually independent of the Russian government and the broader world. When demographic growth made it difficult for young people to establish farms, colonies established daughter settlements that replicated these same basic structures.

Mennonites farmers focused their initial efforts on vegetables and wool production. Over time, however, they diversified their agricultural practices to adjust to changing market conditions. For example, as ports opened along the Black Sea, Mennonites began to raise a hard winter grain for distribution to European markets. The new strain of wheat was so successful that the region quickly became known as the "breadbasket of Russia." Some colonies developed special breeds of cattle and draft horses, others became known for their fruit orchards, and for a time, several even found a niche in silkworm production to meet expanding demand in the European luxury market. Parallel to this agricultural growth, Mennonites also began to make a name for themselves as manufacturers of agricultural implements. By the end of the nineteenth century, large factories in the Mennonite colonies were mass-producing high-quality farm machinery, some of it invented by local entrepreneurs.

Johann Cornies (1789-1848) was the central figure of this economic transformation. In 1817, acknowledging his reputation as an industrious and successful farmer, colony leaders appointed Cornies as the chairman of the Agricultural Improvement Society. During the course of his life, Cornies leveraged this position into a powerful force for change. His master plan included a series of reforms aimed at rationalizing agricultural production, including crop rotation, the introduction of fertilizers, new breeds of cattle, and new strains of wheat. He diversified production within the colonies so that they could better respond to the shifting demands of external markets, and he encouraged gifted young people to pursue specialized training in agriculture and industry.

In time, Cornies extended the reach of the Agricultural Improvement Society into a host of other cultural and educational activities, resulting in a centralized curriculum for all elementary schools and the establishment of secondary schools and teacher training institutes. By the end of his life, Cornies wielded extraordinary authority within the colonies and served as the main point of contact between Mennonites and the Russian government.

Cornies was a controversial figure. His mandates, often imposed from above, were not always well received. One village reportedly responded to a decree that trees be planted along the road leading into every community by obeying the letter but not the spirit of the law: they planted the trees upside-down! Nonetheless, his far-sighted reforms laid a foundation for steady economic growth within the Mennonite colonies that continued into the second half of the nineteenth century. By the end of the century, the colonies had moved through an industrial revolution of sorts and were functioning as small cities. They had hospitals with trained physicians and nurses, firefighting equipment, and music and literary societies; some had even begun to offer insurance plans for widows and orphans. Increasingly, Mennonite youth were attending German universities, returning to the colonies with doctoral degrees in theology, engineering, medicine, and history. Though culturally and politically isolated from the Russian empire, Mennonites were nonetheless economically integrated with the outside world and highly attentive to events in German-speaking Europe.

Challenges Within the Colony System

Beneath the appearance of success, however, the colony system was experiencing a series of internal tensions, many of which remained hidden until a crisis brought them into public view.

Theological dilemmas of self-government. The terms of the 1788 Privilegium allowed Mennonites in Russia to create a kind of "state within a state." On the one hand, this was an ideal arrangement in that it permitted Mennonites to pursue their vision of a faith community unimpeded by outside government intervention. Yet it also brought with it new and unexpected challenges, most of them arising from the conflict between the colonists' religious identity as members of the church and their secular identity within the political structure of the village.

One question had to do with the meaning of voluntary baptism—a central theological principle in the Anabaptist-Mennonite tradition. Because the legal status of Mennonites in Russia had been conferred upon them as a group and because the colonies developed in relative isolation from Russian society, the meaning of a voluntary commitment to follow Christ became increasingly unclear. Did a young person raised in a Russian Mennonite village really have a choice *not* to become a member of the church? If an individual opted out of church membership, what then became of his or her legal identity within the Russian empire? Did that person still have claims to the privileges granted Mennonites under the 1788 charter? Inevitably, the structure of the colony system moved toward a definition of church membership that was shaped at least as much by ethnicity as it was by a voluntary decision to become a Christian.

The competition between secular and religious identities was especially problematic in matters of discipline. If a Mennonite villager committed an infraction, should the discipline be administered by the church (in the form of admonition, exclusion from communion, and possibly social avoidance) or by village administrators serving in their secular function? Such questions became particularly vexing in instances of crime. If a member of the community was caught stealing, should the person be punished by the church or by the mayor—or by both? And what if the crime was more serious? Was it ever permissible for civil authorities to apply corporal punishment? Was there a place in a Christian community for a jail? Or to cite another troubling example, how should the community treat nomadic groups who passed through the area and helped themselves to grain and fruit? How should it respond to roving gangs of bandits who extorted money or goods from the community with blatant threats of violence?

Surprisingly, even though Mennonites in Russia had a perfect opportunity to live out their vision of a church separated from the "fallen world," the problems of coercive power refused to disappear. Indeed, colony life sometimes seemed to replicate the same inconsistencies, albeit on a much smaller scale, of medieval Christendom.

Economic disparities. By the middle of the nineteenth century, the influx of new immigrants combined with steady demographic growth had created an underclass of poor, landless day laborers. The 1788 Privilegium clearly stipulated that Mennonite families were not permitted to subdivide their property—a restriction intended to keep intact a viable farming economy. As a result, however, the children of farm families increasingly struggled to gain access to land. At first, the colonies alleviated the pressure by establishing daughter settlements. And the development of a more diversified economy helped to absorb some of the excess labor.

But by the second half of the nineteenth century, the growing number of landless day laborers was becoming a significant problem. Since voting in village assemblies was tied to land ownership, the propertied class held a political and economic advantage over its landless neighbors. As a result, through intermarriage and political maneuvering, several key families consolidated their wealth and status even further. Officially, of course, the colonists were all part of a church that preached mutual aid and the fundamental equality of all believers. Yet it was obvious that a two-class society was emerging among the Russian Mennonites. By 1870, nearly two-thirds of all family heads were landless.

The situation became even more volatile after 1861, when Tsar Alexander II freed the Russian serfs. Virtually overnight, the decision released thousands of migrant agricultural workers who were available for hire on Mennonite estates and willing to work for cheaper wages than the Mennonite day laborers. Since the former serfs were uneducated, unable to speak German, and loyal to the Russian Orthodox Church, they were clearly not going to be integrated into colony life.

As the gap between the rich and the poor continued to widen and as landless Mennonites competed with emancipated serfs for work, resentments simmered just beneath the surface.

Religious renewal. The first group of Mennonite immigrants to South Russia tended to minimize whatever theological distinctions had divided them in Germany. But the new setting in Russia was ripe for theological conflict. Already in 1812, Klaas Reimer, a minister from the Molotschna colony, encouraged a dissident group to break with the main church out of a desire to maintain stricter standards of personal morality and church discipline. Specifically, Reimer opposed the financial contributions that Mennonites were making to the Russian military in the face of Napoleon's advancing armies in 1812. Reimer also resented the growing authority of the village mayor over church ministers, especially in the practice of corporal punishment, and he called for stricter enforcement of church discipline in general. Although the nickname *Kleine Gemeinde* (the little church) was intended scornfully, Reimer's group claimed the label as an affirmation of their separatist identity. In 1843, the Russian government granted formal recognition to the Kleine Gemeinde. Thirty years later, the entire fellowship emigrated to North America.

An even more serious division rocked the Molotschna colony in the late 1850s. For many years, itinerant Protestant preachers from Germany had visited the Mennonite colonies, hoping to bring about a spiritual awakening through revival campaigns and private prayer meetings. For some Mennonites, the emphasis on prayer, Bible study, and a regenerated Christian life was a welcome alternative to Mennonite church traditions that had come to seem suffocating. In a setting where church membership was easily confused with ethnic identity and cultural tradition, the dramatic experience of a "crisis conversion" seemed fresh, genuine, and personal.

By the 1850s, a renewal movement had coalesced around the

preaching of Edward Wüst, a Lutheran pietist from Germany. Among other things, Wüst and his followers expressed concern that everyone in the Mennonite community, "including lovers of money, drunkards and blasphemers," was permitted to take communion. They also demanded clearer evidence of a Spirit-filled transformation in the lives of believers, and they revived interest in missions as an expression of a living faith. In January 1860, a group of eighteen men in Molotschna signed their names to a document announcing their intention to leave the mother church (*Kirchliche*), thereby marking the birth of the Mennonite Brethren (*Brüdergemeinde*). Over the next few decades, the new fellowship struggled for theological self-definition, but its emphasis on mission yielded steady growth. By 1910, the Mennonite Brethren could claim three thousand baptized members in congregations scattered throughout the Mennonite colonies.

Relations with Russian government. As already noted, the Privilegium of 1788 granted Mennonites almost complete autonomy from the Russian government. In 1800 Tsar Paul had reaffirmed and renewed the generous terms of that charter, and Mennonites, by and large, regarded the Russian monarchy with a deep sense of gratitude and affection. Nostalgic stories of official visits by the tsar to Mennonite colonies were passed down through the generations. The colonies frequently sent formal letters of greeting and thanksgiving to the tsar on state occasions. And they even named the Alexandertal colony after Tsar Alexander I in appreciation for his benevolence. In turn, Russian authorities were grateful to Mennonites for their productivity, their discipline, and their conservative political orientation.

However, these outward displays of mutual warmth tended to mask deeper tensions. During the second half of the nineteenth century, the rapid expansion of the Mennonite colonies and their ongoing identification with German culture made them conspicuous within Russian society. Increasingly, Russian nationalists expressed irritation with the independence Mennonites enjoyed. And they voiced their growing resentment at the Mennonite refusal to be assimilated into Russian culture. By the 1860s these concerns had gained considerable influence. Voices within the government began to insist that the Mennonite colonies teach Russian in their schools, pay more taxes, and contribute more vigorously to the defense of the empire.

Finally, in 1870, Tsar Alexander II reversed the promises of the 1788 Privilegium by introducing universal military conscription. The decree triggered an intense debate between colony leaders and the Russian government, eventually resulting in an agreement that permitted Mennonite conscripts to fulfill their military obligations through an alternate form of service with the forestry department.

Despite this compromise, many colonists found the turn of events very unsettling. In 1874 and 1875, some eighteen thousand Russian Mennonites—approximately 30 percent of the total—emigrated to North America, attracted by the promise of cheap land and a renewed assurance that they would be freed from military obligations. The emigrations helped to ease the land shortage, but deeper questions about future relations with the Russian government remained unresolved.

In the late 1890s a decree that Russian become the official language of instruction in all Mennonite schools provoked a major debate within the colonies between those who sensed that the fate of Mennonite identity was inseparably linked to the German language and those who recognized the necessity of becoming bicultural. One unexpected consequence of the debate was a renaissance of German language and heritage, reflected in the growing number of Russian Mennonite graduates from German universities and a proliferation of German-language newspapers, periodicals, poetry, and fiction. According to one source, in 1909 villagers in Molotschna could choose from no fewer than nine different German-language newspapers.

A deeper consequence of the debate, though far less apparent at the time, was a persistent unease among Russian authorities as to where Mennonite sympathies would lie if Russia should ever come to war with Germany.

By all outward appearances, Mennonites in Russia were flourishing during the early years of the twentieth century. Their farms were among the most productive in the country; their factories—equipped with the latest machinery imported from Germany—were producing innovative agricultural implements; their secondary schools were preparing young people for a diversifying economy; and their colonies boasted an impressive array of well-administered social services.

But tensions were undeniable. Within the colonies, the gap between the rich and the poor continued to widen, and troubling questions about the relationship between faith and ethnicity refused to go away. Outside of colony borders, the Russian elite resented the economic clout wielded by the Mennonites and the steadily increasing amount of land that was coming under Mennonite control. Although Russian peasants were grateful for work on Mennonite estates, they were keenly aware of their status as underpaid outsiders. And peasants and nationalists alike were suspicious of the political loyalties of these German-speaking colonists who refused to swear oaths of allegiance and dodged their obligation to serve in the military. In their eyes, Mennonite wealth and Germanic identity was closely tied to the archaic tradition of "privileges"—a legacy of Russia's feudal past, not its emerging future.

The Collapse of the Colony System: World War I and the Communist Revolution

On June 28, 1914, a young Serbian nationalist in Sarajevo assassinated the Austrian Archduke Ferdinand, setting in motion a chain of events that led to the outbreak of World War I. Two weeks after the assassination, Germany declared war on Russia. By the fall of 1914, both sides were deploying the largest armies the world had ever seen.

In the months leading up to the war, Mennonites had been acutely conscious of the rising tide of anti-German sentiment in Russia, and they tried to respond in ways that would assure the local population of their loyalty. Some colonies sent telegrams to Tsar Nicholas II, promising their support; many raised money for the Russian Red Cross or organized relief efforts to support families whose sons had been sent to the front. Mennonites also declared their readiness to shift their young men out of forestry service into the medical corps, even if it meant serving in battle zones. Nearly absent from these responses was a sustained conversation about the Anabaptist-Mennonite doctrine of nonresistance. For most Mennonites, support for the Russian war effort followed naturally from Christ's teaching that his followers should "render unto Caesar what is Caesar's."

As the war progressed Mennonites in Russia, like the rest of the world, were completely unprepared for the scale of devastation it was to unleash. By 1915 the Russian army had suffered more than two million casualties. Meanwhile, agricultural production in Russia had declined precipitously, leading to rising prices and, in some areas, severe food shortages.

In January 1917, political unrest against the tsar that had been growing for decades finally exploded in St. Petersburg, forcing Nicholas II to abdicate the throne. Shortly thereafter, the Russian army virtually disintegrated as millions of soldiers deserted the frontlines and began the long walk home. In October, as the war effort collapsed altogether along the eastern front, a group of Bolshevik revolutionaries wrested power from the provisional government. In short order, the Bolsheviks assembled the All Russian Congress of Soviets, which formally handed power over to the Soviet Council of People's Commissars headed by Vladimir Lenin.

With the treaty of Brest-Litovsk the following spring, Russia's war with Germany officially came to an end. At home, however, the aftershocks of the war continued to reverberate. Part of the immediate confusion for Mennonites had to do with their legal status. The Bolsheviks—since renamed the Communist Party—demanded that local government be organized into "soviets," or "people's assemblies," leaving the long tradition of Mennonite village self-government in a state of limbo. An even more immediate crisis was the outbreak of a three-way civil war among the White army (those who remained loyal to the tsar), the Red army (supporters of the new Communist regime), and loosely organized bands of anarchists who pillaged and terrorized indiscriminately.

For nearly three years, Mennonite villagers watched helplessly as various armed groups swept through their colonies, demanding food or livestock, extorting money and threatening to kill anyone who stood in their way. Nestor Makhno—a former peasant who had likely worked for Mennonites as a day laborer—was an especially notorious warlord. Head of his own private army, Mahkno seemed to take special delight in preying on Mennonite villages. Early in 1919, as both the German and White armies retreated from South Russia, bandits like Makhno had free reign in the region. When attempts to negotiate proved fruitless, some Mennonites tried to flee. Others counseled patience and endurance. And some began to organize for their own defense.

The story of Mennonite "self-defense" (*Selbstschutz*) during these traumatic years is a controversial chapter in Russian Mennonite history. Surely, any examination of that story must be attentive to the context. By the early twentieth century, Mennonites in Russia still affirmed the principle of nonresistance, though perhaps more as a lingering cultural habit than as a deeply held theological conviction. Now, as Mennonites witnessed the work of generations being wantonly destroyed and watched helplessly as innocent villagers were robbed, raped, and murdered, it is not surprising that they felt compelled to defend their lives and property. When other villages, encouraged by German army officers who temporarily occupied the region, began to form militia groups for self-defense, several Mennonite villages followed suit. The strategy proved to be disastrous, however. The massacre at Eichenfeld noted at the outset of this chapter was carried out in retaliation against that village for harboring men who had been active in the Selbstschutz resistance.

The impulse leading to the Selbstschutz is certainly understandable. What is even more remarkable, given the horror that the

Mennonites in South Russia had endured, was the Russian Mennonite reaffirmation of their commitment to nonresistance almost immediately after the revolution. Already in February 1921, the Union of South Russian Mennonites had formally rededicated itself to the principle of pacifism and entered into risky negotiations with the Communists to reinstate some form of alternative service.

The years of war and revolution were followed by a decade of famine, especially in the Ukraine and Crimea. The anarchy of the post-revolutionary years destroyed barns, depleted granaries, and left fields untilled. Thousands of draft horses had been requisitioned at the outset of the war, further disrupting the local agrarian economy. As a result of the chaos, the central institutions of Mennonite life—schools, churches, factories, and social-service organizations—were almost completely destroyed. Within the span of only a year or two, Mennonite families who had enjoyed a standard of living unrivalled in all of Russia were facing starvation.

In the summer of 1920, Mennonite groups in North America responded to the crisis in South Russia by creating a relief agency: the Mennonite Central Committee (MCC). By September of that same year, with additional financial support from Mennonites in the Netherlands, MCC began sending food and material aid to the suffering people of the Ukraine.

The initial focus of MCC's efforts was on famine relief. In the spring of 1922, their soup kitchens were feeding nearly twenty-five thousand people per day. But the organization also began to offer assistance to Russian Mennonites who wanted to emigrate. The first wave of emigrants left from Chortitza and Molotschna, the areas hardest hit by revolutionary violence, from 1923 to 1925. They were followed by another wave in 1926 through 1929, mostly refugees from the Mennonite colonies in Siberia and eastern Russia. All told, between 1923 and 1929, an estimated twenty-one thousand Mennonites, including many of the most dynamic and gifted leaders, immigrated to Canada, where fellow Mennonites under the leadership of David Toews helped them adjust to a new life.

A later emigration initiative in 1929 and 1930 saw thousands of Mennonites thronging to Moscow in the hope of securing exit visas. Only after a long series of appeals by fellow Mennonites in Germany, Holland, the United States, and Canada were they finally permitted to leave the country, with the majority settling in Brazil and Paraguay. In December 1930, still another group of Mennonites—two entire villages—made a daring midnight escape across the frozen Amur River into northern China. Eventually, the group made its way to Harbin, China, where in February 1932 they too departed for Paraguay.

To all these host countries—Canada, Paraguay, and Brazil—the Russian Mennonite emigrants of the 1920s brought their tradition of hard work, administrative savvy, and communal discipline. And they flourished in their new homes. Although the colony model developed in Russia did not survive in Canada, it continues to live on in modified forms in Mexico, Paraguay, and other South American countries.

Mennonites Under Stalin

The full story of the Mennonites who remained behind in the Union of Soviet Socialist Republics has not yet been told. For them, the painful events of the 1920s were only a prelude to further horrors yet to come. Stories of Anabaptist persecution four centuries earlier would become brutally relevant for these Mennonites during the middle decades of the twentieth century.

In January 1924, Joseph Stalin, Soviet dictator and leader of the Communist Party, embarked on a massive collectivization effort aimed at transforming all private farms into state-run communes. Among the obvious targets of this massive social reengineering project were Mennonite colonies, especially the estates owned by wealthy Mennonites. Resistance to Stalin's program met with arrests, sham trials, imprisonment, and executions. The All-Mennonite Conference that convened in Moscow in 1925 was a portent of things to come. Of the seventy-seven people who participated in this "martyrs conference," twenty-eight are known to have been exiled. The rest were apparently "disappeared"—executed or sent to work camps in Siberia. In the late 1920s, hundreds of Mennonite men, along with thousands of other ethnic Germans in the region, were forcibly separated from their families and sent to Siberia or the Gulag, where many starved, died of disease, or were worked to death.

The years 1936 to 1938 brought another campaign of repression, often called the Great Terror, in which the Soviet government outlawed all public worship and targeted ministers for especially cruel treatment. Night visits by the secret police (*Spetskomandantura*) resulted in the sudden arrest of relatives or neighbors, and an extensive spy network planted a spirit of fear and suspicion in every community. As in the sixteenth century, the Mennonite church was forced to go underground, meeting secretly for worship in private homes or under the cover of weddings or funerals.

With the outbreak of World War II, yet another tragic chapter in the history of Russian Mennonites began to unfold. When Hitler turned his armies on Russia in June 1941, Stalin assumed that anyone in the USSR of German ancestry was a potential Nazi collaborator. Within a year, some eight hundred thousand ethnic Germans—including many Mennonites—were scheduled for deportation to the interior of the Soviet Union, especially to Siberia and the republics of central Asia. There they were to form a workers' army (*Arbeitsarmee*) to support the war effort.

Faced with the prospects of forced deportation, Mennonites generally celebrated the advance of German storm troopers into the Ukraine and Crimea as liberators from Stalin's tyranny. But when the tides of war shifted and the German army was forced to retreat, these same Mennonites found themselves part of a massive group of refugees moving westward, trying desperately to stay ahead of the Red army.

Given the horror of their recent experience under Communist rule, the impulse of Russian Mennonites to identify with the German cause is understandable. Yet the support that many expressed for National Socialism and their general willingness to fight in Hitler's army added another layer of complexity to an already painful story.

The Mennonites who remained in the USSR after World War II found themselves reliving an all-too-familiar nightmare of destruction, plunder, rape, and despair—of families torn asunder, of fathers and brothers dead or missing, of a future filled with unknowns. Those who escaped the USSR as war refugees—perhaps twelve thousand in all—eventually settled in Canada and Paraguay. Those who remained behind were forced to endure another round of reprisals, forced relocations, and arbitrary prison sentences.

Some Mennonites in the post-World War II era departed from Christianity altogether, retaining the memory of their Mennonite past only in their family names, a few cultural traditions, and remnant phrases from the German language. Other Mennonites found a new spiritual home among the Russian Baptists or other evangelical groups. Still others experienced a revival of Mennonite identity in the 1950s and 1960s, focused primarily on such distinctives as nonresistance or believers baptism.

All Christians in the USSR during the 1950s and 1960s struggled with the decision about whether or not to officially register with the government by joining the All Union Council of Evangelical Christian Baptists. Some Mennonite congregations did; others, like the Karaganda congregation in Kazakhstan, refused. The stories of Mennonite faithfulness and endurance during these years have only now started to be told. A full history of Mennonites in the Soviet Union in the years after World War II remains to be written.

Glasnost and the Aussiedler Exodus

There is good reason to anticipate that such a history will indeed be written, thanks to a remarkable sequence of events that has brought the story of Mennonites in Russia full circle—namely, back to Germany. Between 1987 and 1993, more than one hundred thousand people of Mennonite origin left the former Soviet Union to settle in Germany. It was the largest migration in all of Mennonite history and, as with all such upheavals, the transition has been rich with possibilities and fraught with challenges.

In the late 1980s, Soviet leader Mikhail Gorbachev introduced a series of internal reforms that allowed for greater individual freedoms, more autonomy to the Soviet republics, and increased political openness (*glasnost*). The reforms, which led to the fall of the Berlin Wall in 1989 and the collapse of the Soviet Union two years later, allowed ethnic Germans living in the USSR to take advantage of a standing offer of citizenship and financial assistance from the German government if they chose to relocate in the West. Thus thousands of Russian Mennonite descendants joined in a massive exodus of other ethnic Germans out of the former USSR and into Germany.

The integration of these so-called *Aussiedler* (re-settlers) into German life has posed a series of fascinating challenges, especially for those who wish to remain linked in some way to the Anabaptist-Mennonite tradition. During the preceding seventy-five years, remnants of Mennonite communities had been scattered in places as diverse as Kazakhstan, Kyrgyzstan, Armenia, and central Siberia, resulting in a colorful variety of Aussiedler congregations and coalitions, often gathered around the charismatic leadership of a key minister.

Many Aussiedler groups have experienced culture shock as they adjusted to life in western Europe. On the one hand, they have been deeply grateful for the material assistance offered by the German government, along with the many freedoms afforded by the rule of law and a democratic state. The Aussiedler have been quite ready to embrace modern conveniences, to build new homes, and to establish thriving businesses. Many, perhaps the majority, have little interest in religious matters and are simply eager to enjoy the benefits of an affluent society.

At the same time, those Aussiedler who have retained a religious identity find much in western culture and in the practices of European Mennonites to be quite alien. Their survival as Christians in the Soviet regime under the constant shadow of persecution reinforced a religious identity that is deeply suspicious of government, strangers, and "the world" in general. They are troubled by the theological liberalism of European Mennonites and other German Christians that seems to blur gender roles, confuse lines of church authority, and shrink from clear pronouncements on ethical boundaries, especially those regarding sexuality. They are concerned about maintaining a strong sense of group identity amid the individualism of western culture and have done so by preserving a distinctive style of dress, limiting their exposure to the media, and promoting educational and service programs for their youth. Many of the Aussiedler groups are enthusiastic about missions and wonder why Mennonites in the West seem so reluctant to share the gospel with their neighbors.

All this has made the Aussiedler reluctant to associate too closely with existing Mennonite groups. Instead they have created a parallel set of institutions. In scarcely more than a decade, various Aussiedler groups established their own seminary and mission training school, along with elementary and secondary schools, relief organizations, mission societies, publishing concerns, and social-service outreach programs. Today the Aussiedler Mennonites in Germany dwarf all other European Mennonite groups in size, though the exact nature of their theological and historical kinship with these groups has not yet been fully defined.

Conclusion

The Russian Mennonite story is a narrative rich with paradoxes. In few settings have Mennonite communities been more isolated and self-contained, yet nowhere has the drama of national politics—dominated by Russian tsars, Communist revolutionaries, and Soviet commissars—intruded so profoundly into their daily life. Mennonite colonies in Russia sought to live by a set of religious convictions that placed the congregation at the center of their community life, yet it was this very fusion of religious and cultural identities that blurred the meaning of believers baptism and threatened to make the church an ethnic enclave. Mennonites in Russia desired to live in disciplined church-communities that were visibly separated from the world, yet in spite of their best intentions, the realities of sin—the fallenness of the world—stubbornly refused to disappear.

Throughout their history, Russian Mennonites struggled with the question of their relationship to this "promised land." Were the truly faithful ones those who risked all by emigrating in times of trouble or those who risked all by remaining behind?

These questions point to a theme repeated again and again in the Anabaptist-Mennonite story. How do believers live like Christ in the world of time and space? What shape will the faithful church take within a changing context? How does the "word become flesh"?

Mennonites in Russia struggled earnestly to answer those questions. Mennonites elsewhere, drawing on a similar theological heritage, faced similar questions. To be sure, Mennonites in North America were generally spared the trauma of anarchy, dislocation, and persecution, yet they too faced the challenge of living out their convictions in a complex and changing national context.

7

Mennonites in North America I

Negotiating the New World

On October 19, 1745, six Mennonite ministers from the Skippack congregation in eastern Pennsylvania composed a letter to the "ministers and elders of the nonresistant Mennonite congregations of God in Amsterdam and Haarlem," asking their Dutch cousins for assistance in translating the *Martyrs Mirror* into German. At first glance, the request seemed rather odd. Why would a frontier congregation, meeting in log cabins at the edge of the wilderness, go to the Herculean effort and expense of translating and printing a 1,400-page tome? And why choose a book focused so narrowly on the themes of persecution, suffering, and martyrdom? After all, such topics were hardly relevant for Mennonites in the New World who, as the authors of the letter acknowledged, were permitted to live "unhampered in freedom of conscience" and "in peace and liberty."

Like their Mennonite counterparts in Europe who would soon be moving to South Russia, the Swiss Brethren and Amish colonists had come to America in search of a "promised land." And, for the most part, they had found it. Here, free from the religious intolerance and feudal restrictions of Europe, they had been granted the liberty to create their own communities, to worship as they saw fit, and to become farmers, artisans, merchants, or whatever they pleased, just like their neighbors.

As the Skippack ministers went on to explain, the reason for their ambitious project was exactly the same as that put forward in the preface of the *Martyrs Mirror* by the book's compiler, Thieleman van Braght. He had written at the height of the Dutch Golden Age, "These times are certainly more dangerous . . . than the times of our fathers, who suffered death for the testimony of the Lord." During the time of the martyrs, van Braght observed, "Satan came openly . . . as a roaring lion [whose] chief design was to destroy the body." Now Satan comes "in a strange but pleasing form," he wrote, for now the world "reveals itself very beautiful and glorious, more than at any preceding time . . . in the lust of the flesh, the lust of the eye and the pride of life."

Like van Braght, the Pennsylvania ministers hoped that a translation of the *Martyrs Mirror* would keep alive the memory of persecution—not because Mennonites were suffering, but precisely because they were enjoying the security, prosperity, and freedoms of their new environment. In particular, they hoped that the book would inoculate colonial Mennonites against the fever of militarism. "The flames of war seem to be mounting higher and higher," the ministers worried. "It therefore behooves us . . . to make every preparation for steadfast endurance in our faith."

Although the Dutch were not forthcoming with much help, the ministers pressed forward. By 1748, copies of the enormous volume of Anabaptist martyr stories were coming off the press at the nearby Ephrata Cloister. Bound with leather-covered oak boards and weighing some thirteen pounds, the 1748 *Martyrs Mirror* was the largest book published in colonial America to date. Its appearance in a country where Mennonites would experience more freedom and opportunities than perhaps anywhere else in the world was an indication of the central challenge for Mennonites in America: how to remain faithful in a setting where Satan comes not "as a roaring lion," but "in a strange and pleasing form."

The Mennonites who migrated to America hoped to escape the

religious intolerance, the political restrictions, and the economic burdens of Old World feudal Europe. And they largely succeeded. Yet they found that they could not finally escape the snares of "the world." As in Russia, the Mennonites who immigrated to America were confronted with a beguiling paradox. The very features of American life that most attracted them to the New World also posed a threat to their faith and identity, often in subtle ways. How, for example, was the American celebration of rugged individualism to coexist with Mennonite virtues of humility and communal accountability? How could the materialism and the competitive nature of market-oriented capitalism be integrated with Mennonite values of simplicity and mutual aid? How would Mennonites in America negotiate their new status as citizens of a democratic society rather than as subjects of a feudal prince? The answers to these questions would not come easily.

Immigration to North America

The first Mennonites to establish a permanent home in North America set out from the German city of Crefeld aboard the *Concord.* In the fall of 1683, they landed in Philadelphia where, with the help of several Quaker families, they settled on a small plot of land called Germantown just north of the city. Over the next fifteen years, dozens of other Mennonite families from North Germany and the Palatinate joined the community. In 1708 the group constructed the first Mennonite church building in North America, a log meeting-house that still stands today. The first Amish families arrived shortly thereafter, in 1714, settling in Berks County, Pennsylvania.

During the century that followed, some seven thousand additional Mennonites and Amish immigrated to North America. Initially, Mennonite settlements clustered in the rich farmland of Skippack, northwest of Germantown, then about fifty miles west in Lancaster between the Pequea and Conestoga creeks. Following the general westward migration of the eighteenth century, Mennonites and Amish could be found in the Shenandoah Valley of Virginia as early as the 1720s, in Maryland by the 1750s, and in Mifflin County, Pennsylvania, by the 1790s.

The same steady westward trend continued into the nineteenth century, as Mennonites and Amish pushed into Wayne and Holmes counties, Ohio (1810s), before buying up land in Indiana, Illinois, and Iowa (1840s), and then in Missouri (1860s) and Kansas (1870s). With the exception of a northward migration into "Upper Canada" (eastern Ontario) beginning in the late 1770s, Mennonite and Amish congregations could be found in a consistent arc that stretched from eastern Pennsylvania to northwest Ohio and on into the Midwest.

The influx of some eighteen thousand Russian Mennonites in the 1870s introduced a new dynamic into this settlement pattern. Slightly more than half of the 1870 immigrants settled on prairie land along the railroad lines that ran through Kansas, Oklahoma, and South Dakota; the rest established homesteads in the eastern reserve of Manitoba, forming the nucleus of the city of Winnipeg. These Canadian Mennonite communities were supplemented in the 1920s by another wave of refugees fleeing from South Russia— the so-called *Russländer*—many of whom eventually settled further west in Saskatchewan and British Columbia.

Despite their differences, both the Swiss-German and the Russian Mennonites established flourishing religious communities strengthened by in-group marriage, close kinship ties, congregational patterns of mutual aid, and a strong sense of cultural separation from the world around them.

Family lore often suggests that Mennonite immigrants came to North America primarily for religious reasons: to escape religious persecution or to avoid military conscription. This is true, but only in part. The first Mennonite and Amish migrants in the early eighteenth century were indeed persecuted Swiss Brethren refugees. With the generous help of the Dutch Committee on Foreign Needs, many of these refugees resettled in the Palatinate; but a significant number continued their journey down the Rhine River to seaports like Rotterdam or Le Havre, where they found passage to the New

World. And the massive immigration out of South Russia in the 1870s was clearly triggered by the fear that Mennonites were about to lose the exemption from military service that had been promised them in the Privilegium of 1788.

But the motivations of other immigrants were more complex. In 1773, for example, a group of four Mennonite ministers in Pennsylvania explained in a letter to Dutch Mennonites that they were indeed grateful for the "freedom to serve God according to the considerations of their conscience." But they also acknowledged that immigrants in the New World paid fewer taxes than they did in Europe and "that the land is fruitful . . . to overflowing, for those who are willing to work." Here, they continued, "we have no want of food or raiment, and there are among us even people who are rich." The ebb and flow of Mennonite migration to the United States largely coincided with broader immigration patterns, suggesting that Mennonites made the decision to emigrate for similar reasons as their neighbors: land shortages, over-taxation and poverty at home, combined with the promise of cheap land, the lure of adventure, and hopes for a brighter economic future abroad.

Mennonite settlers in North America followed closely on the heels of the pioneers who were dispossessing the native inhabitants of their land, frequently with violence. Thus early Mennonite homesteaders frequently encountered Native Americans with mixed outcomes. In one memorable instance in 1757, Delaware Indians attacked the cabin of Jacob Hochstetler. Hochstetler's wife and two of his children were killed, in part because Jacob refused to allow his sons to defend the family with their hunting rifles. Jacob and two sons were taken into captivity. Although they eventually returned to their Mennonite communities in Pennsylvania, other settlers—and many more native peoples—lost their lives in the struggle to possess the land. In general, Mennonites were more inclined to be passive recipients of land taken from the natives than they were aggressive frontiersmen, but they offered almost no prophetic witness against the injustices and cruelties imposed on the native peoples.

The Promises and Perils of Prosperity

The Mennonites and Amish who settled in America brought with them a long tradition of agricultural success. Correspondence among the early settlers makes it clear that what Mennonites migrating westward wanted more than anything was land—better land, in greater quantities, and at cheaper prices. They had an eye for fertile farmland and extensive experience in making marginal land more productive. Wherever they settled, they quickly set about to drain swamps, clear fields, and plant their crops, often with a view to marketing their produce rather than simply farming for their own subsistence.

In addition to their agricultural skills, Mennonite traditions of mutual aid gave them another advantage over their neighbors. By the mid-eighteenth century, a system had developed whereby European Mennonites who provided a letter of good standing from their home congregations could count on a Mennonite from Pennsylvania or Virginia to pay their passage in exchange for several years of farm labor.

Along with the standard examples of shared labor—at harvest time, community husking bees, or barn raisings—mutual aid among Mennonite settlers also included a generous spirit of hospitality. Newcomers to America could count on spending the first few weeks adjusting to their new homeland in eastern Pennsylvania at the tables of other Mennonites who were already well established. As they passed through various Mennonite communities in search of a homestead, they could count on receiving free exchange of information about available land, advice on the details of currency exchange, warnings against unscrupulous land dealers, and counsel on dealing with local grain merchants and horse dealers. In an 1831 letter to his friends in the Palatinate, for example, Jakob Krehbiel described how Mennonites in Pennsylvania had offered interest-free loans to a group of immigrants who had fallen on hard times and were struggling to establish a settlement in Canada. Within a few years, the loans were paid off and the community was prospering.

Mennonite immigrants who settled in isolated homesteads, apart from the ties of community, tended to lose their distinctive religious identity rather quickly. At the opposite extreme were congregations such as the Swiss Brethren from the Jura region or the Alexanderwohl congregation from Molotschna, who transplanted their entire communities virtually intact. The former settled in Ohio (Sonnenberg) and Indiana (Berne) and the latter in central Kansas; both clung fiercely to their Germanic dialects, folk customs, and distinctive religious practices until well into the twentieth century.

Traditionally, Mennonite communities were overwhelmingly rural, closely tied to the rhythms of the seasons and the fortunes of agricultural markets. Mennonites in these farming communities tended to be wealthy but not conspicuously so, since so much of their capital was invested in land or set aside to purchase new farms for the next generation. The deep rootedness of these Mennonite settlements was a powerful source of stability and enduring community identity. At the same time, however, Mennonite attachment to the land complicated their even deeper identity as "pilgrims and strangers," a people whose loyalty was first and foremost to the body of Christ and only secondarily to the political authorities.

Between Loyalty and Nonresistance

"It is our fixed principle," wrote a group of Mennonite ministers in 1755 as many colonial Americans were forming militias in response to the French and Indian War, "rather than take up arms in order to defend our King, our country or ourselves, to suffer all that is dear to us to be rent from us, even life itself." The ministers were quick to add that this refusal to participate in military service came "not out of contempt to authority" but from a desire to act in accordance "to what we think is the mind and will of our Lord Jesus."

The statement aptly articulated a tension in Anabaptist-Mennonite theology that can be traced all the way back to the Schleitheim Confession of 1527. In article 6 of that statement,

Swiss Brethren leaders agreed that "the sword is an ordering of God outside the perfection of Christ"—an ambivalent phrasing that attempted to affirm the legitimate authority of the state while rejecting the notion that Christians should participate in the coercive violence that governments would inevitably use to carry out this role.

This ambivalence—respecting the role of government while rejecting Christian participation in its policing or military functions—has characterized Mennonite attitudes toward the state throughout their sojourn in North America. On the one hand, Mennonites were quick to recognize the advantages of a political system that granted them full religious liberties based on a rule of law. In their correspondence with family and friends back in Europe, Mennonite immigrants to America frequently contrasted the arbitrary rule of privilege and nobility in the Old World with the democratic principles of liberty and freedom they experienced in their new homeland. "In Europe," wrote a group of ministers in 1773, we "did not enjoy sufficient freedom to serve God according to the considerations of [our] conscience." But here we "enjoy unlimited freedom in both civil and religious affairs. We have never been compelled to bear weapons. With yea and nay we can all testify before our praiseworthy magistrates." Louis Jüngerich wrote fifty years later, "Here in America, equality and freedom reign. Even the President of America, the Head of State, is our equal." And in another letter, he said, "America is indisputably a good country where freedom flourishes."

On the other hand, Mennonite immigrants were traditionally hesitant about appealing to the court system to defend their legal rights and cautious about participating in electoral politics. In times of war, Mennonites in North America have generally sought exemption from military conscription by appealing directly to the executive branch of government (like subjects seeking a privilegium from the feudal lord), rather than lobbying legislators or pursuing their cause through the judicial system on the basis of their constitutional rights.

This ambivalence toward the state became especially problematic in times of war. The outbreak of the Revolutionary War raised a host of questions that Mennonites had not previously encountered. To the extent that colonial Mennonites had a political ethic, it tended to be conservative and oriented to the British crown. Yet the strongest advocates of religious liberty were often ardent defenders of the American Revolution. When Mennonites petitioned for exemption from service in the local militias, they brought down the wrath of loyalists and revolutionaries alike. In the end, some did serve as teamsters, while others agreed to pay war taxes or hire substitutes.

But most Mennonites drew the line when pressured to swear oaths of allegiance, and almost all refused to report for duty when conscripted. John Newcomer, a Mennonite gunsmith from Lancaster County, turned down requests that he make muskets for the war effort. Other Mennonites in the region were known to give food and shelter to needy people on both sides of the conflict, regardless of their political allegiances. The experience in the Revolutionary War sobered Mennonites in the New World. It isolated them in a new way from their patriotic neighbors, and it reminded them that their religious convictions might be in tension with the many benefits offered by their new homeland.

Later wars revived similar tensions. Although their official statements consistently defended their commitment to biblical nonresistance, actual practice among Mennonites proved more complicated. The Civil War sparked a vigorous debate about the appropriateness of "purchasing substitutes," that is, paying for someone else to fight in your place. Most Mennonites refused to enlist in the Union or Confederate armies, but they were nonetheless torn by competing allegiances and far less clear about whether or not they should pay war taxes, serve as teamsters, or sell produce that was clearly intended for the war effort.

America's entry into World War I caught Mennonites and other peace churches unprepared. The conscription legislation of 1917 made no provision for conscientious objection. All able-bodied young men, without exception, were required to report to military training camps. In those camps, Mennonite and Amish young men came under intense pressure—both psychological and punitive—to wear a military uniform and to participate in training exercises. Though the government eventually permitted some Mennonite conscripts to serve their terms as farm laborers, other young Mennonites who refused to cooperate were threatened, humiliated, and even imprisoned. Two Hutterite youths, Joseph and Michael Hofer, died in Fort Leavenworth, Kansas, as a result of this abuse. More broadly, Mennonites and Amish throughout the country who refused to buy war bonds or to otherwise support the war effort were subject to ridicule, threats, and physical mistreatment.

The experience prompted church leaders in the years following the war to develop a more coherent plan. In cooperation with representatives from the Church of the Brethren and the Quakers, Mennonites negotiated an understanding with government officials that future draft legislation would allow Mennonite conscripts to perform alternative forms of service, provided that the work was of "national importance." Further negotiations gained concession from the government that this alternative service—eventually called Civilian Public Service (CPS)—would be under the administrative oversight of the churches rather than the military.

When the United States entered World War II in 1941, a surprising number of Mennonite youth—perhaps as many as 41 percent in the Mennonite Church and 73 percent in the General Conference—enlisted in military service, albeit many of those in noncombatant roles. Thousands of other conscripted Mennonites entered CPS and spent the war years working in national parks, mental hospitals, and public health projects. Much like the forestry service of the Russian Mennonites, the CPS camps allowed Mennonites to participate in the national cause without directly supporting the armed forces.

Since World War II, understandings of nonresistance among Mennonites have continued to be a source of conversation and conflict. The Civil Rights Movement of the late 1950s and 1960s, followed by popular protests against the Vietnam War in the 1960s and 1970s, persuaded a number of young, educated Mennonites that traditional Mennonite approaches were too passive in their witness to peace. Advocating more visible, politically engaged forms of public involvement, a new generation of Mennonite activists insisted that peace cannot be achieved without also working for justice. In contrast to traditional understandings of nonresistance, activists began to call for an end to all forms of state violence, and they were willing to use confrontational tactics of direct protest to make their voices heard.

Today Mennonites in North America are divided on the principle of nonresistance and the appropriate relationship of the Christian to the state. Some have come to regard the United States, especially in its foreign policy, as imperialistic and exploitative of the powerless. For them, faithfulness to Anabaptist-Mennonite convictions demands a consistent witness against the symbols of U.S. national identity and resistance to all expressions of military power. Others, who are grateful for the religious liberties and economic opportunities in the United States, remain willing to pay taxes that support the military and perhaps even to pledge allegiance to the flag, recognizing the legitimate authority of government, even though they retain strong reservations about participating in military service. For many contemporary Mennonites, the line between an appropriate biblical respect for those in authority and the Constantinian impulse to blur church/state allegiances remains difficult to define.

Religious Worldviews

The Mennonites who immigrated to North America in the eighteenth century were not theologians. If asked to describe their faith in doctrinal language, they likely would have stammered a bit and simply quoted a verse from Scripture or possibly pointed to the Dordrecht Confession. If pressed further, they would eventually have explained their commitment as a decision to follow Christ's teachings and to abide by the discipline of the church. The hymns they sang, the devotional literature they read, and their favorite passages from Scripture all pointed toward a view of faith as a choice between two paths—a broad one and a narrow one. Many will travel down the broad path of selfishness, sin, and violence; followers of Christ, however, will pursue the narrow road—a pilgrim journey that will almost certainly lead to suffering. Memories of persecution, kept alive in texts like the *Ausbund* and the *Martyrs Mirror,* were still fresh in the eighteenth century.

Gradually, however, the language of "narrow paths" and suffering began to sound anachronistic in the New World. After all, religious minorities of all sorts were welcomed here; Mennonites enjoyed the same political rights as their neighbors, and they were free to worship (or not worship) exactly as they pleased. Moreover, despite their language of being a separate people, there was little in Mennonite practice—apart from the principle of nonresistance—that distinguished them from the thousands of other German-speaking immigrants passing through the eastern seaports. In Europe, hostile authorities had once defined Mennonites from without as a distinct people; in this new setting of religious freedom, those boundaries would need to be created from within. As a result, references to suffering—so prominent in European Mennonite literature and thought—gradually gave way among Mennonites in North America to a new language of humility and nonconformity.

The theme of humility had its basis in the teachings of Jesus that affirmed such qualities as meekness, gentleness, and servanthood. The model of humility was Christ, who, in the words of the early Christian hymn, "being in very nature God, did not consider equality with God something to be grasped, but made himself nothing, taking the very nature of a servant, being made in human likeness. And being found in appearance as a man, he humbled himself and became obedient to death—even death on a cross!" (Philippians 2:6-8).

Mennonites gave humility ritual expression in such practices as foot washing and in the use of a lot—a procedure for leadership selection by random drawing rather than self-promotion. Among Swiss-German Mennonites in the United States, humility also took the form of modest dress, a plain aesthetic, and simple forms of speech. Thus, as American dress became more refined, Mennonite groups tended to resist modern fashions, initially with a general emphasis on the principle of simplicity, but increasingly with explicit prohibitions against certain "worldly fashions" and greater attention to what became known as "regulation garb" (devotional coverings and cape dresses for women; plain cut suit coats for men).

While their Reformed, Lutheran, and Episcopalian neighbors were building impressive stone churches in the centers of towns, Mennonite meetinghouses tended to be simple structures with two exterior doors on the gable end, few windows, and roughhewn benches that seated men on one side and women on the other. While many immigrant groups quickly adopted English, Mennonites maintained their distance from public culture by continuing to speak a German Palatine dialect, known colloquially as Pennsylvania Dutch. During the course of the nineteenth century, many Mennonites became fluent in English but continued to reserve German as a language for prayer, hymnody, worship, and Bible study.

While most Swiss-German Mennonites affirmed the principles of nonconformity and humility, they were less united in their understandings of exactly how these convictions should be expressed, especially in the midst of a rapidly changing culture. At the heart of the debate was an ancient tension: granted that the "word" must in some way "become flesh," exactly what form should the Spirit assume? How should that form be discerned? How should it be enforced? Efforts to resolve these questions have been the basis for numerous conflicts within the Anabaptist-Mennonite tradition.

Some of these conflicts have prompted Mennonites to leave their tradition, finding other denominations that offer a more attractive resolution to these questions. Other attempts to resolve the tension between Spirit and form have fundamentally altered the shape of Anabaptist-Mennonite theology. Yet for most of Mennonite history, earnest engagement with these questions has been a crucial source of renewal, revitalizing the tradition and recovering aspects of Anabaptist-Mennonite faith that have been underemphasized or ignored.

Negotiating Conflicts and Renewal

The five themes of renewal summarized below are not an exhaustive accounting of Mennonite religious identity during their three-century sojourn in North America. But they do point to certain recurring dynamics that have been present in the tradition almost from the beginning and that continue to find expression among Mennonites today.

Revivalism. In 1753, Martin Boehm, a twenty-eight-year-old Pennsylvania farmer, was chosen by lot to become a minister in the Byerland Mennonite congregation near Lancaster. But Boehm had deep reservations about the authenticity of his calling. He was especially haunted by a sense of his unworthiness before God. One day, unable to bear the weight of his doubts any longer, he stopped his plowing and knelt in the field to pray. To his amazement, Boehm suddenly experienced a moment of pure joy. "It seemed as if I had awoke," he wrote later, "to new life, new thoughts, new faith, new love."

Boehm immediately began to tell others of his experience. But not everyone shared his enthusiasm. By 1777, Mennonite bishops in the area had grown so weary of his fervent and persistent preaching about the experience of personal grace that they removed Boehm from his ministerial office. Undaunted, Boehm struck an alliance with a like-minded Reformed minister, William Philip Otterbein, and the two men established the United Brethren church.

Whereas Mennonites had traditionally emphasized the themes

of ethics, suffering, humility, and church discipline, the United Brethren had all the hallmarks of early American revivalism: an emotional recognition of one's sinful character; a dramatic sense of conversion, often evoked by fiery preaching and accompanied by weeping; and a strong emphasis on missions, all framed within the intimate language of a personal relationship with God. For Mennonites who felt trapped in a joyless, rule-driven tradition, revivalism offered a more personal and Spirit-centered understanding of faith.

It is not surprising, then, that Mennonites became the prime targets for revivalist forms of outreach and renewal. For example, Christian Newcomer, once a baptized member of the Groffdale Mennonite Church, became one of the United Brethren's most effective itinerant evangelists, focusing his ministry especially on the Mennonites. By the same token, other revivalist-inspired groups such as the Dunkers, Brethren in Christ, Church of the Brethren, Methodist, and United Missionary churches have filled their pews with former Mennonites and Amish who found in their warm, heartfelt sermons a welcome alternative to the sober, moral earnestness of their own tradition.

Even Mennonites who did not convert were affected by the revivalist or Pietist movements. At the turn of the nineteenth century, for example, Mennonites in the Lancaster region published a new collection of songs to supplement, and later replace, the ponderous martyr hymns of the *Ausbund.* Only 17 percent of the hymns in the new Lancaster songbook—significantly titled *A Nondenominational Hymnal* (*Ein Unpartheyisches Gesangbuch*)— came from the *Ausbund;* the rest were borrowed from other traditions, with a strong preference for Pietist hymns. Other Mennonites developed a keen interest in the writings of Pietist authors such as Gerhard Tersteegen, whose devotional booklet *A Spiritual Flower Garden* (*Eine Geistliches Blumengärtlein*) could be found in many Pennsylvania Mennonite and Amish homes.

Martin Boehm's story was repeated dozens of times in the following centuries, albeit in many variations. Sometimes—as in the case of revivalist preachers such as John S. Coffman in the early 1900s, George R. Brunk in the 1950s, and Myron Augsburger in the 1960s—a more experiential form of spirituality served to reawaken a fresh sense of religious energy and fervor within the Mennonite church, providing an antidote to the routines and habits that threatened to stagnate the faith.

More often, however, revivalist preaching has encouraged Mennonites in North America to leave the Anabaptist tradition and join with other denominations or parachurch movements. In communities with heavy concentrations of Mennonites and Amish, the neighboring Pentecostal, nondenominational, or charismatic congregations are often filled with former Mennonites. Nearly always, this transition also signals a theological trade-off, in which an appeal to the movement of the Spirit coincides with a rejection of traditional ethical concerns emphasized by Mennonites, especially the principle of nonresistance.

Progressivism. In 1847, John H. Oberholtzer (1809-1895), a gifted, self-educated preacher at Swamp Mennonite Church, headed a division of Mennonites in eastern Pennsylvania that eventually led to the creation of the General Conference Mennonite Church in 1860. Oberholtzer and his followers were frustrated by the conservatism of Mennonites in his community, especially the restrictive cultural habits that governed church practices. Specifically, Oberholtzer called for greater liberties in matters of dress, clearer lines of church organization (including a formal constitution and regular minutes of church meetings), the creation of new institutions that would promote higher education, a stronger mission program, and better church-related publications. In short, Oberholtzer wanted a more progressive church, one that was attuned to the shifting cultural realities of the world around it.

Oberholtzer's primary area of influence had been in eastern Pennsylvania, but in 1860 his initiative was taken up by progressive-minded Mennonite immigrants in the Midwest, leading to the formation at West Point, Iowa, of the General Conference of Mennonites in North America. The General Conference might have remained a small splinter group were it not for the wave of Russian Mennonite immigrants in the 1870s who embraced it. The newcomers from Russia brought with them skilled leaders and a long tradition of institutional experience that quickly transformed the General Conference into a dynamic body. Within a decade, the General Conference had established an orphanage, an educational program (the Wadsworth Institute at Wadsworth, Ohio), and a mission outreach to Native Americans in the western plains states.

During the century that followed, the General Conference encouraged a strong congregational polity among its member churches. These congregations formed regional districts that together provided support for a dynamic mission outreach, several colleges, a seminary, a publishing house, and denominational offices in Winnipeg, Manitoba, and Newton, Kansas. Before merging again with the Mennonite Church in 2002 to form Mennonite Church USA, the General Conference had some sixty-five thousand members in more than four hundred congregations in Canada, the United States, and South America.

A similar progressivist spirit found expression within the larger Mennonite church—sometimes called the (Old) Mennonite Church to distinguish it from the General Conference—in the flurry of activities associated with the work of John F. Funk (1835-1930). In 1867, following his conversion at a Moody revival meeting in Chicago, Funk left a flourishing lumber business and moved to Elkhart, Indiana, where he established a printing and publishing business in the service of the Mennonite church. There he attracted other future church leaders to his progressivist cause, including evangelist J. S. Coffman, historian John Horsch, mission advocate George Bender, and H. A. Mumaw, the founder of the Elkhart Institute (later Goshen College). Funk not only published the leading Mennonite church paper of the day, *Herald of Truth* (German edition, *Herold der Wahrheit,* 1864-1902), but he also promoted a host of theological, historical, doctrinal, and devotional books that solidified a sense of Mennonite identity amid the rapid economic and cultural changes at the turn of the century.

Shortly thereafter, Mennonites began to establish dozens of institutions: Sunday schools (1880s), Mennonite Aid Plan (1882), Young Peoples' Meetings (1890s), mission ventures (1890s), a relief agency (1897), and Goshen College (1904), to name only a few. In 1920, five different Mennonite groups joined together to form the Mennonite Central Committee (MCC) as a compassionate response to the famine and devastation in the Ukraine following the Russian Revolution. At about the same time, women across the church began to organize sewing circles to support overseas relief work, an outreach that pulled thousands of Mennonite laywomen into the larger mission and service outreach of the church.

These initiatives and dozens more that emerged in the following decades all expressed a similar desire to make the principles of Mennonite faith more relevant to the changing realities of the world. Yet these institutions also introduced new tensions into the church, especially with regard to the ideals of nonconformity and humility. The new organizations fully embraced the progressivist spirit of the broader American culture. As such, they reflected the busyness, hierarchies, marketing demands, and budget-conscious strategic planning characteristic of modern institutions in ways that could easily become more focused on their own survival than on the priorities of the larger church. Critics sought for renewal in a different direction.

Old Order movements. In the summer of 1862, a group of Amish ministers gathered in the barn of Samuel and Lydia Schrock in Wayne County, Ohio, for a series of meetings about church practices. The specific question up for debate had to do with baptism and whether it was permissible to baptize in a stream or pond rather than inside a house, as was traditionally the case. Soon the agenda opened up to other kinds of questions, especially those related to the rapidly changing nature of American culture. What was the Amish position, for example, on voting or lotteries or lightning rods or photographs or marriage outside the church or dress restrictions or meetinghouses?

Some in the group, which continued to meet almost every year until 1878, advocated a greater openness to change. Like Oberholtzer and Funk, they were ready to adjust the boundaries separating the church from the world. But others insisted that the line be firmly held. The result was a division within the Amish church between the more progressive group, which adopted the label Amish-Mennonite and eventually joined with the larger Mennonite body, and the so-called Old Order Amish, who were committed to holding firm to the traditional practices.

In the face of the broader progressivist movement, similar divisions were emerging within the Mennonite Church as well. In the 1870s, for example, Jacob Wisler (Indiana and Ohio) and Abraham Martin (Ontario) led Old Order movements out of the Mennonite Church in protest against such innovations as Sunday school, revival meetings, and the growing use of the English language. A similar set of disagreements prompted Jonas Martin to part ways with the Lancaster conference in the 1890s. All of these, and other Old Order divisions that followed, reflected concerns analogous to those that led to the Amish break from the Swiss Brethren in 1693 or the Kleine Gemeinde division of 1812—the impulse deep within Anabaptist-Mennonite theology to define the church as a body visibly separated from the surrounding culture.

It is a fiction of the popular imagination that these Old Order groups are frozen in time or pathologically resistant to change. Passing on a tradition, even a tradition committed to stability, is always a dynamic process, dependent on gifted leadership to negotiate the complex balance of cultural change and continuity of conviction. Old Order groups are not so much opposed to innovations as they are committed to asking critical questions about how such changes will impact their values of humility, family life, and community relationships, and the clarity of the church as a body separated from the world. In the face of intense pressure to conform to contemporary culture, the Old Orders represent a creative form of resistance to modernity and, with it, an alternative vision of church renewal.

Fundamentalism and evangelicalism. If the Old Order movement was a reaction to progressivist initiatives, the fundamentalist movement among Mennonites was a theological response to the liberal tendencies of some Mennonites in the first half of the twentieth century. Like the Old Orders, Mennonite fundamentalists hoped to find a firm place to stand amid the shifting sands of modern culture. They did so by borrowing heavily from sources outside the Anabaptist-Mennonite tradition. In 1909 a series of booklets called *The Fundamentals* appeared that defined the essentials of the Christian faith in a series of succinct doctrinal principles. For many American Christians, these "fundamentals" became the litmus test of genuine Christianity and a powerful antidote to the strains of liberalism and modernism that seemed to be infecting the church.

For some Mennonites, the clarity of the fundamentalist worldview, which divided the world into distinct categories of good and evil, seemed to fit well with their own tradition of nonconformity. The confident, often polemical, tone of fundamentalist theology provided a sense of reassurance in a time of rapid cultural change. So some Mennonites borrowed heavily from the language of fundamentalism—the inerrancy of Scripture, for example, or the substitutionary atonement, or the imminent return of Christ—while adding several additional Mennonite "fundamentals," such as nonresistance or plain dress.

Today Mennonites who might have been interested in fundamentalism in the 1940s have tended to shift their attention to conservative evangelical theology. Evangelicalism shares many of the theological concerns of the fundamentalist movement but is generally more optimistic about the Christian calling to transform society, culture, and politics.

Thus contemporary Mennonites inclined toward a conservative theology have borrowed heavily from evangelical radio and television ministries, educational institutions, books, and seminars for counsel on how they might engage American mainstream culture with a new sense of confidence. These congregations may continue to affirm Mennonite convictions like believers baptism or even nonresistance, but their members are also likely to listen regularly to Focus on the Family radio programs, read the books in the Left Behind series, support the Promise Keepers movement, and make financial contributions to the ministries of popular television preachers.

Historical memory. On the evening of December 29, 1943, Harold S. Bender, professor of church history at Goshen College and editor of *The Mennonite Quarterly Review,* delivered the presidential address to the American Society of Church History. At the time, there was little to suggest that his speech would become one of the most significant statements for the Mennonite church in the last half of the twentieth century. Bender had written the address in great haste; he presented it to a very small, albeit prestigious, audience of academic historians; and he departed almost immediately after the address for more pressing church-related business elsewhere. Nevertheless, "The Anabaptist Vision" has proved to be an enduring and influential symbol of twentieth-century Mennonite renewal through the conscious recovery of historical memory.

In his essay, Bender argued that North American Mennonites were the heirs of a deep and rich theological tradition. Whereas most academic historians had dismissed the Anabaptists as wild-eyed fanatics, Bender insisted that they were the true heroes of the Reformation. Unlike Luther and Zwingli, who allowed political concerns to override their early theological insights, the Anabaptists had held firm to biblical principles and had carried the ideas of the Protestant reformers to their logical conclusion in their emphasis on discipleship, the church as a disciplined and visible community, and an ethic of love in all human relationships. Not least, Anabaptist ideas had inspired themes at the heart of the U.S. Constitution. "There can be no question," Bender argued, "but that the great principles of freedom of conscience, separation of church and state, and voluntarism in religion, so basic in American Protestantism and so essential to democracy, ultimately are derived from the Anabaptists of the Reformation period."

By the middle of the twentieth century, the fabric of rural Mennonite communities was beginning to unravel. The Great

Depression strained the farm economy, and in the aftermath of World War II an entire generation of young people moved off the farm to the cities and suburbs, taking jobs in the manufacturing, business, and service occupations. At the same time, soaring land prices, especially along the eastern seaboard, made it difficult for young Mennonites to establish themselves as farmers. It became all the more tempting to sell the family farm and invest the profits in more lucrative business ventures.

For a generation of Mennonites in the process of leaving their tightly knit farm communities for the world of suburbia, university training, and the professions, Bender's "The Anabaptist Vision" and the larger effort to rehabilitate Anabaptism as a respectable field of historical and theological study were reminders of the best features of their religious tradition. Not only did it describe Anabaptist history in the context of modern scholarship, but it did so in clear, understandable language while offering upwardly mobile Mennonites a tradition worthy of pride and admiration.

In the second half of the twentieth century, the "recovery of the Anabaptist vision" has been an important source of renewal in the Mennonite church. The Anabaptist commitment to nonresistance has sparked a great deal of careful reflection on Mennonite peace theology; the egalitarian emphasis in early Anabaptist congregations has raised new questions about the meaning of ordination and given a higher status to lay leadership; the practice of mutual aid among sixteenth-century Anabaptists has inspired some Mennonites to live in community or to adopt a simpler lifestyle; and communal approaches to reading Scripture evident among some Anabaptist groups, and their concern for church discipline, have prompted a renewed interest in group Bible study and discernment. Some Mennonites have embraced this conscious appeal to historical memory as a form of renewal—one that affirms, rather than rejects, the deep roots of the tradition.

Denominational 'Transformation' for the Twenty-First Century

In July 1989, representatives from the Mennonite Church of Canada, along with their counterparts from the two major Mennonite groups in the United States—the Mennonite Church and the General Conference Mennonite Church—initiated a series of conversations to explore the possibility of integrating their church bodies. Since the founding of the General Conference in 1860, the two groups had maintained a parallel set of congregations, conferences, and denominational agencies, both of which extended across the border into Canada.

The differences between the groups were cultural as well as theological. Most members in the General Conference traced their history back to the emigrations from South Russia to the United States and Canada in the 1870s and, to a lesser extent, to the migration of the 1920s. The majority of General Conference congregations were located in Canada. The culture of the Mennonite Church, by contrast, was deeply shaped by the Swiss-German immigrant streams, reflecting the traditions of the Swiss Brethren and Amish.

In contrast to the strong conference identity in the Mennonite Church, General Conference Mennonites tended to affirm a church polity that granted more authority to individual congregations, leading to somewhat greater diversity in matters of faith and practice. Traditionally, General Conference congregations also tended to be more affirming of North American culture and were more likely to embrace higher education and participate in political affairs than Mennonite Church congregations.

However, these differences had diminished over time. Members of newly formed congregations, especially urban fellowships composed of people largely new to the Anabaptist-Mennonite tradition, had little awareness of these divergent traditions. Indeed, a growing number of congregations had adopted joint membership in both the General Conference and the Mennonite Church, and young people—even those raised in traditional congregations—showed little interest in embracing the traditional distinctions.

Early in the process of exploring the possibility of integration, the two groups agreed to cooperate in writing a joint confession of faith. In 1995, after a long and deliberative process lasting nearly fifteen years, the Mennonite Church General Assembly and delegates of the General Conference Mennonite Church approved the twenty-four articles of the "Confession of Faith in a Mennonite Perspective" by majority votes of more than 98 percent.

At the same gathering, delegates voted to merge the two groups and at the 1999 assembly approved a new integrated structure of church organization. When the Mennonite Church of Canada opted for a merger within its own national context, the result of the lengthy process became clear. The two groups, the General Conference Mennonite Church and the (Old) Mennonite Church, would join to become two new national groups: Mennonite Church Canada (MC Canada) and Mennonite Church USA (MC USA).

By many accounts, the merger was a success. The integration process healed a division among Mennonites nearly 140 years old; it streamlined two sets of overlapping, sometimes redundant denominational agencies; and it recalibrated the theological center of the church around a new confession of faith that both groups enthusiastically affirmed.

But the merger also raised a number of additional questions that are not fully resolved. Although the agreement did bring together portions of the General Conference and Mennonite Church bodies, it also resulted in the creation of two nationally organized Mennonite bodies, raising questions about the theological symbolism of Anabaptist groups defining their church structures along territorial boundaries. Efforts to unify a divided church also resulted in the decision of dozens of congregations—generally those with a more conservative orientation—to break from both bodies. And grassroots loyalty to the newly created MC USA and MC Canada groups remains tenuous, at least if measured by the initial decline in giving to church agencies and support for denominational periodicals and programs.

But the impact of another less visible transformation may be even more profound. As local mission efforts have taken root among Mennonites beyond the Swiss and Russian ethnic traditions, the larger church is being transformed and renewed. In the end, the future of the church is likely to reside less in the maintenance of Germanic cultural traditions than in the integration of new worship practices, spiritual insights, and leadership gifts from a broad mix of racial and ethnic groups—at home and around the world—that are relatively new to the Anabaptist-Mennonite tradition. It is to that story that we now turn

Worldwide Baptized Anabaptist-Related Members	North American Anabaptist Groups Adult Members	
1,400,000	Amish	116,000
	Beachy Amish Mennonite	8,000
(Mennonite World Conference 2005)	Brethren in Christ	24,000
	Church of God in Christ (Holdeman)	18,000
	Conservative Mennonite Conference	11,000
	Hutterian Brethren	16,000
	Mennonite Brethren Church	64,000
	Mennonite Church Canada	34,000
	Mennonite Church USA	111,000
	Old Order Mennonites	22,000
	Other Mennonites	34,000
	Total	458,000

8

Mennonites in North America II

A New Mosaic

In June 2004 the Central Plains Mennonite Conference celebrated the addition of a new congregation to its fellowship. On the surface, Christ Community Church of Des Moines appeared to be an unlikely candidate for entering the Mennonite fold. Virtually none of its participants had German-sounding family names; most members regarded the acronyms of Mennonite institutions as an alphabet soup of random letters; and their style of worship, which included the celebration of the Lord's Supper every Sunday, borrowed more heavily from the ancient liturgies of the early church than from the practices of sixteenth-century Anabaptism.

Yet members of this small congregation saw something in the Mennonite tradition that was attractive. "It's hard to find a church these days that is willing to live out the truth that community is important," one member of Christ Community noted. Another leader added, "We have benefited from the gift [of the Mennonite church], and we are persuaded that you owe that gift to all of God's people." The new congregation recognized in the Mennonite church a body of believers who cared about discipleship and following Christ's way of peace, and they wanted to become part of that body.

However, that is only half the story. If Christ Community Church has gained something from its association with the Mennonites, the broader significance of their decision is the gift that this new congregation and dozens of other new congregations across North America have brought to the larger tradition. The desire of Christ Community Church to pursue "whole life discipleship," for example, should prompt other Mennonite congregations to think more carefully about how they are putting their faith into practice. The congregation's process for inviting, teaching, and forming new members—a highly intentional program that extends over two years—highlights a part of Mennonite baptismal theology that is sometimes neglected in established churches, and its liturgical worship style is a much-needed reminder that the focus of our worship should be on God rather than on ourselves.

The story of Christ Community Church is unique in its details. But the broader theme of mutually enriching encounters that cut across culture, theology, and history has been a significant development in the story of North America Mennonites during the twentieth century.

Mennonite "home missions" in the United States began in the 1880s with an outreach by the General Conference to several Plains Indian tribes. Shortly thereafter, Mennonites extended their mission efforts, tentatively to be sure, into a number of urban settings and then wholeheartedly in the establishment of several hundred rural mission congregations during the first half of the century. At the same time, Mennonite initiatives among African-American and Latino communities were slowly taking root. In more recent decades, the rapid growth of multicultural urban Mennonite congregations are invigorating the whole church with a new vision for missions and a rich variety of worship styles.

To be sure, the history of Mennonite home missions in the twentieth century has not been without its problems. Sometimes racial prejudices, unspoken cultural expectations, and the hidden rules understood only by church "insiders" have made it impossible for newcomers to find a genuine home in Mennonite congregations. Sometimes well-intended initiatives have felt heavy-handed and paternalistic to those on the receiving end. And sometimes the gap between the professed ideals of Mennonite theology and the messy realities of actual Mennonite practice has become so wide that new members turn away in frustration and disappointment.

But the overall impact of these encounters on the Mennonite church has been profound. As Mennonites of Russian and Swiss-German descent have shared the gospel with people of other cultures, they have been forced to distinguish between their faith convictions and their cultural identity. Today the "typical" Mennonite congregation in North America is no longer a rural community church steeped in European cultural traditions but rather an urban or suburban fellowship whose members speak a wide variety of languages, trace their ancestry back to numerous countries, and worship in many different styles.

As Christ Community Church can testify, the Anabaptist-Mennonite tradition has frequently been a gift that others have received with gratitude. Yet, in the process of receiving that gift, these newcomers have also brought gifts of their own, which have enlivened, enriched, and sustained the Anabaptist-Mennonite tradition in unexpected ways.

Mennonite Missions to Native Americans

Lawrence Hart has told the story many times, but it is never worn from the telling. A Cheyenne peace chief, Hart grew up steeped in the religious traditions of his people. His grandfather, John Peak Heart, had been a central figure in the renewal of Cheyenne religious practices during the first half of the twentieth century; his father, Homer, was a gifted lay pastor long associated with the Red Moon Mennonite mission church in Hammon, Oklahoma. Hart himself is an articulate Mennonite minister, a tribal chief, and a bridge-builder between the Mennonite church and the traditional practices of his Cheyenne people. One of Hart's many stories tells of a transformative moment in his understanding of how such boundaries might be crossed.

In November 1868, Black Kettle—a friend of Hart's great-grandfather and a Cheyenne peace chief—had traveled to Fort

Cobb, seeking assurance from Colonel William Hazen that the Cheyenne people would find safe haven along the banks of the Washita River in the Indian Territory (later known as Oklahoma). Angered by reports of recent Cheyenne raids, Hazen had refused their request. The news was disappointing, but Black Kettle could never have anticipated what was to happen next.

On the night of November 27, the U.S. Seventh Cavalry, led by Lieutenant Colonel George Custer, approached the Cheyenne encampment. At the signal of the army's marching song "Garry Owen," the troops attacked, killing or capturing virtually the entire group, women and children included. The Massacre of Washita has lived on in Cheyenne memory as a day of infamy.

One hundred years later, the so-called Grandsons of the Seventh Cavalry arrived in the Oklahoma town of Cheyenne to participate in a centennial event that included a reenactment of the Washita massacre. As the tribal chiefs gathered for a ceremonial reburial of an infant victim of the event, the Grandsons of the Seventh Cavalry marched once more to the tune of "Garry Owen," shooting blank cartridges as they replayed the horrific scene of the slaughter. The Cheyenne were terrified and stunned by the realism of the reenactment and outraged once more by the memories of the tragic day. Again, no one could have anticipated what was to happen next.

According to Cheyenne custom, a new woolen blanket that had been part of the burial ceremony was to be presented later in the day to an honored guest chosen by the peace chiefs. Lawrence Hart, then a young chief, assumed that the blanket would go to one of the many tribal dignitaries who had gathered for the occasion. To his shock, however, the older chiefs asked Hart to present it to the captain of the Grandsons of the Seventh Cavalry. As the captain stepped forward, saber raised to give a military salute, Hart asked him to turn around. And then, in a gesture of vulnerability and reconciliation, Hart draped the blanket over the shoulders of the captain.

The gift stunned the captain and all those in attendance. Shortly thereafter, the captain removed the "Garry Owen" pin from his uniform and gave it to Hart. "Accept this on behalf of all the Cheyenne Indian people," the captain said. "Never again will your people hear 'Garry Owen.'"

The story is only one example of a reality that has occurred again and again in the history of Mennonite missions. Lawrence Hart joined the Mennonite church as a result of missionary efforts among the Cheyenne people. But it was ultimately the Cheyenne peace chiefs, not the Mennonite missionaries, who taught Hart the principle of nonresistance, a gift that he has since returned to the Mennonites as a faithful teacher of peace. Through Hart's willing-ness to cross the boundaries of culture, the Mennonite tradition has been renewed and God's Spirit made visible in a new way.

The larger story of Mennonite missions to the Plains Indians is a complex, sometimes painful history filled with good intentions, destructive mistakes, and the steady reality of God's grace amid human frailties and failures. When Samuel and Susanna Haury arrived in Darlington, Indian Territory, in May 1880 as the first missionaries of the General Conference to Native Americans, they described their work as "foreign" missions. And perhaps with good reason. The cou-ple had trained for overseas missionary work at mission schools in Germany, and they encountered the Cheyenne as a people whose cul-ture and language were almost completely alien to them.

By 1875 the steady westward migration of white settlers, whose way had been cleared by the U.S. Cavalry, had forced both the Cheyenne and the Arapaho off their traditional hunting lands and onto a reservation in Indian Territory. When Mennonite mission-aries like the Haury's arrived five years later, the tribes were in cul-tural turmoil. Reservation life had brought an end to buffalo hunt-ing, introduced new diseases, and led to the forced enrollment of Cheyenne and Arapaho children in government schools. Initially, the work of the missionaries seemed to be fully aligned with the interests of the U.S. government. For example, Samuel Haury served not only as superintendent of the mission but also as the principal of the Indian school and as a government sub-agent for the Darlington district.

The first significant step toward greater cultural sensitivity came with the arrival of Rudolphe Petter in 1891. An energetic and gifted linguist, Petter committed himself to an intense study of the Cheyenne language. Along with his wife, Bertha, he established a phonetic system for writing in Cheyenne, an effort that eventually culminated in a massive Cheyenne-English dictionary, along with the translation of the Bible into Cheyenne. At about the same time, J. A. Funk completed a similar undertaking as a missionary to the neighboring Arapaho tribe. In 1916, Petter and his wife refocused their energies on a new mission undertaking in southeast Montana—following the movement of the Northern Cheyenne— where they remained until 1947.

A second major General Conference mission effort among Native Americans focused on the Hopi of northern Arizona. H. R. Voth began his missionary career among the Cheyenne in Darlington, but in 1893 he and his wife, Martha, relocated to Arizona and set about learning the Hopi language and culture. The Hopis had lived among the mesas of Arizona as desert farmers for nearly 1,300 years. Isolated from the immediate impact of the westward migrations, they had kept their traditions relatively intact.

Like Petter and Funk, Voth took a keen interest in Hopi customs and religious ceremonies, gathering artifacts and recording the details of Hopi ceremonial practices. Although his passion for collecting has had an enduring value for anthropologists, Voth aroused significant controversy among both the Hopi and the General Conference mission board when he sold many of his Hopi artifacts to the Field Museum in Chicago and agreed to work as a hired agent of the museum. J. B. Frey, a gifted preacher who had also mastered the Hopi language, left a somewhat more positive legacy among the Hopi, although his work was called into question over accusations that he believed in the doctrine of universal salvation.

In the end, after more than a century of dedicated missions among the Cheyenne, Arapaho, and Hopi, the results in terms of actual converts and self-sustaining congregations were rather meager. Native peoples tended to regard Mennonite missionaries—

sometimes quite correctly—as a part of the U.S. government's campaign to pacify and "civilize" them. Although several missionaries were deeply interested in local language and culture, most made a sharp distinction between Christian faith and tribal practices, a strategy that inevitably pitted Christian converts against traditionalists who were intent on preserving their culture. Competition with other missionary organizations and internal controversies, such as the forty-year theological debate that swirled around Frey's teachings, further complicated matters.

Yet the consequences of Mennonite missions among the Plains Indians were by no means entirely negative. The dedicated work of several key individuals had resulted in the creation of dictionaries in Cheyenne, Arapaho, and Hopi, and eventually the translation of the Bible into these languages. Through the teaching and example of Mennonite missionaries, numerous native leaders served faithfully in positions of congregational leadership. And the pioneering work of the General Conference paved the way for later mission initiatives by the Mennonite Church and the Mennonite Brethren to other Native American groups, including the Choctaw (Mississippi), Métis (Manitoba), Cree (several Canadian provinces), Creek (Georgia and Alabama), Navajo (Arizona, Utah, and New Mexico), Lakota (South Dakota), and Ojibway (Great Lakes region).

During the second half of the twentieth century, Native American concerns gained a more visible structural presence within the General Conference and Mennonite Church through the creation of two councils (the Mennonite Indian Leaders Council and the United Native Ministers Council) that have cultivated Native American leadership and served as advocates for native congregations. Now combined as the Ministries of Native Congregations, these councils played an important role in educating the broader church on Native American concerns and in nudging Mennonites to take greater ownership of their complicity in the larger historical drama that forced native peoples off their lands.

In 1991, just prior to the sesquicentennial recognizing Christopher Columbus's landfall in the Americas in 1492, the

Mennonite Church passed a resolution formally acknowledging the "displacement and oppression of the native populations," and calling on members and congregations to the following:

1. Refrain from a triumphalist spirit in celebrating this event [the Columbus sesquicentennial] *in favor of humble gratitude for the benefits experienced in these new lands.*

2. Recognize the greed and devastation that characterized the coming of the Europeans, and repent of our participation in the unjust exploitation of native peoples.

3. Seek to understand more accurately the rich history of native peoples, hear their stories, feel their pain, and learn from their values and patterns of life.

4. Rejoice that even through suffering many Native Americans received the gospel message and share in the body of Christ.

5. Recognize the leadership of the United Native Ministries Council (UNMC), and learn to know and support in love and prayer the member congregations and congregations eligible for membership in the council.

6. Advocate for appropriate redressing of injustices done to native people in the past, and for just and constructive programs of human betterment for native peoples now and in the future. We would welcome guidance from UNMC on how to work at this. A first suggestion from the council is the building of relationships with Native Americans in our home communities.

7. Renew a commitment to the mission of Christ in North America that is sensitively inclusive of peoples of all nations, tribes, peoples, and tongues.

8. Reaffirm the global nature of the church and its mission and resist the provincial attitude characteristic of nationalistic celebrations.

More recently, MCC has also supported an initiative called "Return to the Earth," which is committed to reburying with dignity the remains of native peoples exhumed by archaeological digs.

None of these efforts can undo the wrongs of the past. But they serve to remind the church that the sufferings of a part of its body—in this case, those of Native American ancestry—cause the entire body to suffer and dare not go unacknowledged.

Home Missions in Urban and Rural Settings

As a young Mennonite girl growing up in Holmes County, Ohio, Ella Shoup had lofty dreams. She hoped to study at Goshen College and then devote the rest of her life to missionary work in South America. The first part of her dream came true. Ella graduated from Goshen Academy in 1920 and then spent two years at Goshen College. But a chronic asthma condition made it impossible for her to pursue her ambition to serve the church as an overseas missionary. So she and her husband, Norman Bauman, a farmer from Ontario, settled near Youngstown, Ohio, where she turned her attention to raising a family.

In the late 1940s, Ella began a practice of taking along a bag of Christian books to Youngstown during her regular visits to the doctor. There she would go door-to-door, offering the books for sale. One day a sudden rainstorm drove her to find shelter in the overhang of an empty storefront. When several children joined her there, also seeking refuge from the rainstorm, Ella passed the time by telling them Bible stories. The children were captivated and begged her to return to tell them more stories. Over the next five years, Ella spent numerous hours establishing friendships among the families in the neighborhood around West Federal Street. Along the way, her weekly Bible-story hour for children gradually expanded into a Sunday-afternoon worship service, now held in a vacant building and attended by adults as well.

By 1952 the impromptu outdoor story session on a rainy afternoon had become a functioning congregation. Ella's dream to serve as a foreign missionary in South America did not come to fruition, but the families who became part of the little congregation she helped to establish in Youngstown were transformed by her witness.

The congregation on West Federal Street was one of dozens of Mennonite church plants started by ordinary people in a burst of missionary zeal around the middle of the century. Ella was part of a generation of Mennonite young people who had been deeply shaped by the introduction of Sunday schools, revival meetings, young people's meetings, and the inspiring stories of returned overseas missionaries—all emphasizing the importance of sharing the gospel with a lost world. By the middle of the century, Mennonites who had traditionally looked on "the world" as something to be feared or avoided now began to refer to the world as a mission field "white unto harvest."

Between 1860 and 1960, the (Old) Mennonite Church began nearly six hundred local missions in the United States. Some of the earliest of these mission projects were urban initiatives. The Chicago Home Mission, for example, begun in 1893 at the instigation of Menno S. Steiner, an Ohio Mennonite evangelist, initially took the form of several Sunday school conferences with an outreach focused especially on children. Reorganized in 1896 more firmly under the control of the Mennonite Church, the mission broadened its program to integrate mother's groups, sewing classes, and a nursery with more explicit forms of evangelism. Similar mission efforts soon followed in Philadelphia; Kansas City; Fort Wayne, Indiana; and Lima, Canton, and Youngstown, Ohio.

In 1908 General Conference Mennonites also created a Home Mission Board and sent their first urban missionaries, Elmer and Esther Grubb, to Los Angeles. Shortly after, with the help of General Conference students attending Moody Bible Institute, a mission congregation emerged in Chicago, with other church plants eventually established in Altoona, Pennsylvania, and Hutchinson, Kansas.

Although the intentions of these early mission efforts to the city were unquestionably noble, the short-term results were marginal, especially if judged by any numerical standard. The history of these pioneering ministries were often clouded with tensions, especially over issues of ownership, funding, and focus, and conflicts between the charismatic personalities in the field and the more sober-minded inclinations of the sending agencies. Frequently, both missionaries and agencies expressed uncertainty about the place of Mennonite "theological distinctives" in mission settings, especially those related to plain dress or nonresistance.

Mennonites were more successful in their efforts to plant rural congregations. Between 1930 and 1960, approximately 430 new congregations entered the (Old) Mennonite Church, many of them the result of a local outreach by established churches. Under the banner "Every Congregation an Outpost," churches would identify several families who agreed to move or commute to a neighboring town as church planters. Typically, they would rent a building and hold Bible school during the summer months before starting regular weekly worship services with a special emphasis on Sunday school classes for the children. Pastors were typically bivocational, eking out a living with odd jobs and the ongoing support of the sending church.

Although these rural church plants rarely grew very large and often reflected a paternalistic spirit of charity, they represented a remarkable outpouring of energy, often at great personal sacrifice to those most closely involved. A significant number of later Mennonite leaders gained valuable training in these outposts. Moreover, the rural missions provided sending congregations with an opportunity to break down some of the cultural barriers that had long separated them from their local community.

In venturing beyond traditional borders, these early mission efforts opened the Mennonite church to still another, largely unintended, consequence—an encounter with the profound challenges of race, prejudice, and structural injustice, along with new possibilities of transformation and renewal.

Outreach to African-Americans

In the course of his ninety years, James Lark lived through the long, often painful, trajectory of twentieth-century race relations in the United States. Born in Savannah, Georgia, in 1888, Lark had witnessed the lynching of his uncle and endured the persistent reality of racism during his military service in France during World War I. In the 1920s James and his wife, Rowena, moved to the outskirts of Quakertown, Pennsylvania, where they first encountered Mennonites. Persuaded more by the example of practical discipleship and the teachings of nonresistance than by the obligations of plain dress, the couple joined the Rocky Ridge Mennonite Church and quickly moved into positions of leadership. During the 1930s and 1940s, the Lark family led numerous Bible school ministries in black communities in Maryland, Virginia, and Illinois, drawing heavily on Rowena's gifts as a soloist and children's storyteller. In 1946 James accepted ordination as a Mennonite minister at the Bethel congregation in Chicago; eight years later he became the first African-American bishop in the Mennonite church.

Throughout the remainder of his long career, Lark worked tirelessly to establish urban ministries that addressed the physical as well as spiritual needs of the African-American community. Before his death in 1978, he had been instrumental in establishing at least four integrated Mennonite churches and several summer-camp programs. Along the way he also challenged Mennonite church leaders to take seriously a model of urban ministry that connected evangelism with community development, including daycare centers, leadership training, healthcare, and job opportunities for young people.

Lark was a visionary and an entrepreneur, prone to impatience with those who were slow to catch the full scope of his vision. Frustrated at the disproportionate amount of resources the Mennonite church was devoting to overseas missions, he frequently likened his role to that of a tugboat—a tiny force of movement trying to nudge the larger body of the Mennonite church into uncharted and deeper waters of urban ministry among African-

Americans. In many ways, James and Rowena were ahead of their time—pioneers in their prophetic insistence that the gospel would inevitably call Christians to ministries of racial integration and reconciliation that addresses the needs of the whole person.

As with the mission outreach to Native Americans, the history of Mennonite relations with African-Americans has been mixed—an occasion for confession as well as celebration. Mennonites were among the signatories of the first petition against slavery in North America, issued in 1688, and few, if any, appear to have owned slaves. Nevertheless, the Mennonite church as a whole has not had a particularly distinguished record in terms of its outreach to the black community or initiatives on behalf of racial reconciliation. For the most part, Mennonite congregations were segregated well into the twentieth century, and several early integrated mission churches reportedly held separate services for communion and foot washing.

Still, the vision for home missions that gripped the church in the early twentieth century included several initiatives that crossed the color line. Between 1898 and 1950, the Mennonite Church established thirteen predominantly African-American congregations. The first of these efforts emerged among Mennonites in Lancaster County, Pennsylvania, directed to a rural black community in the eastern part of the county called Welsh Mountain. The initial focus of the Welsh Mountain Industrial Mission was less on saving souls than on social reform: improving nutrition, hygiene, and living conditions, and instilling a work ethnic through a job creation program. Over time, however, attention gradually shifted to spiritual and educational needs. By the 1930s, this outreach had broadened to Bible study, Sunday school, and the formation of the first African-American Mennonite congregation.

The Welsh Mountain mission was followed in 1933 by the Lancaster Colored Mission and a church plant in Philadelphia in 1935 that eventually became the Diamond Street Mennonite Church. Although ten additional African-American congregations were established during this early phase of activity, by 1950 the total number of African-American Mennonites probably did not exceed several hundred members.

In the early 1960s many young African-American Mennonites hoped that the larger Mennonite church, given its deep memories of suffering and persecution, would rally to the cause of the Civil Rights Movement. By and large, however, the church was hesitant, not only out of a latent racism but also because of deeper reservations about participating in confrontational political activities that involved the demanding of legal rights. Nonetheless, the 1960s and 1970s witnessed a slow shift within the church in terms of its social and political witness.

Inspired by the vision of Martin Luther King Jr., at least some Mennonites began to reframe traditional Mennonite nonresistance into more activist forms of political engagement that included an acknowledgment of structural injustices and a willingness to engage in nonviolent resistance to racism and oppression. Vincent Harding, a gifted African-American Mennonite preacher, civil rights leader, and historian, was a prophetic voice of conscience within the church during those tumultuous years. Harding, who had served alongside King, inspired numerous young Mennonites to rethink the radical faith of their Anabaptist forbearers in light of the contemporary social and political realities and to bring issues of racial injustice to the forefront of the church's agenda.

These were minority voices within the broader Mennonite church, to be sure, but such voices eventually found greater hearing in the form of the Urban Racial Council, created in 1969, and in its later organizational incarnations (the Black Council; the Afro-American Mennonite Association; and the Office of Black Concerns). Currently, the African-American Mennonite Association provides workshops, consultations, and biennial assemblies for African-American and integrated congregations. In 1995 the Damascus Road Anti-Racism Process, an initiative of Mennonite Central Committee, emerged as an Anabaptist antiracism training program whose long-term goal is to dismantle racism, especially in churches and faith-based organizations.

A photo taken in 1952 depicts a church building in Cleveland, Ohio, bearing a large sign. Beneath the name of the congregation— Gladstone Mennonite Church—three additional words boldly identify the character of the congregation as "biblical," "interracial," and "evangelical." The Lee Heights congregation that succeeded Gladstone went a long way to embody those three adjectives, but the broader hope expressed in that sign—a vision of a Mennonite church grounded in the biblical conviction that the proclamation of the gospel will inevitably form congregations in which people of all races gather for worship—has yet to be realized.

Hispanic Missions

As Saulo Padilla and his wife, Wilma, packed their U-Haul in preparation to leave their home in Calgary, friends who came by to help them begged the couple to reconsider.

By all accounts, Saulo was living out an immigrant success story. In 1980 Saulo's father, a university teacher and labor organizer in Guatemala City, had fled to Canada, where he was granted asylum as a political refugee. Six years later, his father sent for the rest of the family.

Saulo arrived in Calgary as a fifteen-year-old, speaking no English. The transition was difficult for the whole family. Within a year, Saulo's mother had returned to Guatemala, and Saulo dropped out of school to take on a series of low-paying jobs. The one stable point in his life was the local Spanish-speaking congregation. He had begun attending the First Hispanic Mennonite Church of Calgary not because it was Mennonite but because the worship service felt familiar and the people of the congregation treated him and his siblings like family.

Then, in 1992, Saulo entered an MCC job-training program. It was a life-changing experience. "They treated me with respect," Saulo recalled. "They not only prepared me for a job, but they helped me believe that I had a future."

Over the next decade, things fell into place for Saulo as he pursued the immigrant dream. He married, found a good job, and moved his growing family into a brand-new home. All the while Saulo continued to be actively involved in the congregation, serving as a regional youth leader and leading a men's group. On the surface he "had it made."

But underneath the appearance of economic success, Saulo was haunted by a sense that he "was not doing enough to live out his beliefs." A stint on the board of MCC Alberta triggered his curiosity about Mennonite history and theology, themes not strongly emphasized in his Spanish-speaking congregation. Finally, the combination of a revival meeting, an invitation to consider church leadership, and the offer of a scholarship in the Hispanic Ministries program at Goshen College, brought new clarity. So in the spring of 2001 Saulo and his family left a new home in Calgary, a good job, healthcare benefits, and the familiarity of friends and family to follow God's calling.

That sense of call has deepened since then. Saulo and Wilma quickly plunged into the congregational life of a local Hispanic church. Within a few months, they began a weekly radio ministry aimed at the growing Spanish-speaking community. And Saulo, who had never graduated from high school, immersed himself in the rigors of college course work. Four years later, Saulo is continuing his studies at Associated Mennonite Biblical Seminary, while Wilma is completing her degree. The specific details of their future ministry remain uncertain, but for Saulo one thing is clear: "I don't know what form it will take, but I see my future as working within the Mennonite church. My heart has become part of the Mennonite church and its mission."

Saulo's journey is only one of many such stories of individuals emerging as leaders of the Hispanic Mennonite community, one of the fastest-growing segments of the Mennonite church during the last decades of the twentieth century.

The Mennonite outreach to the Hispanic community was not the result of a strategic plan or a vision for a multicultural Mennonite church. Yet good things come from accidental beginnings. In the late 1920s, children of Manuel and Ignacia León, recent immigrants from Mexico, began attending a Bible school organized by the Chicago Home Mission. Impressed with the biblical instruction that their children were receiving, Manuel and Ignacia expressed interest in the mission and started coming to its Sunday-morning service.

In 1932 several missionaries on home leave from Argentina began to hold services in Spanish. Not long thereafter, the emerging congregation came into contact with David Castillo, a gifted Pentecostal preacher who agreed to take several theological courses at Goshen College before assuming leadership of the congregation. In 1940 Castillo left to pastor a Hispanic Mennonite mission in La Junta, Colorado, but the fledgling Iglesia Evangélica Menonita continued to thrive. Eventually known as the Lawndale Mennonite Church, the small congregation that began by accident went on to nurture many future Hispanic leaders of the Mennonite church.

As with most Mennonite mission congregations, initial church growth among Hispanics was slow. By 1955 there were still only four Spanish-speaking Mennonite congregations in the United States. Fifteen years later, a dozen more had emerged in scattered locations such as Texas, Pennsylvania, New York, and Ohio. In the 1980s, however, growth among Hispanic Mennonites accelerated as a result of gifted leadership, an infusion of resources from the church and a wave of new immigrants from Central America and Mexico.

From a community of less than two hundred members in 1955, Hispanic Mennonites had grown to fifty-two congregations with a membership of 1,500 in 1982. Twenty years later, the number of Hispanic Mennonite churches in the United States had doubled and its membership nearly tripled.

Included under the umbrella of Hispanic Mennonites are a significant variety of groups who do not all share the same history, culture, or religious assumptions. Some have lived in the United States for generations, such as Mexican-Americans in the Southwest. Many Hispanic Mennonites are the second- and third-generation offspring of Spanish-speaking immigrants who represent various stages of cultural assimilation.

Probably the largest group is first-generation immigrants, mostly from Mexico but also with representation from virtually all the Spanish-speaking countries in the world. How to integrate differences in culture, dialect, and personal experiences while also responding to the basic needs of the immigrant groups, presents a significant pastoral challenge.

Relating to the culture of the broader Mennonite church is another ongoing challenge. Long-time pastor and administrator José Ortiz has commented that being a Hispanic Mennonite "requires the ability to function in not only two, but three cultures—Hispanic, Mennonite, and American."

The National Council of Hispanic Mennonite Congregations has worked creatively to address these issues. Their Office of Literature and Congregational Education, for example, has translated numerous materials on Mennonite history and theology into Spanish, created a quarterly publication called *Ecos Menonitas,* and nurtured fifty-five students successfully through the Hispanic Ministries program (1979-2004) as part of a larger commitment to leadership training. More recently, a new model of extension classes has emerged that is proving to be more convenient for bivocational pastors.

Still, the results of these efforts are not yet clear. One Hispanic historian concluded reluctantly, "The development of considerable literature and educational material has had little discernible impact on the development of a Hispanic Mennonite identity." And Gilberto Flores, director of leadership development for Mennonite Mission Network, has commented, "The name 'Mennonite' is not a word that generates passion among the Hispanics," in part because it "is associated with ethnocentricity rather than with the Christian gospel."

Yet even if Mennonite identity among many Hispanic congregations remains shaky, the deeper themes of the Anabaptist tradition continue to hold an ongoing appeal—especially those aspects of the early Anabaptist movement that emphasized the living presence of the Holy Spirit, a concern for those at the margins of society, and a deep sense of urgency about sharing the good news of salvation with others.

The Urban Explosion

If the focus of growth among Mennonites in the United States during the 1970s and 1980s was primarily among African-American and Hispanic congregations, the story of cross-cultural dynamism in the Mennonite church of the 1990s was among new urban immigrant groups, especially within the Ethiopian, Taiwanese, Vietnamese, Korean, Laotian, and Cambodian communities.

Southern California offers the best example of this new development. By the middle of the 1980s, Anabaptist-Mennonite congregations in the Los Angeles area were in serious decline. Children in the handful of older congregations in the region were frequently not returning to the church, and the shifting demographics of the neighborhoods no longer reflected the ethnic composition of the congregation. In the late 1980s, a small group of pastors in the Los Angeles area began meeting for prayer. Gradually, they formed a network, staffed largely by volunteers, for training, consultation, and mutual encouragement. In 1992, following the riots in the wake of the Rodney King trial, the network took bold steps to create a new model of congregation-focused mission outreach.

The Center for Anabaptist Leadership (CAL) they established has since blossomed into a vital hub for numerous ministries in the region. An associate from each of the Asian, African, Spanish, and African-American communities provides training for missions and pastoral ministry, and all the emerging leaders are required to take several basic courses at CAL on themes related to Anabaptist-Mennonite theology.

Church growth in the region since then has been nothing short of astounding. The Los Angeles area currently has thirty-two Mennonite congregations with members from at least forty-one different countries. Some 90 percent of Mennonites in the region are people of color, 95 percent are first-generation Mennonites, 60 percent are new Christians, and 75 percent were born outside the United States.

A very similar phenomenon, albeit on a smaller scale, has unfolded in the Hampton, Virginia, area around the various ministries of Calvary Community Church; in the Dade County-Miami region of the Southeast Mennonite Conference; and among Mennonites in the Philadelphia region where, on any given Sunday, Mennonites in Philadelphia gather for worship in at least a dozen different languages (none of them German!).

From 'They' to 'We'

During the past century, Mennonites in the United States stumbled toward a rediscovery of the great commission. No doubt, part of this newly awakened interest in mission simply reflected the broader currents of American Protestantism, influenced by late nineteenth-century revivalism and the confident institution-building spirit of the early twentieth century. But even if the mission impulse among Mennonites reflected the spirit of their times, it also emerged out of a genuine desire to share the good news of the gospel beyond the boundaries of traditional Mennonite communities.

Mennonites crossed those borders in the United States—encountering cultural diversity among Native Americans, rural poor, and urban minority groups—confident that they had a gift to share. Many new believers were attracted to the Mennonite church by the integrity they witnessed in the lives of the mission workers—common, ordinary folks who treated them with dignity and modeled Christ's love with gentleness, consistency, and humility.

At their best, Mennonite missionaries communicated an understanding of the gospel that refused to separate the gift of God's forgiveness from the call to follow Christ as his disciples. At their best, Mennonite missionaries taught that the good news of the gospel always finds expression in the gift of Christian community, so that the churches they planted became vibrant gatherings of people whose lives intersected not only on Sunday morning but also during the week in the concrete practices of mutual aid and mutual accountability. At their best, Mennonite missionaries taught and modeled the love of Christ that flows outward to the world in vulnerable and risky acts of reconciliation. Clearly, there is much to celebrate in a century of Mennonite home missions. Their efforts have clearly born rich fruit.

At the same time, it is equally clear that some encounters between Mennonites and people of other cultures can only be regarded as occasions for confession and repentance. Even the best intentions of mission workers often fell far short of the goal. Sometimes Mennonites have been guilty of overtly racist attitudes and actions. More often they were unable to see beyond the perspective of their own culture and exercised more subtle forms of oppression in their insistence on retaining control or in their paternalistic posture as a dispensers of charity. At times the gospel that Mennonites presented was far too thin—sustained more by human efforts than by the power of the Spirit. More often, their gospel was much too thick—laden by a heavy burden of ethnic and cultural forms. Church leaders often found it easier to relate to minority groups as a focus of mission rather than as full-fledged brothers and sisters in the church, a habit evident in the ongoing language of "we" and "you." For all of these shortcomings, those representing the larger Mennonite tradition can only repent and ask for forgiveness—of God and of those brothers and sisters who have been offended.

In the end, however, the most significant outcome of the mission encounter is neither the worthy efforts of Mennonite missionaries nor the corporate confession of failures—important though these may be. Rather, the most significant impact of missions has been the gift of renewal that cross-cultural encounters has offered the Mennonite church by unsettling, transforming, and renewing the tradition.

One expression of that gift has become evident in worship. New Mennonites have awakened a fresh awareness of the gifts of the Spirit and a deeper sense of exuberance and joy in worship that has impacted the larger church. To be sure, not all Mennonite congregations have embraced these new worship styles with enthusiasm, but a greater attentiveness to the presence of the Spirit in corporate worship has been a powerful gift to the larger tradition.

New Mennonites have also raised a healthy critique about theological trends in the church that threaten to erode the radical claims of the gospel. Some traditional Mennonites, especially those who have been shaped by the refinements of modern culture, express an attitude of doubt about the authority of Scripture; a reluctance to speak about faith in public settings; a skepticism about the transforming power of the Spirit to heal broken bodies or troubled minds; and a perspective on social ills and the human condition that draws more from the social sciences than from the gospel. New Mennonites, by contrast, are often ready to testify without hesitation to the depths of sin, the power of God's transforming love, and the joy of the Christian journey—all gestures that run against the grain of a certain kind of cultural assimilation. In so doing, they call the church back to an Anabaptist form of witness that traditional Mennonites are sometimes tempted to keep hidden.

Finally, new Mennonites have helped traditional congregations to gain a healthier perspective on culture. Of course, faith is always expressed in particular forms, whether it be Swiss Mennonite traditions, Russian Mennonite folkways, or the rich variety of cultural expressions found in Native American, African-American, Hispanic, and Asian communities. But the temptation is powerful, especially among those in the dominant culture, to confuse form with substance and to elevate one's own cultural tradition above all others. Cross-border encounters push all of us to pursue a delicate balance between affirming our distinct cultural identities while not allowing those identities to overwhelm the more fundamental unity that we have together in Christ. Encounters among Mennonites representing different cultures remind all of us that culture is a necessary medium for God's Spirit to take form—but not an end in itself.

This call for humility works in both directions. Newcomers to any existing tradition recognize that they will be asked to reshape fundamental aspects of their identity to conform to the tradition they have chosen to join. But in that very process, the larger tradition is renewed as well, as old customs are seen in a new light and habitual assumptions renegotiated.

Only if this happens can we make the transition in identity from "they" to "we." This transformation does not happen easily or immediately; indeed, it requires a great deal of patience, forbearance, mutual hospitality, trust, vulnerability, and openness on the part of everyone to the new thing that God is doing in our midst. But the very future of the Anabaptist-Mennonite tradition depends on a capacity to embrace those beyond ourselves, knowing that the Spirit of God hovers at the borders of that cross-cultural encounter.

9

Mennonites Around the World

To the Uttermost Parts of the Earth

Workinesh Bantiwalu had been warned by her Ethiopian friends to steer clear of the missionaries and their house fellowship on the Wonji Sugar Estate, seven miles south of Nazareth, Ethiopia, where she and her husband worked. Yet the singing attracted her, she said, "especially the song that says 'the door to life is narrow; strive hard to enter it.'" As she listened to the messages, her "heart was touched." Finally, after much deliberation Workinesh made a break with the Orthodox Church and was rebaptized as a member of the Meserete Kristos Church (MKC), an indigenous renewal movement that emerged out of a Mennonite mission initiative in the late 1950s.

What Workinesh did not know is that the church she joined was about to enter a period of intense tribulation. In 1974 Marxist revolutionaries came to power in Ethiopia and imposed restrictions on all forms of evangelical Christianity. Soon after, authorities began harassing and arresting MKC leaders, sometimes beating them or holding them in custody for long periods. Still, the members of MKC continued to gather for prayer and worship.

In 1982 the Marxist government of Ethiopia officially closed MKC and for the next four years held six of its key leaders in prison. For nearly a decade, MKC congregations went underground, determined to remain faithful despite persecution. By now an older women, Workinesh was arrested and accused of owning a pistol. "My only weapon," she answered, "is my Bible. . . . I don't protect myself; God is the one who protects me." Even after a fierce beating, her answer remained the same.

Workinesh was not alone. Between 1974 and 1991, hundreds of MKC members endured similar persecution. Remarkably, the church did not die; instead, precisely the opposite occurred. With their leaders imprisoned and their churches closed, members of MKC developed a new model of church life. Small cell groups began to form, meeting secretly in homes for prayer and Bible study. These groups, many of them led by women, quickly reorganized when they grew to ten or twelve participants. As new people joined, specially appointed teachers led them in an extended period of instruction to nurture their faith and ensure that their confession of faith was genuine. Above all, the underground MKC church was sustained by prayer—regular sessions of intense intercession to God that often lasted for hours. Even though their gatherings were illegal, those who participated in the movement later recollected that "no one was afraid."

Before the period of persecution, there were fewer than ten thousand members in the MKC. By 1991, when persecution came to an end, it had grown to a fellowship of fifty thousand baptized members. There are now more baptized believers in the Meserete Kristos Church in Ethiopia than in any other national Mennonite church in the world. In 2003, Mennonite Church USA (MC USA), then the largest Mennonite church, reported 110,253 baptized members while MKC membership stood at 98,025. Only two years later, the Ethiopian church had grown by more than ten thousand new members, well surpassing membership in the MC USA.

It is difficult to read the account of the MKC during the period of Communist persecution without thinking of the Anabaptists of the sixteenth century. Like those Anabaptists, MKC began as a small fellowship of believers committed to following Jesus in daily life. Like the Anabaptists, MKC faced fierce opposition. And like the

Anabaptists, MKC survived persecution by developing strategies for survival and growth that depended heavily on lay ministry, friendship evangelism, a commitment to discipleship training, and above all, a deep attentiveness to the presence of the Holy Spirit.

The story of the persecution and survival of the Mennonite church in Ethiopia in the 1970s and 1980s and of its astounding growth in the decades since was not an isolated event. During the twentieth century, the Mennonite church around the world grew rapidly, from some 225,000 members living in seven countries in 1900 to some 1.4 million members in more than sixty countries and speaking nearly eighty languages. Although the largest Mennonite institutions and the strongest concentration of financial resources are still found in North America, the rapid numerical growth of the Mennonite church in the twentieth century has come overwhelmingly from countries in the Southern Hemisphere. Today more than 60 percent of all Mennonites live in countries outside Europe and North America, with the fastest growth coming in Ethiopia and the Congo. Although the Mennonite churches in the north have done much to keep alive a historical memory of the Anabaptist movement, it is Mennonites in the Global South who are reliving that sixteenth-century experience of renewal, persecution, suffering, and growth.

This transformation of the Mennonite church from a tiny European fellowship to a global communion has unfolded in several steps. It began in the second half of the nineteenth century with a renewed commitment among Mennonites—first in Russia and the Netherlands and then in North America—to missions: the imperative of the great commission to take the good news of the gospel to the "uttermost parts of the earth."

The shift to a global church was further encouraged by the growth of relief and service organizations that helped connect European and North American Mennonites with hungry and homeless people in other parts of the world. It continued in the course of the twentieth century as Mennonites from Russia and North America migrated to the Southern Hemisphere in search of greater religious freedoms and new economic opportunities, and it took on concrete form in the creation of the Mennonite World Conference, an international body committed to holding the global Mennonite church together in a worldwide communion.

More than anything else, however, the remarkable growth of the Mennonite church around the world is the result of local initiatives—the emergence of indigenous congregations who have creatively translated an Anabaptist understanding of the gospel into the idiom of their own cultures.

Globalization Through Missions and Service

In January 2003 nearly 2,500 people gathered in the pavilion of the Sultan's palace in the central Javanese city of Solo. For years, the city had been the site of religious, ethnic, and economic tensions that frequently teetered into violence. Following an economic crisis in July 1997, rioting in the streets left hundreds of people dead and dozens of stores looted or destroyed. Since then, Muslims, Christians, Hindus, and Buddhists lived uneasily side-by-side. Chinese-Indonesians, generally among the wealthier inhabitants of the city, feared to travel in public, and relations between security forces and jobless youth were stretched to the breaking point.

Paulus Hartono, pastor of the small Mennonite congregation in Solo, recognized that something needed to be done to defuse the tension. Working with an interfaith committee that included Muslims, Catholics, Buddhists, and Hindus, Hartono conceived the idea of declaring 2003 as the year of the Peoplehood for Peace in Solo and of holding a public rally to celebrate this public commitment. As threats of violence escalated, rally organizers patiently continued to arrange conversations among antagonists and to extend invitations to alienated groups, including the city's police department. At the opening event, a representative of a fundamentalist Muslim group begged the gathering to avoid false rumors and to reject all acts of violence. Then Mesach Krisetya, president of the Mennonite World Conference, addressed the crowd.

Mesach had been raised in a Confucian family. As a young man he had become a Christian, and soon thereafter he began attending seminary. In 1967, when the Indonesian government demanded that all Indonesians of Chinese ancestry select an Indonesian name, Mesach chose his name because he was fond of the Old Testament story of the three young men in the fiery furnace— Mesach was one of the "fireproof" men. His last name combined the Indonesian word for "Christ" (Kris) with the Sanskrit word for "loyal" (Setya). In a country where Christians could expect to experience persecution, Mesach's name identified himself as a person loyal to Christ regardless of the cost.

After serving as a pastor in the Mennonite church in Indonesia, Mesach studied at Associated Mennonite Biblical Seminary in Elkhart, Indiana, and then offered his leadership gifts to the Mennonite World Conference. Now, facing a crowd of frustrated people in Solo, Mesach offered a testimony to the gospel of peace. Five times the crowd interrupted his speech with enthusiastic applause. Then a group of Mennonite laypeople, Chinese businesspersons, Muslim teens, and Catholic nuns joined hands across the pavilion and declared their commitment to become a "peoplehood of peace."

The story behind the peacemaking efforts of these Indonesian Mennonites in Solo began almost 150 years earlier. In 1851 Mennonite congregations in the Netherlands pooled their resources to support the first overseas Mennonite missionaries, Pieter Jansz and his wife, on a journey to the Netherlands East Indies (Indonesia). There the Janszs and their co-workers established a mission church in north central Java and set about translating the Bible into Javanese and Malay. The missionary model they introduced was based on small, self-sufficient agricultural colonies that could better support new converts in a Muslim setting hostile to Christianity.

Over the next century, the Javanese Mennonite church grew slowly, reaching a total of 1,200 people by 1940. In the 1920s another Mennonite church emerged among Indonesians of Chinese descent, founded by the visionary leader Tee Siem Tat. By mid-century, both groups had developed their own internal leadership, which often creatively fused Mennonite theology with insights from other Christian churches in the region. Today Indonesia has three Mennonite synods. The 15,200-member United Muria Indonesian Christian Church (GKMI) and the 12,000-member Jemaat Kristen Indonesia (JKI) are predominantly of Chinese ethnicity, while indigenous Javanese make up the majority of the Evangelical Church of Java (GITJ), which numbers around 48,000 members.

Over the past decades Indonesian Mennonites have survived repeated waves of persecution triggered by both religious and ethnic hostility. Chinese Indonesians have been the particular target of rioters in recent years, suffering the loss of numerous stores and several churches. "When at the same time you are Chinese, Christian, and rich you are a triple minority," observed Mesach. "In a very uncertain situation, we know that it is God who holds the future." Yet the Mennonite church in Indonesia continues to thrive, bearing witness to the gospel of peace in settings fraught with tension.

The mission initiative that brought Jansz to Indonesia in 1851 has been repeated many times in countries throughout the world.

In 1866, General Conference Mennonites in North America—with financial support and expertise from Mennonites in Prussia—founded the Wadsworth Institute in northern Ohio with the goal of training future church leaders. Although the school closed after only ten years, many of the General Conference's pioneer missionaries received their training there, going on to serve in its first foreign mission fields in India (1900) and China (1914).

In the 1880s the Mennonite Brethren in the Ukraine started their own overseas mission initiative, sending a couple who had spent the previous four years in training at the Hamburg Baptist Seminary to India. The Mennonite Church entered overseas missions in 1899, sparked in part by reports of widespread famine in India. Like many later Mennonite Church mission projects, the initial Mennonite presence in India began with a relief effort—the construction of an orphanage and school—that served as the basis for more explicit evangelistic outreach. Other Mennonite Church mission efforts soon followed: to Argentina (1917), East Africa (1934), Puerto Rico (1945), Ethiopia (1948), Japan (1949), and a host of other African, East Asian, and South American countries in the 1950s.

Once established, the various Mennonite mission boards and agencies took up their tasks with energy and optimism. According to mission historian Wilbert Shenk, European and North American Mennonites created twenty-five new missions between 1850 and 1945. Following World War II, mission initiatives increased exponentially, with fifty-two new ministries begun between 1945 and 1959, and well over a hundred during the second half of the twentieth century.

In both Europe and North America, Mennonites tended to borrow heavily from the strategies and methods of the broader Protestant mission movement. For example, Mennonites in the Netherlands and the Palatinate consciously modeled their early efforts after the Baptist Missionary Society in England. In Russia, Mennonites followed the lead of Lutheran Pietists and German Baptists; and in North America, the revival meetings of Dwight L. Moody, the YMCA movement, and texts like John R. Mott's *The Evangelization of the World in This Generation* (1900) left deep imprints on Mennonite mission strategies. This borrowing was undoubtedly a catalyst for early Mennonite missions, but when it was done uncritically, the gospel preached by Mennonites on the mission field tended not to differ in any meaningful way from that of other Protestant groups.

The relief and service ministries of Mennonite Central Committee (MCC) provided North American Mennonites with another important connection to the worldwide church. Established in 1920 to provide relief supplies to famine-stricken Russia, MCC quickly extended its outreach to other countries offering "a cup of water . . . in the name of Christ." Through MCC and the opportunities for service in the many ancillary agencies spun off from it (Teachers Abroad Program, PAX reconstruction work in post-war

Europe; Inter-Mennonite Trainee program; Mennonite Economic Development Agency, to name a few), thousands of Mennonites, especially young people, gained direct exposure to the emerging international church.

In the years following World War II, MCC also helped hundreds of young Mennonite men complete their alternative service overseas, far from the rural communities of their childhood. Deeply shaped by their experiences, this generation of service workers returned to their home congregations with a new awareness of the world's needs.

The commitment to international mission and relief efforts also reflected the growing affluence of Mennonites, along with an emerging expertise in organizational management, and rising levels of education in occupations like linguistics, healthcare, and tropical agriculture. Finally, improved communication between the missionaries and their sending congregations—in the form of newsletters, brochures, and curriculum materials—further solidified a sense of ownership among Mennonite congregations in the widening scope of the church's work.

Globalization Through Migration

In May 2003 the citizens of Paraguay elected a new president. Because Paraguay is a small country with little economic or political significance to the United States, the major news networks barely took notice of the event. Yet for the Mennonite church in Paraguay, the election of Nicanor Duarte Frutos was unprecedented. The new president's wife, Gloria, was an active member in a Spanish-speaking Mennonite congregation in the capital city of Asunción; Duarte Frutos himself, though technically still a Catholic, also regularly attended the church, along with the couple's children.

In the weeks after the election, the Mennonite connection to Paraguayan politics became even more visible. By the summer of 2003, Duarte Frutos had persuaded four Mennonites to serve in high-ranking positions in his government, and newspaper editorials were speculating in worried tones about his capacity to serve as commander-in-chief of the country's armed forces, given the non-resistance position of the Raices congregation.

The fascinating story of Mennonite involvement in Paraguayan politics illustrates a second way in which the Mennonite church has become a global body: migration. Most of the thirty thousand Mennonites now living in Paraguay are descendants of Russian Mennonite immigrants who came to South America seeking refuge from repressive governments in the first half of the twentieth century.

The ancestors of the Old Colony Mennonites in Paraguay—so named because they originally came from Chortitza, the oldest of the Mennonite colonies in South Russia—had moved to Canada in the 1870s in the hopes that they would be allowed to worship as they pleased and to educate their children in their own schools. Their hopes were short-lived. In 1916 the Manitoba government introduced compulsory public education and insisted that all schools be conducted in English (rather than in German). In protest, a sizeable group of Old Colony Mennonites, perhaps half of their membership in Canada, once again packed their bags, immigrating this time to an isolated region in the province of Chihuahua, Mexico. Soon thereafter, in 1927, several related groups (*Sommerfelder* and *Bergthaler*) moved to an equally remote spot in the Chaco region of Paraguay. Based on government assurances that they would be granted exemption from military service and complete freedom in matters of religion, they founded the Menno Colony there.

At about the same time that Old Colony Mennonites from Canada were settling in Paraguay, the lingering chaos of the Communist revolution triggered another mass exodus of Mennonites out of the newly formed Soviet Union. Some were able to relocate in Canada. Most were forced to seek asylum elsewhere. From 1930 to 1932, following lengthy negotiations with the governments of Germany, Brazil, and Paraguay, some two thousand Mennonites established the Fernheim and Friesland colonies in

Paraguay. Another three hundred Mennonite families were granted asylum in Brazil, where they settled in Curitiba and Witmarsum. In the late 1940s, still more Mennonites from the USSR—some 4,500 war refugees—immigrated to Paraguay, where they became the nucleus of the Neuland colony.

This pattern has been repeated many times since then in numerous countries. In 1948, for example, Kleine Gemeinde Mennonites from Canada established a settlement close to the Old Colony groups in Chihuahua, Mexico, while Mennonites from the USSR planted colonies in Uruguay, Argentina, and Bolivia. Since the 1960s, Mennonites from Mexico have been relocating to countries like Costa Rica, Bolivia, Paraguay, and Argentina, while Beachy Amish and Conservative Mennonite groups in the United States have established small settlements in Costa Rica, Nicaragua, and Paraguay. These various groups often settled in close proximity, intermingling in a colorful blend of Mennonite ecumenicity.

In 1978, some seventy-five Old Colony families from Chihuahua, frustrated by land shortages and new social welfare laws, relocated to Belize, where they established the Spanish Lookout Colony. Since then, Mennonites in Belize have thrived, and their agricultural productivity has had a major impact on the Belizean economy.

Wherever they went, Mennonites cultivated a distinct communal identity reinforced by characteristic dress, colony-run schools, intermarriage, and the preservation of the German language. In recent decades, however, the boundaries that isolated Mennonite settlements from the surrounding people and culture have begun to break down, especially in those communities that have initiated mission and service projects among the indigenous population. As younger generations become fluent in local languages, attend state universities, and adopt the local culture, enduring questions of faith, identity, and witness come to the surface again. In these new settings, how does the "word become flesh"?

The struggle to answer that question is one reason the Mennonite story in Paraguay is so fascinating. The story of Mennonite survival in what came to be called the "green hell" of the

Paraguayan Chaco is a testimony to their hard work and the grace of God. The first settlers faced daunting obstacles of disease, hunger, crop failure, a border war, and uncertain relations with their indigenous neighbors. Yet they persevered. With financial assistance from Mennonites in North America and a well-organized system of cooperative governance and industry, the colonies in Paraguay survived and began to flourish. In the 1960s, the construction of the Trans-Chaco Highway gave the colonies direct access to markets in the capital city of Asunción. Since then, Mennonites have become a major economic force in Paraguay. Today the colonies produce more than 70 percent of the dairy, 20 percent of the grains, and almost half of the meat for the entire country.

As this economic revolution was taking place, Mennonites in Paraguay were also undergoing a political transformation. In 1954, a general named Alfred Stroessner led a successful military coup and began a thirty-five-year dictatorial rule over Paraguay. Stroessner appreciated the role that Mennonites played in the Paraguayan economy; he himself was of German background, and he admired Mennonite discipline and productivity. Recalling the horrors of anarchy in Russia, Mennonites were grateful for the order Stroessner imposed on the country and for the fact that he allowed them to worship as they pleased. So Mennonites stayed out of politics as much as possible, ignoring the fact that other Paraguayans lived in fear and opposition leaders were disappearing under Stroessner's reign of terror.

All that changed in 1989 when a bloodless revolution removed Stroessner from power and replaced his dictatorship with a democratic government. Suddenly, Paraguayan Mennonites found themselves living in a country that desired a constitution, the rule of law, and regular elections. Since then, they have been forced to reflect on the intersection of faith and politics in new and unexpected ways. Should they, for example, play a role in shaping the new constitution in order to protect their status as conscientious objectors? Should they participate in Paraguayan politics?

The democratic reforms of 1992 created a system of provinces, each with its own governor and legislature. As it turned out, the boundaries of one of the newly created provinces, Boquerón, happened to coincide with a large portion of the Mennonite colonies in the Chaco region. So for the first time, Mennonites found themselves forced to address new questions about political parties, campaign ethics, and the corrosive nature of corruption.

Initially, ministers and colony leaders resisted the idea of political participation. But following the election of the first Mennonite governor of Boquerón in 1993, that resistance has diminished. Church and colony leaders have worked out a statement of basic principles to guide Mennonite politicians and voters. Today the idea of a Mennonite running for public office in Paraguay has become almost routine.

With the election of Duarte Frutos in 2003, Mennonite involvement in national politics took on a new dimension. In a public effort to root out corruption, the president appointed Mennonites to several key government positions, including health services, commerce, internal revenue, and international economic relations. Initially, the Mennonites were reluctant to serve in these roles. But Duarte Frutos persisted, arguing,

> Imagine trying to place soccer on a field that is littered with broken bottles, cement rubble, construction debris. For fifty years that's what politics in Paraguay has been like. It's impossible to participate without getting injured. We're not asking you Mennonites to play on this field. But up until now, you've just been sitting in the stands, watching from a safe distance. What I'm asking you to do is to get out of your seat and come down and help me clean up the field so that we can play in a safe, decent, and fair way.

By all accounts, the Mennonites who have served in these positions have done well, remaining committed to the church even as they help to run the government of Paraguay. Along the way, the church has grown too, thanks to an energetic series of missionary and development projects among indigenous people of the region, numerous social-service projects in Asunción, and several Spanish-language mission churches, including the one that introduced Gloria Duarte Frutos to the Mennonites. What started as a migrant church of refugees now has a powerful witness that extends far beyond the colonies themselves.

The Spanish-speaking Raices congregation in Asunción is another example of the globalization of the Mennonite church and a church body established and sustained by indigenous Mennonites.

Emergence of Indigenous Mennonite Churches

In February 1960, a delegation of administrators from Congo Inland Mission joined with North American Mennonite missionaries from Djoko Punda Station for a momentous meeting with indigenous leaders of the Congolese Mennonite churches. Mennonites had first come to Djoko Punda in 1912—intrepid pioneer missionaries from the newly formed Egly Amish Church (Defenseless Mennonites) in central Illinois. On the banks of the Kasai River in south central Congo, they had established a mission station that would serve as the hub of their outreach to five ethnic groups in the region.

From the beginning, the missionaries were committed to learning local languages as the basis for their evangelistic and educational work. Through the years, that sensitivity to local context enabled the steady growth of the church. In the 1950s generous government subsidies opened the way for dozens of young North Americans to complete their alternate service work in the Congo through MCC's PAX or the Teachers Abroad Program. In addition to agricultural programs, Mennonite missionaries created a training school that prepared new Christians for service as pastors and evangelists. The church grew rapidly, increasing by more than 270 percent in the 1950s alone.

Until 1960, Mennonite missions in the Congo looked much like any other mission program. But all that changed at a meeting in Djoko Punda Station in February 1960. "From the early days," the North American representatives said to the Congolese leaders, "our missionaries have lived and worked among you. By God's help, a large and growing church has been planted. It is now time that the mission and the missionaries step back and make a larger place for you, our African brothers and sisters."

The delegation went on to make it clear that the missionaries serving in the region would be happy to remain, but only if the indigenous Mennonite church of Congo invited them to do so. And if they did remain, they would be serving under the authority of the Congolese.

The Congolese Mennonite experience since then has been a story of intense suffering and pain. Decades of revolutionary violence, corrupt dictatorships, and a devastating civil war have left the country in ruins. Since 1998 at least four million Congolese have died in the fighting, making it one of the deadliest conflicts since World War II. But through these difficult times, the Mennonite church has remained a strong and vibrant presence. Amid unimaginable hardships, the church has continued to be a place of refuge and hope long after most missionaries have fled the country. Today, the three Congolese Mennonite denominations—the Community of Mennonite Brethren Churches in Congo, the Evangelical Mennonite Community, and the Mennonite Community in Congo—number nearly 200,000 members and are among the fastest growing Mennonite churches in the world.

The emergence of an indigenous Mennonite church in the Congo was not an isolated or unique phenomenon. In some places—such as Japan, the Argentine Chaco, and Ivory Coast—Mennonite missionaries consciously adopted a model of missions that envisioned local converts in control of the church from the very beginning. In other places—Ethiopia and Somalia, for example—the process of indigenization was imposed on the church when anti-colonial governments forced the eviction of all foreign missionaries. And in still other parts of the world—India, Puerto Rico, and many countries in Central and South America—local control has come about as a slow evolutionary process.

But in every instance the pattern is the same. Mennonite congregations around the world today are looking less and less western and reflecting more of the nuances, customs, and cultural realities of their local settings. Today many of the churches in the Global South are themselves sending out missionaries, some of them to the United States.

Mennonite World Conference: Joining the Local and the Global Church

Social philosopher Mikhail Bakthin has correctly noted that humans beings are physically incapable of seeing their own backs. In other words, there are parts of ourselves that we are unable to perceive without the benefit of another person's perspective. To truly know ourselves, we must listen to others, trusting them to see us as we are. Bakthin's insight is especially relevant for local congregations.

Mennonites have traditionally placed a very high value on face-to-face relationships within a small gathering of believers. In a healthy community, our lives intersect with each other not just in worship on Sunday morning but also in many other contexts during the week. For most Mennonites, local friendships count for more than abstract relationships on a global scale.

Yet for all the gifts of the local congregation, no single gathering of Christians can claim to be the full body of Christ. The Bible frequently describes the church not only as a local fellowship but as an international body as well. According to the witness of the apostles, Christ's reconciling presence unites Jew and Gentile, slave and free, male and female, east and west. The book of Revelation envisions a coming time when people "from all races and tribes, nations and languages" will gather for a great wedding banquet.

In an era of hypernationalism and ethnic warfare, the witness of the church as an international body that transcends human divisions has never been more relevant. If congregations do not cross national barriers, they are missing out on an essential feature of the gospel.

Since 1925 the Mennonite World Conference (MWC) has helped Mennonites reclaim this aspect of the gospel by connecting local bodies of believers to the global Mennonite fellowship. Initially, MWC served simply as a forum for regular conversations among interested, mostly European, Mennonite groups. Christian Neff, chairperson of the South German Mennonite Conference and organizer of the first gathering, envisioned the 1925 meeting as a celebration of the four-hundredth anniversary of the first adult baptisms in Zurich and as an opportunity to better coordinate Mennonite relief efforts in South Russia. Delegates from five countries met in Basel, Switzerland, for the first "Mennonite World Conference." Five years later, another small group of delegates met again, this time in Danzig, to discuss practical matters related to the emigration of a group of Russian Mennonites from Moscow.

The events of World War II disrupted whatever progress might have been made toward a deeper sense of shared identity among Mennonites. When MWC reconvened in North American during the summer of 1948, delegates were forced to deal openly with these painful realities. The gathering proved an important occasion for extending mutual forgiveness to former national enemies and taking steps toward reconciliation. It also served as a forum for theological conversations, with particular attention given to the question of church-state relations and biblical nonresistance.

The next several MWC gatherings were dedicated to European and North American themes. But by the early 1970s, Mennonite church leaders had begun to shift to a more global perspective. In 1972, an MWC gathering in Curitiba, Brazil, brought into sharp, often uncomfortable, focus the realities of U.S. armed intervention in the Southern Hemisphere and the challenges facing Brazilian Mennonites under a repressive military government. Since then, MWC assemblies have consistently met in southern settings—in Calcutta, India (1997), Bulawayo, Zimbabwe (2003), and in Asuncíon, Paraguay (planned for 2009)—with the explicit goal of educating the broader Mennonite church about the life, witness, and challenges of the host group.

Today membership in the MWC has expanded to include churches in some sixty-six countries. Its executive committee, with offices in Strasbourg, France, has shifted its energy away from conference planning to cultivating face-to-face relationships among Mennonite communities around the world so that they can give and receive gifts as equals. In recent years, MWC has published a series of books—mostly on theological topics—that attempt to bring Mennonites around the world into conversation on a common theme.

In 2006, representatives from several regional bodies completed a joint Confession of Faith. The Global Mennonite History project, also nearing completion in 2006, has sought to cultivate a deeper historical identity throughout the church by encouraging Mennonites around the world to write their own histories. Increasingly, MWC is moving in the direction of becoming a Mennonite World *Communion,* a way of describing its goal of nurturing a sense of the global church as a body of believers living in fellowship with each other.

Mennonite World Conference has helped Mennonites around the world move beyond the self-sufficiency of the local congregation to recognize a deeper sense of connectedness with the global Mennonite fellowship. Those congregations that have established intentional relations with sister churches in different countries—nurtured by a visits, correspondence, service trips, and a commitment to prayer—almost always speak of the blessings that result from such exchanges.

What Does It Mean to Be Anabaptist-Mennonite in a Global Context?

The movement that began with a handful of youthful reformers in Zurich in January 1525 has taken root, first in Europe, then in Russia and North America, and now in the "uttermost parts of the earth." Today the "typical" Mennonite is better described as a Congolese woman or an Ethiopian lay pastor rather than a Pennsylvania farmer with a German family name. There is much to celebrate in this global transformation of the Mennonite story. But these new realities also raise a number of significant questions.

Political and economic realities within a global fellowship. In comparison with Mennonites in Europe and North America, the majority of Mennonites today live in countries of relatively little wealth or political influence. When visiting North American Mennonite congregations in the spring of 2006, Congolese church leaders Adolphe Komuesa Kalunga and Matthieu Shimatu Kapia could not help but think of church members who were starving to death at home as they met with local Mennonites in luxurious church buildings. "It is understandable that people in a culture of abundance worship in costly surroundings," Komuesa said, "but please listen to those of us who live in miserable conditions. We celebrate our global Mennonite community but there is still a lot of work to do."

So questions for North American Mennonites inevitably arise. As citizens of wealthy and powerful nations, what responsibility do they bear to brothers and sisters in the church who live in great need? And how might those Mennonites in relatively poor countries share their gifts with those from more affluent regions?

The challenge of transcending our economic and political differences is not a simple one. In the 1970s, for example, Christians in many Central and South American countries discovered in the witness of the sixteenth-century Anabaptists a clear message for the poor and the politically oppressed. Here was a group committed to making Scripture available to ordinary people on the assumption that the gospel was relevant to their social, economic, and political situation. Here was a radical Christian movement that stood in solidarity with those at the margins of society. Inspired by the Anabaptist story, these new Mennonites assumed that their sisters and brothers in North America would support them in a theology of liberation, speaking out against the oppression of the poor and using their influence to oppose the military presence of the U.S. government in their countries. More recently, the Congolese Mennonite church has requested Mennonites in the United States to support legislation that would increase aid to their country. Persecuted Mennonite pastors in Vietnam have appealed to the worldwide fellowship of Mennonites to protest against their mistreatment, and representatives of the Mennonite church in Colombia have called on U.S. Mennonites to lobby against military aid to their country.

Such requests for political intervention have left U.S. Mennonites uncertain and divided. Yet history offers a reminder that this is not a new phenomenon. In 1659, at the height of the Dutch Golden Age, Hans Vlamingh, a wealthy Dutch merchant and treasurer of the Dutch Mennonite Committee for Foreign Needs, began a tireless campaign on behalf of the Swiss Brethren, who were experiencing intense persecution. Vlamingh corresponded regularly with their persecuted leaders, raised funds among the Dutch congregations, and distributed that money to refugees who were seeking asylum in the Palatinate.

But he also took his cause directly to the political authorities. Along with other Mennonites, Vlamingh persuaded the Dutch Estates General to issue a formal letter of censure against the Bernese government for its mistreatment of the Swiss Brethren; he encouraged Dutch Reformed pastors to write letters of admonition to their Swiss counterparts in Bern; and he himself wrote numerous letters, made several visits, and even sent gifts of rare tulip bulbs, newly fashionable eyeglasses, and a barrel of fresh oysters— all of which could have easily been interpreted as bribes!—to Swiss authorities whom he hoped might intervene on behalf of his persecuted brothers and sisters.

How contemporary Mennonites in the United States respond to requests for political intervention on behalf of their brothers and sisters in other countries will be an ongoing matter of discernment. But Vlamingh's example suggests that already in the seventeenth century Dutch Mennonites recognized a deep spiritual kinship with others in the Anabaptist tradition, and they were willing to use their political influence and economic resources to support their oppressed sisters and brothers.

Theological identity. Most Mennonites living in North America today have some awareness of the basics of Anabaptist-Mennonite theology. If nothing else, the visibility of the Amish in popular culture has helped to solidify a general self-perception of Mennonites as a denomination that cares about peace, affirms a simple lifestyle, and values community. Although any given individual might not be able to offer a theological basis for these themes and might not even personally embrace them, the average Mennonite would still likely have some understanding that they belong to the Anabaptist-Mennonite tradition.

It is far less clear, however, what it means to be a Mennonite within the global context. For example, what associations does a new convert in the Republic of Congo have with the word *Mennonite*? What do Indonesian Mennonites hold in common with emerging Mennonite cell groups in South Korea? How is the Mennonite church in Bogotá, Colombia, connected with Dutch Mennonites in Amsterdam?

The question of identity is never fully resolved for any Christian group. But identity for Mennonites—especially in a global context—is somewhat more complicated than it is for other Christians. Catholic bishops the world over are ultimately accountable to the pope in Rome for their theology; if their public teaching runs contrary to official doctrine, they can be disciplined or removed from office. The sixty-six million Lutherans around the world whose congregations are part of the Lutheran World Federation all recognize the authority of the Augsburg Confession of Faith as a basis for interpreting Scripture. Pentecostals in every country share a belief that a personal encounter with the Holy Spirit, probably associated with the charismatic gift of tongues, is essential to the Christian experience.

The global Mennonite church, by contrast, does not have anything quite comparable to this. In many of the Mennonite colonies, religious identity has been carried—and sometimes overshadowed—by cultural markers like language, food, dress, family systems, leadership structures, hymnbooks, and catechisms. In reaction to this,

Mennonite missionaries have been quick to warn against the dangers of confusing such cultural markers with the gospel. But there is also a powerful reverse tendency in mission settings to present the gospel in a very general or abstract language, so that the only thing that really matters is "conversion," while teachings on Christian discipleship or ethical practices such as peacemaking or mutual aid are relegated to secondary, "denominational" concerns.

Although specific Mennonite groups around the world might be ready to define what it means to be Mennonite, no single authority controls a Mennonite "trademark," defines the formal requirements for membership in the global Mennonite fellowship, or is ready to enforce those requirements, even if the global Mennonite church could reach some agreement.

At the same time, it is undeniable that new Christians around the world have discovered in the Anabaptists of the sixteenth century a story that speaks to their own setting. And clearly, local Mennonite conferences are addressing the challenge of theological education. Thus Mennonites in Indonesia, Guatemala, India, Paraguay, and Zaire have established seminaries that offer historical and theological training for future leaders. In other countries, such as Korea, Japan, England, and Brazil, local Mennonites have created study centers that offer printed resources and occasional seminars on Anabaptist-related topics. And the recently formulated MWC Confession of Faith may also help to address these questions.

A gathering of Congolese and other African Mennonite church leaders in 1994 resulted in the formulation of the following affirmations, an example of how one group of Mennonites has worked at defining their shared theological convictions. Among the understandings shared by the group were the following:

> *We affirm our spiritual connections to the Anabaptists of the sixteenth century; we want to live as they lived.*

> *We believe the Bible is the sole Word of God for all times and situations.*

> *The church's center is Jesus Christ our Lord, and the community of faith is a global family of peace, mission, sharing and deeds of mercy.*
>
> *We are in a context of suffering but we will be faithful to God's principles.*
>
> *We understand that peace is not a technique but a style of life—Christ is our peace.*
>
> *As Mennonites in Africa we recognize that we are bridge people, people who need to act as agents of reconciliation across cultural lines and at times in the midst of conflict.*
>
> *Even if the situation in Africa seems hopeless now, we believe there is hope; and the transformation we are experiencing will make Africa the hope of the world (Psalms 68:31).*

Conclusion

In his landmark book *The Next Christendom: The Coming of Global Christianity,* Philip Jenkins documents a dramatic shift now taking place within the Christian world. Whereas church membership in Europe and North America continues to decline and church leaders lament the secularization of modern culture, the Christian church in the Southern Hemisphere is experiencing exponential growth. In 2000, there were about two billion professing Christians in the world, of whom 560 million reside in Europe. Latin America is close behind with 480 million, Africa has 360 million, Asia has 313 million, and North America claims about 260 million.

But soon, according to Jenkins' calculations, a dramatic reversal will have taken place. By 2025 there will be roughly 2.6 billion Christians, of whom 640 million will live in Latin America, 633 million in Africa, 555 million in Europe, and 460 million in Asia.

By 2050, only about one-fifth of the world's Christians will be non-Hispanic whites. What is true of the broader Christian church is evident among Mennonites as well. If demographics matter, the future of the Mennonite church is clearly in Africa, Asia, Central America, and South America.

The opening years of the twenty-first century mark an exciting moment in the history of the Anabaptist-Mennonite tradition. Although the story is now nearly five hundred years old, the fact that its newest chapters are being written in Latin America, Asia, and Africa suggests that the story we tell fifty years from now will be very different from the one we tell today.

At the same time, the worldwide Mennonite church faces profound challenges of identity. Across the political and economic chasms dividing north and south, will the church find ways to become a genuine community? How will dramatic demographic shifts affect the relationship between North American Mennonites and the much larger body of believers outside the traditional centers of power? As indigenous Mennonite churches continue to confront the challenges of their local contexts, will the theological center be strong enough to hold the global Mennonite church together?

All these questions suggest that the future is rife with the potential for conflict but rich with possibilities for new expressions of faithfulness within the Anabaptist-Mennonite church as the Spirit moves to renew the tradition once again.

10

Mennonites in the World

Relations with Other Christians

Late in the afternoon of January 5, 1527, a small group of Zurich offi-cials shepherded Felix Mantz into a boat in front of the fish market on the Limmat River, a waterway that ran through the heart of the city. A well-educated native of the city, fluent in Latin, Hebrew, and Greek, Mantz had grown up only a few hundred yards away in the shadows of the Grossmünster church, where his father served as a well-known canon. Now, however, he was a prisoner. His bound hands had been forced over his knees and a pole thrust between his arms and his legs, contorting his body into a hunched and helpless posture.

Only hours before, the Large and Small Councils of Zurich had condemned Mantz to death. "Contrary to Christian order and cus-tom," the charge read, "he had become involved in Anabaptism, had accepted it, taught others, and become a leader." Furthermore Mantz had raised questions about whether one could be both a magistrate and a Christian, and he had "condemned capital pun-ishment." Since his teachings would lead to "offense, insurrection, and sedition against the government, to the shattering of the com-mon peace, brotherly love, civil cooperation and to all evil," the council had concluded that Mantz must be put to death immedi-ately.

As his executioners rowed the boat to the middle of the river, Mantz reportedly praised God in a loud voice and announced to the onlookers that he was about to die for the truth. Some along the bank of the river implored him to recant. But above those voices, the cries of his mother and brothers could be heard urging him to be faithful. Just before he was pushed into the waters to be drowned, Mantz prayed the words of Jesus at the crucifixion: "Into thy hands, Lord, I commend my spirit."

Mantz was not the first Anabaptist to die for his convictions. But he was a highly educated humanist and a well-known citizen of the city who had been Zwingli's intimate friend. His public execution was a defining moment in the history of the Anabaptist movement, marking the end of any hope that the radical reformers might be reconciled with Zwingli and the city council.

Several months later, Mantz's friends drew up a statement of unity that clarified in unmistakable language the enormous chasm separating the Anabaptists from the rest of the Christian world. "Truly all creatures are in but two classes," read article 4 of the Schleitheim Confession, "good and bad, believing and unbelieving, darkness and light, the world and those who (have come) out of the world, God's temple and idols, Christ and Belial; and none can have part with the other."

Against that backdrop, the scene that unfolded along the Limmat River nearly five hundred years later was truly remarkable. On a late Saturday afternoon in June 2004, representatives of both the Zurich city council and the regional Reformed church stood at the same riverbank where Mantz had been drowned. Expressing the hope that these two religious traditions—divided for nearly five centuries—might be reconciled, Zurich authorities publicly asked forgiveness from their "brothers and sisters in the Mennonite faith" and dedicated a commemorative marker to honor the life of Mantz and five other Anabaptists who had been executed in Zurich.

The event in Zurich was actually only one of a series of dramatic gestures extended by other Christian denominations to the Mennonites in recent years, all of them seeking forgiveness for the persecution and division of the sixteenth century. Five years of conversations between the Roman Catholic Church and the Mennonite World Conference, for example, culminated in 2003 with a joint statement titled "Called Together to Be Peacemakers." Participants in the Catholic-Mennonite dialogue acknowledged a tradition of "mutual hostility and negative images" between the two groups, but outlined steps toward a "healing of memories" that could contribute to "reconciliation between divided Christians." Such a healing would need to include an understanding of each other's history, a spirit of repentance, the recognition of the many areas of theological and ethical convergence between Catholics and Mennonites, and an honest acknowledgment of ongoing differences.

Two years later, the Lutheran World Federation and the Mennonite World Conference began a series of formal conversations on the meaning and relevance of the "condemnations" of Anabaptists that appear in the Augsburg Confession, an authoritative statement of faith shared by some sixty-six million Lutherans around the world.

Meanwhile, a grassroots organization called Bridgefolk has brought Mennonite and Catholic laypeople together for discussions of wide-ranging topics including martyrdom, liturgy, and understandings of war and peace. Still another grassroots initiative has recently emerged between charismatic Mennonite-Amish groups in the United States and a coalition of radical Swiss Reformed pastors. In addition to baptism, the special concern of this group has been focused on the concept of "generational sin" and the need for spiritual healing between an "abusive Swiss Reformed father" and a "disobedient Anabaptist child."

These ecumenical encounters—focused particularly on the themes of forgiveness, reconciliation, and the "healing of memories"—suggest that something new is happening in the history of the Mennonite church. The hostilities that led authorities to execute Anabaptists five hundred years ago are giving way to a new willingness to revisit the past and to acknowledge publicly the shadows that have lurked there for centuries.

Mennonites and the ecumenical movement. U.S. Mennonites have traditionally been skeptical about ecumenical relations. Apart from a short period (1908-1917) when the General Conference joined the Federal Council of Churches in America, the Mennonite church has generally shied away from formal associations with other Christian denominations. Although Mennonite church bodies have occasionally sent observers to the World Council of Churches, the National Council of Churches, or the National Association of Evangelicals, they have steadily resisted membership in such organizations.

The reasons for this reluctance are varied. Mennonites are a tiny group, only a fraction of the size of the Catholic, Reformed, and Lutheran churches in terms of numbers and resources. Memories of past disputations have made Mennonites wary of conversations with the more powerful denominations, fearing that those in charge will drive the dialogue to a predetermined outcome. And Mennonites' commitment to the "gospel of peace," combined with their insistence that allegiance to the church transcends loyalty to the nation, has triggered fears that ecumenical conversations will inevitably lead to a watering down of doctrine and the loss of distinctive identity.

Yet continuing invitations from the Catholic, Reformed, and Lutheran churches have prompted contemporary Mennonites to rethink their history, faith, and practice, and have raised challenging questions about their relationship to the broader Christian community.

Identity and Divisions in Church History

From the Old Testament stories of Abraham and his descendants to the account of the early church in the New Testament, the biblical narrative tells of the ongoing struggle of God's people to remain faithful to their calling. What teachings and practices were essential and what traditions could be set aside as times and circumstances changed? The Old Testament suggests a number of different responses to that question. Faithfulness could mean a strict observance of ritual ceremonies—obeying the law and the commandments of God—or it could mean a more elusive quest for justice, mercy, and love in human relationships. In either case, God expected the children of Israel to maintain visible boundaries with other groups; those who offered sacrifices to false gods or failed to honor the Law of Moses or married spouses from other cultures could expect to incur the wrath of God.

In the New Testament, followers of Jesus struggled mightily with the same questions of faithfulness and identity. In John 17, Jesus offered a passionate prayer for the unity of the church. His prayer seemed to suggest that the integrity of the church's mission to the world was dependent on its unity. Yet that unity could not come cheaply—certainly not at the price of easy compromises. After all, Jesus himself had spoken of the "narrow path" for his followers and of a judgment day in which the "righteous" would be separated from the "unrighteous." As Jesus said, "Not everyone who says to me, 'Lord, Lord,' will enter into the kingdom of heaven" (Matthew 7:21).

So leaders of the early church struggled to define the boundaries of their new movement in relation to the Jewish tradition from which it had emerged and the many other quasi-Christian groups that sprang up around the leadership of charismatic individuals proclaiming a new gospel. The showdown between Peter and Paul described in Acts 15 helped to resolve some of the questions of Christian identity vis-à-vis Judaism. But as we have seen, debates over definitions of orthodoxy and heresy have persisted.

The group of Christians that eventually emerged with its spiritual center in Rome defined itself as the "catholic" (or universal) church representing Christ's living, undivided body here on earth. But even this "universal" body struggled to define the nature of church unity. In 1054, for example, the Catholic Church in Rome was forced to acknowledge a major division with the eastern "Orthodox" church, which had its spiritual center in Constantinople. The Reformation era witnessed a further disintegration of church unity as Christians condemned fellow Christians with such labels as "the Antichrist" and "spawn of Satan," and defended their own convictions by going to war with each other.

As we have seen, the Anabaptists emerged within the context of a fracturing church. Like Luther and Calvin, the first generation of Anabaptists was born and raised as Catholics, steeped in a thousand years of church history and practice. Yet these Anabaptists had determined, on the basis of their reading of Scripture, that church tradition was deeply flawed. So, like the other reformers, they defined themselves in opposition to other Christians. In their rejection of the papal hierarchy, the Mass, and the veneration of saints, for example, the Anabaptists knew that they were *not* Catholics. In their rejection of infant baptism, the marriage between church and state, and a doctrine of grace that seemed to justify sinning, Anabaptists knew that they were *not* Protestants.

The painful reality of persecution only strengthened the Anabaptists' sense that a clear boundary separated them from the broader Christian church. After all, it was not the invading Turkish sultans or Muslim caliphates who were torturing and killing them. It was the Christian princes of Europe, whose actions were vigorously defended by the Catholic, Lutheran, and Reformed theologians serving in their courts.

The Council of Trent (1543-1565) reinforced the claims of the Catholic Church that its unity would be maintained on the authority of the church fathers and the pope's claim of "apostolic succession." Followers of Luther codified their theology in 1530 with the carefully worded Augsburg Confession—a statement that still defines Lutheran orthodoxy today. Similarly, the Reformed church settled on its authoritative statement of faith with the Heidelberg Catechism of 1563. Such claims did not inoculate these groups against further internal divisions, but they did establish a standard by which those in authority could vigorously defend "orthodoxy" against "heresy."

By contrast, the Anabaptist tradition refused to define orthodox beliefs through institutional hierarchies or doctrinal propositions. Instead groups in the Anabaptist-Mennonite tradition have generally insisted that faith is properly understood only as it is embodied in the practices of daily life—offering hospitality to a stranger or visiting a prisoner. This approach has proved to be something of an obstacle to ecumenical conversations. If faith is primarily a question of doctrine, then theological arguments can be resolved by gifted theologians from each side who hammer out the details of church unity in ways that conform to their basic confessions of faith. By contrast, the Anabaptist-Mennonite concern with right living—what has sometimes been described as *orthopraxis*, in contrast to orthodoxy—has made it more difficult to reach agreement on differences, not only in relation to other Christian groups, but also within the Anabaptist movement itself.

Anabaptist-Mennonite perspectives on unity and difference. The Amish division of 1693 is a helpful case in point. When Jacob Ammann and his fellow ministers from Alsace met with Swiss Brethren leaders from the Emmental, they were concerned by rumors that the Bernese Swiss Brethren had stated that the Truehearted would be saved. The Truehearted (sometimes also called "half Anabaptists") were Reformed villagers who had lived alongside the Swiss Brethren for decades and had forged friendships with their persecuted neighbors. Over the years, some of the Truehearted had placed themselves at great risk by providing their Swiss Brethren neighbors with food or by warning them of the arrival of the "Anabaptist hunters." Some had even hidden Swiss Brethren refugees in their homes.

As Ammann pointed out, the Truehearted were not actually Anabaptists. They persisted in baptizing their babies; they continued to attend the state church; they swore fealty oaths; and they supported the local militia. In this sense, they were still part of the "fallen world." And there was the rub. Since they were not willing to take the step of believers baptism or commit themselves to the discipline of the gathered church, they must still be—in the strong language of the Schleitheim Confession—part of the "kingdom of Satan." That, at least, would have been a consistent interpretation of Swiss Brethren theology.

But when Ammann pressed the Bernese Brethren on this issue, most of the ministers in the region were not ready to describe their non-Anabaptist neighbors—generous people who had shown them such compassion—as being outside of God's salvation.

Still, Ammann had a point. Even if the Truehearted were good neighbors, to state publicly that they were "saved" seemed to make a mockery of the Swiss Brethren understanding of adult baptism and their long history of suffering and persecution.

The deep division that unfolded among the Swiss Brethren in the fall of 1693 is only one example of a tension that runs like an iron thread throughout much of Anabaptist-Mennonite history—indeed all of church history. How important are differences in doctrine and practice among people who claim the name "Christian"? Which teachings are *essential* to the integrity of the gospel and which can be regarded as human innovations, however important they might seem to a particular group?

For contemporary Mennonites, the question has two basic components: a theological one and a practical one. First, how should members of the Anabaptist-Mennonite tradition understand their distinctive doctrines and practices in relation to the broader church? Are Mennonites teachings basically variations on a set of doctrines held in common by all Christians, or should Mennonites think of their theology as coming directly from the life and teachings of Jesus, quite independent of the larger Christian tradition?

The second question is closely related. How should Mennonites relate to Christians of other denominations? Should Mennonites seek to "convert" others to their understanding of Christianity? Should they avoid theological conversations with other Christians, leaving all these matters in God's hands? Or should they aggressively pursue ecumenical conversations with the goal of reuniting the various denominations into a single body?

Mennonite Distinctives and the Broader Christian Tradition

If the story of Mennonite relations with other Christians were only one of persecution, it would be easier to argue that Mennonite doctrine and practice are irreconcilable with the broader Christian tradition. Yet for most of their history, descendants of the Anabaptists have lived alongside other Christians in relative harmony, borrowing freely from the hymnody, devotional literature, and spiritual traditions of their neighbors. As the Swiss Brethren in Bern discovered in their relations with the Truehearted, defining clear boundaries becomes more difficult when Christians in other traditions turn out to be good people, no less sincere than Mennonites in their efforts to take Scripture seriously and to follow Jesus in their daily lives.

Moreover, Anabaptism was not born in a vacuum. As a renewal movement within the broader church, the sixteenth-century Anabaptists owed much to both the Catholic and the Protestant traditions. From late medieval Catholic spirituality, for example, the Anabaptists inherited an appreciation for the principles of "yieldedness" (*Gelassenheit*) and humility (*Demut*), and they drew deeply on the traditions of Catholic lay piety that were dedicated to the "imitation of Christ." The Catholic tradition also imparted to Anabaptism the conviction that each person could respond freely to God's initiative, accepting or rejecting God's gift of grace.

With Protestants, the Anabaptists shared an affirmation of the centrality of Scripture in the Christian life, along with an emphasis on the priesthood of all believers and an awareness that we are saved by God's grace not by our own merits. With both traditions, Anabaptist-Mennonite theology has affirmed the basic themes in the creeds of the Christian church. During their interrogations and the recorded disputations of the sixteenth century, Anabaptists frequently cited the Apostles' Creed as the basis of their theology; and their later confessions of faith, such as the Dordrecht Confession of 1632, were written within a theological framework of the Trinity, sin, redemption, and the work of the Spirit, which would strike most people in the Christian world as highly orthodox.

Mennonites have sometimes described their identity in the history of the Christian church as if the 1,200 years stretching from Constantine to the first adult baptisms in Zurich are of no relevance to them whatsoever. Yet this tendency to emphasize what makes them different from the Catholic or Protestant traditions can easily blind Mennonites to the debt they owe to the broader Christian tradition. If Mennonites have any interest in engaging in conversations with other Christians, they will need to be more attentive to the history and convictions that they hold in common with the broader church.

Mennonite "harmlessness"—the desire to assimilate. At the same time, the persistent tendency among Mennonites to minimize their differences with other Christians—less out of a concern for the unity of the church than a desire to assimilate into the religious mainstream—is also a matter worthy of careful consideration. Some contemporary Mennonite congregations have adopted a Protestant view of salvation as a discrete moment or "event" that is somehow prior to, and separated from, all other theological concerns. In this view, the core of Christian faith is often framed in the general language of "accepting Jesus into your heart as your personal Savior." This moment, the argument suggests, is what *really* matters for the Christian. All other theological distinctives—including believers baptism, nonresistance, and discipleship—may be important to the custodians of denominational identity, but they are not essential to the Christian life. Instead they are matters of secondary concern—doctrinal teachings about which Christians of goodwill are likely to differ but not having any real bearing on salvation itself.

For those Mennonite congregations that have habitually defined themselves in terms of cultural traditions and family heritage, this appeal to a "generic" Christian core—accepting Jesus as your personal Savior—holds out the promise of a more inclusive faith and seems to lower the barriers that have historically separated

Mennonites from other Christians. The argument is especially compelling in mission settings. "Just preach the gospel," mission-minded advocates are tempted to argue, implying that any association of specific doctrines or ethical practices with the good news will only bog the church down in petty differences and divisions.

These arguments raise important questions about the nature of Christian truth that are not easily resolved. However, the impulse to downplay distinctive Mennonite doctrines in favor of a kind of generic Protestantism often reflects an effort by Mennonites to convince their neighbors of their "harmlessness," a desire to assure others that Mennonites pose no threat to social or political order. For example, frequently, Mennonites have adopted a theology of "generic Christianity"—faith in Jesus' saving blood is all that really matters—in settings where teachings on nonresistance have brought into question their loyalty to the state. Thus Mennonites in Prussia and Poland, for example, who were eager to assimilate into the newly unified German state in the late nineteenth century, insisted to their Lutheran and Reformed neighbors that they were not a sect but essentially Protestant in their theology. By World War I, they, along with most European Mennonites, had lost the principle of nonresistance altogether. By World War II, many—though by no means all—German Mennonites supported National Socialism.

In a similar way, Mennonites in North America during the closing decades of the twentieth century have also been eager to shed their image as a fringe group associated with the conservative Amish or liberal peaceniks. They have increasingly borrowed a theological vocabulary from conservative evangelical Protestantism that has eased their transition into the public Christianity of American culture. As a result, such teachings as believers baptism, nonresistance, a life of discipleship, and a disciplined church recede to the background, and a growing number of Mennonites are unwilling (or unable) to state what it is—other than the name on their church sign—that distinguishes them from anyone else.

An Argument in Defense of Mennonite 'Distinctives'

For all the superficial appeal of "generic Christianity," closer reflection suggests that such an approach to faith is not biblical or, strictly speaking, even possible. Biblical faith is never "generic" or reducible to an abstract statement about "accepting Jesus into your heart." In the Bible, faith is always embodied. When the "word was made flesh" in Jesus, God entered this world as the son of a Jewish carpenter. In his native language of Aramaic, speaking mostly to Jews, Jesus told parables about seeds and fish. He walked the dusty roads of Judea, sailed on the stormy waters of the Sea of Galilee, and participated in the religious rituals of his day. In the manner of a common criminal, Jesus died a real death. To be sure, Christ's message is timeless, but he delivered it in a very specific context, and ever since, the gospel has found expression with specific cultural forms, even as it has challenged and transformed those forms.

To claim a Christian faith that is somehow generic—based on the "Bible alone" or on some very general claim about "being saved"—is simply an illusion. It means that one is *willfully* blind to the doctrinal filters that one is using (and *must* use) to read Scripture. Indeed, it is precisely those groups who claim to offer a pristine form of Christianity, untainted by doctrine, who are in the most danger of reflecting the prejudices and limitations of their own culture. After all, so-called nondenominational congregations always get their Sunday school curricula from *somewhere,* and their pastors are trained—formally or informally—by *some* theological tradition.

Ultimately, any version of Christian faith that minimizes doctrinal differences in the name of "generic Christianity" is in grave danger of losing its identity as a distinctively Christian witness to the world. Why? Because to do so implies that theological, ethical, and ecclesiological differences are ultimately irrelevant. It implies, contrary to Jesus' own words, that whether or not we offer a cup of cold water to thirsty people, clothe the naked, or attempt to reconcile conflicts with those who have hurt us has no connection to our salvation. Yet what we believe does matter. The teachings we profess, the rituals we enact, the biblical stories we tell, and the meaning we make of them shape our daily lives in profound ways.

So how should those in the Anabaptist-Mennonite tradition relate to the broader Christian world, and especially to contemporary evangelicals? Mennonites can start by affirming points of shared conviction. For example, like most evangelical Christians, early Anabaptists were steeped in a knowledge of the Bible. Even though many were illiterate, they showed a remarkable command of Scripture; biblical language and imagery suffused their worldview. The Anabaptist reformers were deeply biblicist, and the traditions that emerged out of the Anabaptist movement have continued to teach and assume that Scripture is the foundation of the Christian life.

Like most evangelical Christians, Anabaptists reformers also preached the centrality of Jesus Christ to the gospel. But they insisted that the full meaning of Christ's presence on earth could not be reduced to any single image or role. In his life, Christ was a model for how we are to live; in his death, he atoned for our sins; in his resurrection, he proclaimed the victory of love over the forces of hatred and death; in the form of the gathered church, his resurrected body lives on in the world; in his triumph over Satan, he will return as judge and king. The Anabaptists insisted that all these characteristics of Christ were part of the good news, not just his blood shed for our sins and not just taking him into our hearts as our personal savior.

Like most evangelical Christians, Anabaptist reformers believed in the necessity of conversion. They consistently taught that sinful humans come to salvation in Christ when we receive the gift of God's grace in faith and gratitude. In their emphasis on the new birth and their repeated missionary calls to repentance, they echoed the themes of contemporary evangelicalism.

On these points, Protestants of all stripes will likely recognize the Anabaptists as kindred spirits. But the Anabaptist tradition is relevant to contemporary Christianity not because it replicates the doctrines of other Protestant denominations, but because it challenges evangelicals and "generic Christians" alike to examine how basic affirmations find expression in the world of time and space—how the "word becomes flesh." These challenges touch on three points.

1. To a contemporary Christian theology that easily reduces faith to a private, subjective, internal relationship with Christ, the Anabaptist-Mennonite tradition responds that *salvation is insepa-rable from a life of obedience to Christ's teachings;* that is, faith must be expressed in daily discipleship. Throughout their history, Mennonites have stubbornly and repeatedly insisted that the new birth is more than simply the inner experience of God's forgiveness of sins. "No one can truly know Christ," wrote Hans Denck, "unless he follows after him in daily life." The Anabaptist-Mennonite tra-dition thus clearly challenges the temptation of many contempo-rary "generic Christians" to preach a gospel of saving grace as something separate from a gospel of empowering grace: faith *must* be expressed in the concrete acts of daily life.

2. To a contemporary Christian theology that understands the church primarily as a gathering of saved individuals, Anabaptist-Mennonites traditionally respond that *the local, voluntarily gath-ered body of believers is at the heart of the gospel message itself.* For Mennonites, Christian faith cannot be fully experienced apart from the gathered community; discipleship is possible only in fellowship with others. This means that the congregation, rather than the individual, is the primary locus of biblical study. It is within the congregation that the Spirit works most visibly and the will of God is most clearly discerned. It is within the congregation that the practice of mutual discipline can happen in true Christian love.

3. Finally, and perhaps most significantly, to a contemporary Christian theology that is often tempted to reject pacifism alto-gether or to make peacemaking an optional "add-on," the Anabaptist-Mennonite understanding is that *the gospel of peace is the essence of the good news of Jesus Christ.* At the heart of the new birth is a recognition that God granted us the gift of forgiveness and love "while we were still sinners" and "God's enemies" (see Romans 5:8-10). God, having the power to destroy us, loved us

instead. If this is what God did for us, then Christians who have been saved and transformed by God's love must embody that same love in concrete ways, even if that means loving their enemies.

Throughout all of church history, Christians have been tempted to take control of human affairs—to seize the levers of power, to identify their causes with the causes of the nation. Christians have always been tempted to align the kingdom of God with the kingdoms of this world, with force, if necessary. But the Anabaptist-Mennonite understanding of the gospel, shaped by a legacy of martyrdom at the hands of Christian political and religious leaders, challenges Christians everywhere to resist the seductions of righteous violence.

The language of "generic" Christianity can easily lead to a disembodied faith, an abstract Christianity that consists primarily of a private experience with no connection to the way we live on the outside. However, an encounter with Jesus always points us to the incarnation, the "word made flesh." This is not an arrogant assertion intended to defend the narrow interests of a denominational identity, but rather a recognition that God's love for the world becomes real and tangible only to the degree that it transforms how we actually live. Love of enemy, discipleship, and the church as a community are not substitutes for the good news of salvation. They are the good news given shape in the world!

How Should Mennonites Relate to the Broader Christian World?

If the unique themes of the Anabaptist tradition are indeed worth preserving, the question remains: how should Mennonites relate to other believers who also claim the name of Christ?

What is the appropriate image for thinking about their relationship to other Christians? Are Mennonites a different branch off of a single tree? Are they a distinctive species of tree, one of many species within a healthy forest? Are they the prize plant in God's greenhouse, standing tall among the weeds?

Polite coexistence. For much of their history, Mennonites assumed they would always be a minority religious group. Yet even though most would have recognized that the differences between Mennonites and other Christians were real, they were not eager to exacerbate these differences through debate or zealous missionizing. Mennonites almost never make sweeping judgments about the salvation of other groups. If the Anabaptists reminded their persecutors that they would be judged for their actions, as in some passages in the *Martyrs Mirror,* the punishment was understood to be in God's hands, not a task for humans to pursue. Mennonites have frequently established cordial relations with people from other denominations, but for much of their history the divided nature of the church has not been a topic of theological concern.

Informal borrowing. At the same time, despite long-standing reservations about formal ecumenical encounters, Mennonites in North America have frequently engaged in ecumenical borrowing, often without much theological reflection. For example, four-part singing, once regarded by many Mennonites as a worldly innovation sneaking in through Methodist singing schools or the German Lutheran choral tradition, is now widely assumed to be an essential hallmark of Mennonite identity. The colleges, publishing enterprises, missionary boards, relief and service committees, church camps, and mutual aid societies that emerged in the twentieth century and that are now regarded as crucial to the health and well-being of the church were all borrowed from models already existing in other denominations. And more recent interest among Mennonites in the "missional" church, in renewal of worship by drawing on liturgies, or in contemporary praise songs are just a few recent examples of ecumenical borrowing that is intended to enrich and enliven Mennonite faith.

Ecumenical cooperation. Mennonites throughout the world have frequently worked side-by-side with other Christians in cooperative forms of witness. Mennonite ministers routinely participate in community ministerial associations, sharing pastoral insights and collaborating in efforts to address the needs of local people.

Lay Mennonites often work alongside their Catholic and Protestant neighbors in soup kitchens, fundraisers, after-school tutoring programs, and other volunteer initiatives supported by local churches.

For years, volunteers with Mennonite Central Committee who bring a particular expertise to a task or have a long-standing experience in a specific location have been "seconded" to other Christian service organizations. Mennonite Disaster Service coordinates its cleanup operations after natural catastrophes with parallel agencies from other denominations. All these encounters happen so casually that we scarcely think of them as ecumenical events. They rarely have an explicitly theological agenda, and participants are not consciously seeking to bridge doctrinal divides. But these cooperative efforts do point to a "functional ecumenism" that recognizes the richness of God's gifts in other traditions and offers a witness to the church's unity in service to the world.

From reconciliation to full fellowship. Some Mennonites regard the Anabaptist-Mennonite tradition of separatism and the larger reality of denominational distinctions as a theological embarrassment, a scandal within the church. It is not the will of God, they argue, that the body of Christ should be divided into so many competing denominations. Indeed these divisions are more likely to reflect differences in social class, racial identity, or national allegiances than they do differences of conviction.

In John 17, Christ prayed to his Father that his followers would "be one . . . just as you are in me and I am in you" (v. 21). Among those who are baptized in Christ, "there is neither Jew nor Greek, slave nor free, male nor female, for you are all one in Christ Jesus," Paul wrote to the Galatians (3:28). Thus, some have argued, Mennonites should make ecumenical conversations a high priority, with the goal of moving beyond reconciliation of past grievances to the restoration of full communion. It is often less clear whether the conditions for full fellowship with other denominations should include traditional Mennonite understandings regarding, for example, believers baptism and nonresistance. But the urgency of such conversations becomes a theological imperative.

Conclusion: Caution and Confidence in Ecumenical Engagements

In the early 1830s, Leonhard Weydmann, a Mennonite pastor at Monsheim and one of the first seminary-trained, salaried Mennonite ministers in the Palatinate, set out to compose a new catechism for Mennonites in the region. The traditional catechism, he wrote to a friend, was narrow-minded and "outmoded." In the interests of creating a catechism better suited to the realities of the day, Weydmann announced his intention to seek counsel from the Protestant (*Evangelisch*) clergymen in neighboring villages. A decade earlier, the Lutheran and Reformed churches in the Palatinate had agreed to set aside centuries of enmity and to join their two confessions into a "United Protestant Church," repeating a pattern that had become commonplace in churches in many other German territories.

Weydmann's catechism appeared in 1836 and reflected the spirit of his times. The new book eliminated nearly all the traditional theological differences that had formerly distinguished Mennonites from Protestants. Although he retained passing references to nonresistance and adult baptism, he consciously dropped the principle of church discipline, thereby making these themes optional for individual discernment but not a test of church membership. The fundamental organizing principle of Weydmann's new catechism was the atoning blood of Christ and the doctrine of salvation. The traditional Mennonite emphasis on moral regeneration had virtually disappeared, and teachings regarding the nature of the church had become generically Protestant.

Weydmann's catechism undoubtedly eased Mennonite acceptance into mainstream German society. But from a theological perspective, the direction to which it pointed was troubling. By the end of the nineteenth century, the principle of nonresistance had virtually disappeared from the vocabulary of most German Mennonite congregations. Today the cemeteries of many congregations are filled with the graves of those who "died for the Fatherland" in deadly combat with fellow Christians.

Mennonite history is full of similar stories of theological adaptation that led to cultural assimilation. However, the alternative should not be one of defensive retrenchment or erecting higher fences to avoid contact with other Christians. Living traditions must be constantly open to a fresh movement of the Spirit while at the same time resisting the impulse to become reeds blowing in the wind of every new religious fad. This balancing act requires the hard work of discernment—a conscious sifting and sorting through the smorgasbord of ecumenical possibilities to determine which influences strengthen Christian faith and which are distractions. Such discernment raises the following three questions:

First, does the borrowing help us embrace a full, rich understanding of Jesus? If Jesus is God's most complete revelation to humanity, Mennonites should be cautious about drawing on theologies that lead to a partial or truncated view of Jesus and his mission on earth. On the other hand, Mennonites should embrace insights that help maintain a high view of Jesus in which spiritual concerns and ethical practice are never divorced from each other.

Second, does the borrowing promote a view of the believers church as the primary focus of God's saving activity in the world? Mennonites should be cautious about ecumenical borrowing that fosters individualistic understandings of faith or associates the church with the interests of some higher allegiance, be that the nation, economic status, or cultural success. On the other hand, Mennonites should embrace insights that enrich collective worship and keep the gathered church central in its mission outreach.

Finally, does the borrowing strengthen a witness to God's reconciling love in a world that is deeply broken? Mennonites have taught that the Spirit of God is made visible in the world through the miracle of reconciliation: the healing of broken bodies and minds, the restoration of broken relationships, forgiveness in the face of retribution and violence, and a confidence in the power of love over hatred. Thus Mennonites should be cautious about ecumenical borrowing that ignores the profound needs of the world or diminishes the risky work of reconciliation. On the other hand,

Mennonites should embrace insights that strengthen their commitment to testify in word and deed to God's healing love.

Gathered in the unity of the Lord's Supper. Five hundred years ago, the mainstream Christian churches of the day condemned Mennonites as heretics and sought to eliminate them by whatever means possible. Today that is no longer the case. Daily experience has long taught us that we are not the only Christians in our communities and that we do not hold an absolute corner on Christian truth. Our testimony to God's faithfulness has been strengthened through our encounters with other Christians. For this we have reason to be grateful. But even as we borrow, let us be vigilant about the challenge of discernment. For we are inheritors of a treasure—a treasure in jars of clay, to be sure, but a treasure nonetheless. Let us borrow in order to enrich, strengthen, and empower our distinctive contribution. And let us pursue more ecumenical conversations in a spirit of confidence and humility.

In his final supper with the disciples, Jesus told those gathered at the table that when they broke bread and drank the cup, they were to do it "in remembrance of me" (see Luke 22:18-21). When Christians participate in the ritual of Christ's body broken for us, we are reminded that the body of Christ—the church—is indeed broken. But we are not called to remember this broken body only because of our forgetfulness. The opposite of remembering in the Bible is not necessarily forgetting. Rather, the opposite of remembering is "dis-membering," that is, the persistent human impulse to pull apart, to divide. That is why the Bible so often shows us a God who re-members. God is in the business of making things whole—of restoring people, of re-membering communities, of re-membering those who are so often dis-membered.

The Lord's Supper calls us to remember the broken body of Christ even as paradoxically it invites us to participate in his restored and resurrected body. At the heart of the "gospel of peace," so central to Mennonite self-understanding, is a conviction that the fear and violence that led to Christ's death on the cross will not have the last word. Rather, by humbling himself and becoming "obedient to death . . . God exalted him to the highest place" so that "power is made perfect in weakness" (Philippians 2:8-9; 2 Corinthians 12:9).

This is why we gather around the Lord's Table to remember: so that in our remembrance of Christ's body—broken and resurrected —we might find healing for our own brokenness, and together bear witness to a watching world that love is indeed more powerful than death.

Conclusion

Conflict and Renewal in the Anabaptist-Mennonite Tradition

By wisdom a house is built, and through understanding it is established.

—Proverbs 24:3

At first glance the tensions that finally erupted into open conflict among the rural Mennonite churches seemed almost petty: several young pastors, all of them new to the community, determined to invigorate their congregations with fresh ideas about church architecture and worship; an energetic focus on missions that borrowed aggressive strategies and preaching styles from outside the community; and the introduction of a new hymnbook designed to promote contemporary songs that would be sung in an upbeat style.

To anyone who has followed the recent history of Mennonite congregations in North America, these themes of conflict will sound painfully familiar. So it may come as a surprise to learn that the church division described here occurred not in central Illinois or eastern Pennsylvania, but in southwest Germany. And it may be even more surprising to discover that the division occurred almost two hundred years ago in the opening decades of the nineteenth century.

Like all conflicts, the church division in the Palatinate had a context. In the years following the French Revolution of 1789, Mennonites in the region were suddenly granted a new legal status as full citizens, enjoying the same rights as their Protestant, Catholic, and Jewish neighbors. After centuries of living under religious restrictions, they were free to worship as they pleased. Given these new circumstances, it was quite natural, at least to some members, that the church would adopt new patterns of worship.

One of the first innovations introduced by reform-minded leaders in the early 1820s focused on missions. The sixteenth-century Anabaptists had been vigorously committed to missions; but in the centuries that followed, their descendants had become "the quiet in the land," recognized more for their progressive agricultural practices than for the vibrancy of their spiritual commitments. When the new laws made it legal for Mennonites to proselytize, one pastor invited an itinerant Baptist revival preacher to hold a mission rally. Shortly thereafter, some mission enthusiasts began subscribing to Protestant missionary newsletters, collecting money to support overseas mission efforts, and promoting a scholarship fund that would send young Mennonite men to a nearby Baptist mission school to prepare for service abroad.

At the same time, a growing number of voices urged Mennonites to break with the long tradition of a lay ministry selected from within the fellowship on the basis of the lot. "The stutterings of uneducated farmers," one reform-minded leader complained, "are no longer meeting the needs of our young people." So in the mid-1820s, several congregations invited seminary-trained ministers from North Germany as their pastors and began to pay them for their services. Shortly thereafter, to the dismay of the conservatives, the congregation at the Weierhof built a modern-looking church house, patterned after a Baptist structure in England, which soon featured an elevated pulpit and an organ.

Most controversial of all was the publication in the summer of 1832 of a new songbook. For nearly three centuries, Mennonite congregations in the region had sung from an ancient collection of hymns known as the *Ausbund*. Composed in a setting of suffering and persecution, the sixteenth-century songs of the *Ausbund* kept alive the stories of those who had been martyred for their religious convictions. For generations these hymns, sung slowly and in unison, reminded Mennonites that the cost of following Jesus was humiliation, pain, and even death.

Such songs seemed appropriate during the seventeenth and eighteenth century, when Mennonites in the region continued to endure various forms of persecution. With the coming of the French legal reforms, however, many found the *Ausbund* to be utterly outmoded. Compilers of the new hymnal assured skeptics that at least some of the old "core songs" from the *Ausbund* would be retained. But they borrowed freely from contemporary hymns that were being sung in the neighboring Protestant churches, notably songs that emphasized the "saving blood of Jesus."

The new hymnal also featured, for the first time, musical notation to assist those who wanted to sing in four-part harmony, and promoters of the book encouraged congregations to sing the hymns at a faster tempo. When the book finally appeared, one supporter of the project excitedly reported that young people at the Weierhof congregation were gathering every evening to practice the new songs.

Of course, the story is much richer and more complicated than this brief sketch suggests. But the central themes of the conflict have resounded throughout Anabaptist-Mennonite history. How do Christians bear witness to Christ in the midst of a changing culture? How does the faithful church balance the wisdom of the past with a fresh movement of the Spirit "who makes all things new"?

How does the "word become flesh" and dwell among us so that we can behold the glory of the Lord?

This short book has offered only a glimpse into the story of Anabaptists and their descendant groups. I have suggested that the genius of that tradition was its determination to resurrect themes of Christian faithfulness present in the early church but forgotten or repressed in the centuries that followed.

Like the early church, the Anabaptists believed that the decision to follow Jesus should be voluntary, made with a full awareness of the life-changing consequences of that choice. The Anabaptists shared with the apostolic church a commitment to economic sharing and a willingness to engage in mutual accountability with each other. They sought to practice Jesus' teachings in daily life, including the call to love enemies.

The communities they formed sought to be faithful witnesses to the kingdom that Christ had proclaimed—a city on the hill welcoming all those who were prepared to follow in the narrow path of Christ. As in the early church, the first generation of Anabaptists was keenly aware of the presence of the Holy Spirit, claiming its authority over that of the established church hierarchy and yielding to the Spirit's voice in following Christ.

The Anabaptists of the sixteenth century did not live out their convictions consistently; nor do their spiritual descendants today. Indeed, as we have seen, Anabaptist-Mennonite history has been full of detours, disagreements, and divisions. Some of those conflicts, like the Anabaptist Kingdom of Münster, have been the result of outright apostasy; others grew out of petty grievances and mean-spirited attitudes. In retrospect, many of the conflicts seem like they could have been avoided if cooler heads or more gracious attitudes had prevailed.

But there is another theme in the Anabaptist-Mennonite story that is worthy of close attention: a tension that is potentially life-giving. If faith traditions are to be sustained through the ages, each generation must listen anew for the voice of the Spirit and discern how it will be embodied in the current context. Like the spring in a watch, this process of discernment is driven by tension, a tension that, at its best, is also contained within a system of checks and balances that keeps it from becoming destructive.

Finding that balance has never been easy. Without tension, there is no life. Yet the line between faithful continuity and reckless innovation is rarely clear to those closest to the conflict. "We are living in a new age of freedom," wrote a defender of the reforms in the Palatinate, undoubtedly echoing the sentiments of many. "The time has come for us to embrace new forms of faithfulness."

Yet for other South German Mennonites, the innovations were not simply about form; the changes seemed to threaten principles that went to the very core of their faith. "We come to worship God," rejoined a defender of tradition on the question of a professional pastorate, "not the beautiful words of a man who can read Greek." In his mind, the appeal to cultural relevance, so popular among the reformers, had come at the expense of traditional Anabaptist-Mennonite understandings of humility and of a view of the church as a disciplined community rather than merely a setting for Sunday-morning worship.

Where in the midst of honest disagreements is the spirit of truth to be found? How can these conflicts, some of which seem so deeply engrained in the Anabaptist-Mennonite tradition, be transformed from destructive schisms into a life-giving encounter with God?

'By Wisdom a House Is Built'

This book has not offered the final answer to these questions. But it does suggest that congregations in conflict should spend some time learning from the past. An appeal to the past is not always welcome counsel in a culture oriented to the future and infatuated with the new. Yet traditional societies almost always recognize that the wisest people in the village are the storytellers, the keepers of memory. In times of conflict or confusion, the storytellers are the ones charged with the responsibility of bringing a needed perspective otherwise lacking in the group.

Modern societies tend to prefer the technical skills of the experts and the linear clarity of tightly structured arguments to the storyteller's musings. But congregations standing at the intersection between past and future, seeking to hear the voice of God in the midst of conflict, should be attentive to the voices of wisdom that filter down from the past.

Wisdom comes in many forms, of course, but the long arc of history suggests that it almost always includes three elements.

Context. Congregations seeking wisdom will be attentive to their context. The Anabaptist-Mennonite tradition has appropriately described the church as a visible body "separated unto Christ." The temptation of Christians to become chameleons in their culture, imitating the attitudes and assumptions of the broader society, is powerful. Nonetheless, wise congregations recognize that the church can never fully separate itself from a cultural context. After all, we participate in local and national economies, our communities reflect the racial and ethnic diversity of our society, and we are faced with the potentials and perils of new technology. Our children are attuned to fashions in music and clothing, and we share with our neighbors a common cultural vocabulary of images from mass media. If we are going to tell stories wisely, we need to be keenly aware of the context in which those stories are being told.

Tradition. Congregations seeking wisdom will have a deep respect for tradition. We all know people who seem to live their lives like leaves falling in autumn, floating aimlessly, subject to every little gust of wind that comes their way. Stories that preserve the traditions of the past remind us that we are not alone, that the choices confronting us are never made in a vacuum. Instead we are participants in a long and dramatic tradition, a grand story of God acting in human history, patiently, persistently, and lovingly calling a people to faithful obedience. Repeated prayers, the words of a familiar hymn, the savoring of a biblical text, the recollection of a martyr's death, the cadence of the benediction heard Sunday after Sunday—all remind us that we are part of this larger story.

Only if we accept our role as stewards of this tradition will our lives have meaning and purpose. This sense of honor and respect, this debt that we owe to the past should not be understood as "traditionalism," what has been called "the dead faith of the living." Rather, it is tradition in the best sense—the "living faith of the dead." Congregations seeking wisdom will bring the context of their culture into conversation with a living tradition.

The movement of the Spirit. Finally, wise congregations will recount the past in ways that bring their listeners face-to-face with the living God. In the end, the most powerful stories we can tell are not about us, but about encounters with God in which we must take off our shoes because we are standing on holy ground. They will remind us that the in-breaking, transforming movement of the Holy Spirit comes in the form of the One who says, "Behold, I make all things new."

This encounter with the Spirit sometimes comforts, but more often it unsettles us. The Spirit is not easily contained within the finitude of language or institutions or traditions. It defies our efforts to package it or turn it into a system. The Spirit resists our impulse toward nostalgia and sentimentalism. It does not allow us to portray ourselves as we would like others to think of us. It calls attention to the hidden corners and dark attics of our past, places that are full of fear as well as unexpected treasures.

Moreover, stories that bring us face-to-face with God are almost always in tension with our context and our tradition. By its nature, the culture around us is immediate, continually demanding our attention. Likewise, tradition is simply there, "bred in the bone," woven into the language we speak. Stories of our encounters with God remind us that context and tradition are not the final word. Important though they may be, context and tradition always need to be in conversation with the Spirit of God, who comes as a fresh voice, calling us away from the false gods of the culture and reminding us not to make idolatries out of our tradition.

To summarize, congregations seeking wisdom will be insightful observers of their particular time and place. They will listen careful-

ly to the voices among them that call on the church to be relevant—
the voices eager to explore new curricula, design new worship spaces,
implement new programs, and press for changes. Wise congregations will listen carefully to the world beyond their own community.

Congregations seeking wisdom will consciously nurture a
respect for tradition. In a culture addicted to the new, the immediate, and the future, they will offer their members the gift of a living
tradition. Who are the heroes of our past who stand as counterparts to the heroes of Hollywood? What are the stories that have
formed us as a distinctive people of God? Where are the rock piles,
the stone altars erected in our communities that mark the
moments when God intervened in our lives in a surprising and
marvelous way? What are the rituals of confession, of blessing, of
greeting, of singing, of praying, of departing that bring structure
and order to our harried lives?

Congregations seeking wisdom will nurture the gifts of the
prophets, the artists, the poets, and the storytellers in their midst—
those who challenge us to encounter the Divine in a new way. To be
sure, institutions like order, stability, and predictability. Yet if the
prophets and poets and artists are true to their calling, they will
unsettle us, not because they are calling for something new, but
rather because they point us back to the deepest roots, the core principles of our faith. Healthy congregations will be attentive to the
stories the prophets tell.

The Challenge Ahead

These themes of context, tradition, and the Spirit could easily
become a formula for conflict, each claiming priority over the
other. Indeed the conflicts that have torn apart the fabric of community can almost always be described in terms of one voice claiming for itself priority over the other two: progressivists tend to celebrate context; the Old Orders appeal to tradition; the revivalist
claims a unique insight into the Spirit.

Yet the best storytellers know that wisdom is found at the center of this triangle. Wisdom is what keeps the voices of context and tradition and truth in a dynamic ongoing conversation with each other. Wisdom insists that this three-fold conversation happen with mutual respect, even though the three voices may not find themselves in full agreement. Wisdom always comes to the defense of the weakest voice in the conversation, ensuring that every voice gets an adequate hearing.

At its best, past and future meet when congregations become settings where the voices of context and tradition and the Spirit are actively and intentionally cultivated, where the tension between them—like the spring in a watch—drives the community forward toward a shared purpose. At their best, congregations will focus less on cultivating "Mennonite distinctives" than on encouraging the voices of context, tradition, and the Spirit in their midst. They will steadily call on their members—young and old—to put their shoulders to the wheel of wisdom's hard, life-giving work.

The Anabaptist-Mennonite tradition is a gift—a gift precious enough to be lovingly nurtured, resilient enough to be sharply critiqued, dynamic enough to be consistently renewed, and abundant enough to be generously shared. Yet the tradition celebrated in this book is ultimately not ours to possess. Our story is really about a larger story, a witness to the One who has come, has risen, and will come again.

In a short novella titled *Cecelia's Sin,* the Southern Baptist minister and novelist William Campbell tells of a young Anabaptist woman in the Netherlands who is intent on documenting the martyrdoms of her fellow believers. Cecelia writes furiously, determined that no story of faithfulness be forgotten. When the authorities hear of her project and begin a relentless search for the manuscript, she becomes all the more obsessed with gathering stories of Anabaptist martyrs so that their memory will be preserved for later generations.

But then, at the very end of the book, the story takes a very strange and haunting turn. In the last scene of the book we see Cecelia by the fire, burning the manuscript page by page.

Cecelia's sin was that her desire to preserve the story had *become* the story. In the end, she is overwhelmed with the revelation that the Anabaptist story is not a "thing" to be possessed. Rather, it is a life to be lived, sacrificially and joyfully—the word made flesh.

The Author

John D. Roth is a professor of history at Goshen (Indiana) College, where he also serves as director of the Mennonite Historical Library and editor of *The Mennonite Quarterly Review*. He and his wife Ruth are the parents of four daughters and are active members in the Berkey Avenue Mennonite Fellowship. Roth has written and edited numerous books, including *Engaging Anabaptism: Conversations with a Radical Tradition, Beliefs: Mennonite Faith and Practice* and *Choosing Against War: A Christian View*.

"Roth's thought-provoking sketch may emerge as a catalyst for a new vision of what God intends for the global Christian community. This story also serves to remind us of the dangers associated with the church aligning too closely with empire."
—*Keith Weaver, Lancaster Mennonite Conference*

"One of the preeminent Mennonite historians of our time, Roth successfully weaves a complicated set of stories into a fascinating narrative that stretches from the early church to the present, and covers the globe. *Stories* is a remarkable achievement, a must-read for those who don't know the Anabaptist story, and for those who think they do."
—*William Vance Trollinger Jr., Bluffton University*

"Roth has written a lively account of Mennonites—a story that is multi-layered. In a sweeping and engaging way, Roth reviews Christian history and finds the perspective of the Anabaptist/Mennonite people a compelling example of past faithfulness and a contemporary invitation to be Christian."
—*Dorothy Nickel Friesen, Western District Conference*

"Roth finds a balance between historical detail and thematic analysis of Anabaptist history as he demonstrates key connections that illuminate the value of living our story as Mennonites. I plan on drawing heavily on this book as a church-history educator."
—*Ramon Rempel, Rockway Mennonite Collegiate*

"John Roth has written a clear, comprehensive history that condenses a considerable amount of detail into a cohesive, engaging narrative. The book highlights major themes in provocative ways, and with its vibrant vignettes, is recommended reading for both new and long-term Mennonites."
—*Beth E. Graybill, Lancaster Mennonite Historical Society*

"Roth weaves together narrative, biography, and theology in an engaging, compelling, and sometimes provocative fashion. This book is an invitation to consider how what happened back then can illuminate the task of following Jesus now. It will encourage and challenge anyone seeking to be a faithful follower."
—*Jonathan Showalter, Rosedale Bible College*